Screenwriting

FilmCraft

Screenwriting

Tim Grierson

Focal Press
Taylor & Francis Group

NEW YORK AND LONDON

First published in the USA 2013 by Focal Press
Focal Press is an imprint of the Taylor & Francis Group,
an informa business
70 Blanchard Road, Suite 402, Burlington, MA 01803, USA

This book was conceived, designed, and produced by
Ilex Press Limited, 210 High Street, Lewes, BN7 2NS, UK

Publisher: Alastair Campbell
Associate Publisher: Adam Juniper
Managing Editor: Natalia Price-Cabrera
Editor: Tara Gallagher
Specialist Editor: Frank Gallaugher
Creative Director: James Hollywell
Senior Designer: Ginny Zeal
Design: Grade Design
Picture Manager: Katie Greenwood
Color Origination: Ivy Press Reprographics

Notices:
Knowledge and best practice in this field are constantly
changing. As new research and experience broaden our
understanding, changes in research methods, professional
practices, or medical treatment may become necessary.

Practitioners and researchers must always rely on their own
experience and knowledge in evaluating and using any
information, methods, compounds, or experiments described
herein. In using such information or methods they should be
mindful of their own safety and the safety of others, including
parties for whom they have a professional responsibility.

Product or corporate names may be trademarks or registered
trademarks, and are used only for identification and explanation
without intent to infringe.

Library of Congress Cataloging in Publication Data:
A catalog record for this book is available from the Library
of Congress.

ISBN: 978-0-240-82486-4 (pbk)
ISBN: 978-0-240-82485-7 (ebk)

Typeset in Rockwell Light

Table of Contents

Introduction

Of all the crafts associated with the filmmaking process, screenwriting may very well be the most unique—and also the most misunderstood.

The screenwriter is the first person charged with shaping the vision of the final film, the person whose inspiration provides a guiding light for all the artists and technicians who will later add their own individual talents to the project. But when you think of Hollywood films—which often go through several screenwriters, some of whom never receive a screen credit for their work—there's a sense that what writers do is rather disposable. Add to that the public misconceptions ("Writers just write the stuff that the actors say, right?") and the clichéd assumptions ("Anyone can be a writer"), and you can see why screenwriters suffer from an image problem. Just about every creative contributor to a film is regarded as an expert in his or her field—the actor, the composer, the costume designer, the cinematographer—but, sadly, the writer can sometimes be viewed as merely a dime-a-dozen figure. They have the one film job where people are most often fired and replaced. And although screenwriters provide the blueprint for a movie, they are not considered the film's "author:" That honor is bestowed upon the director.

This is the screenwriter's harsh reality, and yet you can easily find dozens of how-to books offering tips on breaking into the business with a high-concept spec script. There are plenty of explanations for this, including the fact that aspiring writers look at the generally mediocre movies put out by studios and assume they can do better. But another reason is that so many still regard cinema as the greatest and most universal art form, and they long to share their stories with the vast audience it affords. It's really no different than the sentiment shared by seasoned, professional screenwriters: Despite the many obstacles to making a great film, they have a burning desire to reveal part of themselves to the world at large.

FilmCraft: Screenwriting seeks to honor those who have taken on that challenge and succeeded. The 15 writers assembled in this book are the best at what they do, but as I hope will become clear from thumbing through these pages, they don't all write the same kinds of films. From the Hollywood blockbuster to the American indie to the international arena, these writers are the people responsible for some of our most indelible cinematic memories of the last 50 years—and most audience members don't recognize their names, let alone know anything about them. *FilmCraft: Screenwriting* aims to give these creators their much-deserved moment in the sun.

For those unacquainted with the *FilmCraft* series, this volume follows a familiar, engaging template: Each chapter is devoted to one writer, letting him or her speak directly to the reader about his or her upbringing, creative philosophy, and career. The *FilmCraft* series takes pains to minimize the presence of the interviewer, thereby allowing the interviewee's personality to leap off the page. If you are looking for how to structure a dynamic three-act script that will make millions, this book will be a disappointment. If, however, you want inspiration and perspective on the writing life, these pages may prove indispensable. And even if you have no interest in writing, but simply harbor a curiosity about how movies arrive on the screen, you will find much that quenches your thirst here.

In addition, this book upends the notion that the film industry is relegated simply to Hollywood—or even to English-speakers. That's why I'm particularly proud of the geographic sweep of these interview subjects. Writers from South Korea, France, Mexico, and Denmark all participated, each providing their own interpretations of what our global cinema means in the early decades of the 21st century. In the American studio system, movies may begin with a screenplay, but decisions made by the producers and executives can soon dilute the quality of the written word, and often commercial considerations are permitted to override artistry. Speaking with writers from around the world, it is striking—if not outright embarrassing—to see how much less of an influence such considerations have elsewhere. No wonder that when you want to see a truly poetic, stimulating piece of cinema, your chances are much better if you opt for a film made outside of Hollywood.

But at the same time, another strength of this book is that it refuses to accept the trite notion that all Hollywood product is automatically substandard. Some of *FilmCraft: Screenwriting*'s best interviews are with writers working in the trenches on big studio projects, and it's incredibly revealing to hear how they approach their work. Mark Bomback, who wrote **Live Free or Die Hard** (2007) and **Unstoppable** (2010), explains his early fascination with wanting to write big Hollywood movies: "A part of me was drawn to that struggle to create something of value in the face of all the obstacles inherent in making a studio picture." As for John August, the writer of **Big Fish** (2003) and **Go** (1999), navigating Hollywood means understanding that you can get your heart broken once passion-projects lose momentum and land in what's referred to in the business as "development hell"—an unhappy limbo where the script has little hope of getting produced. But, according to August, there's also a bright side: ". . . the good thing is that, unlike a lot of other jobs in the film industry, you can always pick up your pen and write something new any time." If anything, these and other writers' comments about studio filmmaking should help increase your respect for the talent, persistence, and patience that are the hallmarks of any good Hollywood screenwriter.

What also emerges in these interviews is the endless work that goes into crafting a superb script. The beauty of the screenplay is in its constant evolution. Before a foot of film is shot, a script has gone through many iterations—subplots abandoned, supporting characters developed, themes strengthened and more deeply explored. "The script is always the dream of the film," Jean-Claude Carrière, the co-writer of such films as **The Discreet Charm of the Bourgeoisie** (1972) and **Belle de Jour** (1967), told me. Further to this theme of constant evolution, the experienced screenwriter recognizes that his or her vocation is not something one can ever fully "master." Even though Carrière is now in his 80s, he acknowledges he still has room to grow. "All the great filmmakers from all over the world have developed the language of cinema," he says. "They have refined it—sometimes they have perverted it—but our main task is not only to know the language we are going to use, but also to try to make it better, if possible." It's a

humbling, but also empowering statement, and it's echoed by other writers in this book who praise their colleagues' contributions to the art of screenwriting. Toward that end, I've also included five "legacy" chapters that celebrate the influential work of legendary writers—everyone from Ben Hecht to Woody Allen to Ingmar Bergman.

While screenwriters may often feel like second-class citizens in the filmmaking community, it was intriguing to hear from my subjects about the sometimes tricky collaboration that goes on between writer and director. Most thought-provoking in this regard was Guillermo Arriaga, who for a time worked side-by-side with director Alejandro González Iñárritu on **Amores Perros** (2000), **21 Grams** (2003), and **Babel** (2006). A strong opponent of the *auteur* theory, Arriaga believes that everyone involved in the process contributes to a film's success or failure. And if writers feel that they're being taken advantage of, Arriaga has some advice. "I've found there are many ways to protect your work," he says. "Everything is negotiable. You can say in your contract, 'No one can change a line'—then it's in your contract. I learned something from the very beginning: People buy what you sell . . . I was very clear from when I was 15: 'This is my work, you respect it. You don't want to respect it, I will not do it.'" Screenwriters who are just starting out in their career may feel that they can't possibly adopt Arriaga's bold stance, but I think that, after reading his chapter, you'll understand that this self-assurance was forged at an early age and has helped make him one of our most distinctive and uncompromising modern-day scenarists.

Perhaps it will be encouraging to readers who want to be writers themselves to know that many of my interview subjects had to take roundabout ways to their ultimate profession. Some were film editors. Some had dreams of becoming athletes. Others grew up in families where art was hardly prized. But what connects many of these individuals is that the wonder of the big screen drew them at an early age. Even now when some of these writers occasionally work in other disciplines—such as the novel or in the theater—screenwriting remains a central focus of their lives. Additionally, a handful of these chapters →

feature writers who are also directors, and I think it's worthwhile to read their comments about how these different aspects of the filmmaking process inform, rather than conflict with, one another.

On a personal note, I was impressed by many of my subjects' willingness to talk candidly about particular projects that ended up being unsuccessful ventures. Take David Hare, a decorated playwright and screenwriter on **The Hours** (2002), and **The Reader** (2008), who tasted disappointment when his extensive work on a film version of Jonathan Franzen's celebrated 2001 novel *The Corrections* fell by the wayside after the producers decided to go in another direction. ("A part of me died when I lost all that work," he confided in me.) If all films are an act of faith, then the screenwriter is among the first in the process to be a true believer, bravely expending immense amounts of creative energy and time to works that may never see the light of day or, perhaps even worse, will eventually only become mediocre movies. Robin Swicord, who adapted **Little Women** (1994) and **Memoirs of a Geisha** (2005), discusses that frustration in her chapter: "I really wish that the great experience that I had writing [the adaptation of] **Practical Magic** had been the audience's experience watching the movie," she confesses. As for her advice on how to cope with the creative misfires, she responds, "You don't look at the [films] that make you unhappy—you just keep moving."

But among these tales of disappointment and lessons learned are also stories of when the fates aligned and acclaimed films came together. Anders Thomas Jensen sheds light on the inspiration behind the Oscar-winning ensemble drama **In a Better World** (2010), while Billy Ray discusses his breakthrough during the writing of **Shattered Glass** (2003) in which he figured out how to make a compelling film about disgraced journalist Stephen Glass. Additionally, there are discussions about working methods, including writers who sing the praises of going somewhere incredibly boring and remote to write a first draft. And then there are the stories of the hours of fruitless toiling that eventually led to the right idea or the right approach. If nothing else, *FilmCraft: Screenwriting* will disabuse you of the belief that writers sit in an ivory tower waiting for the muse to strike. More often, writers just keep writing—waiting, hoping, and praying that something good will emerge.

Happily, I didn't have to wait too long for something good to emerge from the mouths of my interview subjects. I'd like to thank them all sincerely for their time and for their willingness to share a little of their creative and personal lives with me while working on this book. Just as I wanted to make these people come to life on the page through their words, they became three-dimensional figures during our talks, sometimes having to juggle the demands of family and other responsibilities while finding time to speak with me. Even when writers aren't writing, they're thinking about writing, and so getting a chance to eavesdrop on their worlds was a constant delight for which I'll be forever grateful. Likewise, I'd like to thank the writers' agents, producers, and publicists, who helped make these interviews happen. In their own special category are the assistants to these individuals, often serving as tireless, patient point people. This book could not have happened without you, and I offer my appreciation for your kindness and diligence.

The *FilmCraft* series has been expertly shepherded by Mike Goodridge, whom I've had the pleasure of working with since 2005 as my editor at *Screen International*. He is an endless supply of good cheer and biting asides, and I thank him for entrusting the screenwriting edition of this series to me. Thanks also to Tara Gallagher and the other great folks at Ilex Photo who have published such beautiful books.

I could not have made it through life without the generous encouragement of my parents, Bob and Debbie. Like several of the writers in this book, I come from a family without any artists in it, but my parents have always supported my dreams, which has resulted in a road that hasn't always been straight, but has remained richly rewarding. My wonderful sister Lisa and her family are never far from my thoughts, although I don't Skype with them nearly enough.

Which brings me, finally, to Susan, my wife and fellow dreamer. Life is constant change, but you, my angel, have always been there.

Tim Grierson

Cyrano de Bergerac (1990)

Hossein Amini

"The things that I'm drawn to aren't commercial. I don't particularly like happy endings, and I like people who are ambiguous and have contradictions and vulnerabilities—I like my heroes being slightly fucked-up."

Drive (2011)

Born in Iran and currently residing in London, Hossein Amini initially thought that he wanted to be a writer-director after helming a few shorts while at Oxford. But once he started making a living as a writer on other people's projects, he discovered that he enjoyed focusing on screenwriting. His career began with television movies, **The Dying of the Light** (1992) and **Deep Secrets** (1996), but even then Amini knew that his interest was in features. A chance encounter with director Michael Winterbottom at the BAFTA awards in the mid-1990s led to their collaboration on the feature **Jude** (1996), an adaptation of Thomas Hardy's novel *Jude the Obscure* that starred Christopher Eccleston and Kate Winslet. Amini's next adaptation was **The Wings of the Dove** (1997), based on Henry James' novel—the film went on to receive four Academy Award nominations, including Best Adapted Screenplay. Soon after, Amini signed an exclusive overall deal with Miramax Films, working on the independent company's diverse projects like **Gangs of New York** (2002) (for which he didn't receive a credit) and **The Four Feathers** (2002). After his Miramax deal ended, he was approached by Universal Pictures to work on an adaptation of a book by crime author James Sallis about an enigmatic getaway driver. The project, **Drive** (2011), was eventually independently financed and directed by Nicolas Winding Refn, receiving rave reviews in competition at Cannes. Though Amini has primarily written for indie and art-house films, he has recently been involved with some major studio projects, including **Snow White and the Huntsman** (2012) and **47 Ronin** (2013). Currently, he's directing **The Two Faces of January**, his adaptation of the Patricia Highsmith novel, which stars Viggo Mortensen and Kirsten Dunst.

Hossein Amini

So many writers stop at an early age because they're not given encouragement. I was lucky to have parents who were willing to support me for a few years after school until I finally got work. Most Iranian parents want their children to be lawyers, doctors, architects, or engineers—filmmaking is the last thing you'd want your kids to do, because there's no money in it. But luckily, my parents were very supportive—I wouldn't have been able to do it otherwise. So much writing talent is lost because people can't afford to stick around doing it for long enough. I had friends that I started out writing with who eventually had to get a proper job—they became estate agents and this and that—and they were just as good, if not better, than I was. I was lucky enough to be able to do it for longer than they were.

When I was a child growing up in Iran, Bruce Lee movies were my earliest film obsession. My dad was a bit of a film buff, so we had one of those small projector screens, and for my birthday we'd get a Bruce Lee movie. In Iran, there were a lot of outdoor movie theaters—not drive-ins, but just various clubs or whatever that would show movies outside because the weather was usually so hot. But my interest in movies increased when we moved when I was 11, after the Revolution. My parents were separated, so I'd go and stay with my dad in Paris. He didn't know what to do with my brother and I, so he'd take us to movies—he put us in a two o'clock showing, a four o'clock showing, and a six o'clock showing all along the Champs-Élysées. Initially, it was the Hollywood action movies that hooked me, but later I went to Oxford, and there were these two fantastic cinemas that showed older movies. I'd sneak off and see two movies a day sometimes.

JUDE

(01–03) Although Hossein Amini loved Thomas Hardy's novel *Jude the Obscure*, he knew he would need to trim down the story. "If we'd been really faithful to the book," he says, "it would've probably been four or five hours, minimum." Because **Jude** was his first adaptation, Amini needed to come up with a technique for tackling the book. "In terms of approaching an adaptation, I did what I have done ever since, which is to read the book and break it down into every scene that is in the book—every concrete scene. Then I put them all on cards **(02)** and fill in scenes **(03)** where I feel there's something missing. With **Jude**, it was quite easy because Hardy had lots of scenes, so you're taking out ones that make it too long and figuring out how to make the film flow." Asked if he's ever gone back to reread a book he's adapted after the film is completed just to see how different it changed from the source material, Amini replies, "I don't think I've ever gone back and done that. I mean, I read them so closely when I'm working on the script—I read them three, four, sometimes five times before I've finished the first two drafts. I'm really living with that book—I'm reading it every time I get on the bus or the Underground. Once the film's done, I don't go back."

01

"So much writing talent is lost because people can't afford to stick around doing it for long enough."

They'd have a Fellini week or a Tarkovsky week—all on the big screen. In Paris, I remember seeing **Kiss Me Deadly** (1955)—to see a black-and-white *film noir* on the big screen was just such a mind-blowing experience. Those are the things that made me fall in love with film, and that hasn't gone away.

I grew up watching European and American movies rather than British television, which is the traditional thing here in London. So when I started out writing TV movies, that was a problem I had: I was always thinking big-screen. I worked on this docudrama, **The Dying of the Light**, which was about an aid worker in Africa, but it had very little dialogue and it was set on this enormous canvas. I arranged it like a movie, but I didn't realize I was working with a TV budget—I was dreaming of David Lean and trying to write to that scale.

While I was working in TV, I met Michael Winterbottom, and he mentioned he wanted to do a film of Thomas Hardy's *Jude the Obscure*. He asked me, "Is that something you're interested in? Do you know the book?" And I lied and said I did know the book, which I hadn't read at the time. I very quickly went and read it as soon as I could—luckily, it was a book I loved, but honestly, I would've done anything in film. I was excited about working in TV, but the chance to work in film was just a dream.

Michael was pretty vague about how he wanted to approach the adaptation—he knew he wanted to concentrate on the modern aspects of the story. But for me with **Jude**—and I think it's true of all adaptations—you have to have a love affair with the book. You feel like you're the first person to have read this book and this is how you want to tell your friends about it. Also, I tend to fall →

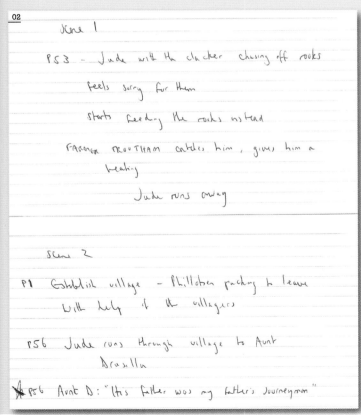

in love with one character initially. With **Jude**, it was obviously the Jude character. I was attracted to the idea of how life defeats you, which is a theme I've subsequently always been interested in. I'm intrigued by people who start off with noble intentions, but then life somehow conspires to turn them into something other than what they wanted to be. The Hollywood version of **Jude** is "He's this guy who comes from nowhere and rises to the top." But what I loved about this book was that it was the guy who comes from nowhere, has these beautiful dreams and ambitions, but eventually life drags him down. I find something very noble about defeat—which is probably not great for Hollywood blockbusters, but goes back to the Greek myths, the ones where the characters rebel against the Gods, but ultimately fail. Something about their failure is so heroic and so human.

In movies, what's always really interested me are the reaction shots and what the person is thinking. Again, it's that big-screen experience of seeing someone's face in a close-up with all that emotion. I want to keep the dialogue as real and conversational as possible—as opposed to using heightened dialogue, where it really is about what people are saying. The favorite scenes that I've written have all tended to be the ones where the dialogue is setting up the best reaction from the actor. I love trying to find the simplest way to say something with the maximum impact on the person who's listening to it. Quite often, the dialogue is almost like background noise, and what's really important is setting up the silent emotions on the faces of the characters.

What tends to happen is a production company has a book, and your agent says, "They're thinking of you for this. Read it, and then go pitch them." With **The Wings of the Dove**, I got to the end of the book, and I had no idea how to do it. But then I got to the very last scene, which is the breakup scene, and then it was really easy to go backwards and create a story out of that. I'd always been a *film noir* buff, so it all clicked into place. My pitch was that this was *film noir*—the only difference is that they don't literally

kill each other; they just break the other girl's heart and kill her that way. Period movies back then were defined by Merchant Ivory—and in a very unfair way to Merchant Ivory, because a lot of their films are classics. But at the time, Merchant Ivory had almost become the cliché, so we were all going, "How do we subvert Merchant Ivory?" And by thinking of **The Wings of the Dove** in terms of *film noir*, it became a really exciting new way to do a period drama.

After the success of **The Wings of the Dove**, I didn't get overconfident, but I think I was naïve about the business. I'd grown up on Hollywood movies, and I wanted to get to America very quickly and do those movies. But when your early films are relatively well-received, it's a dangerous thing—it doesn't go to your head, but you want to say yes to everything and everyone. You spend so long not getting anything made, and then suddenly you're getting offered all this stuff. Part of me wishes I'd spent the next seven or eight years trying to make films like **Jude** or **The Wings of the Dove**, because I think I would have gotten a lot more made, and I would have

01 **Jude** (1996), directed by Michael Winterbottom

> **"I love trying to find the simplest way to say something with the maximum impact on the person who's listening to it."**

probably had a lot more control. But those are mistakes you make—people can be very persuasive when they want you to do something, and the money can be very persuasive, too.

When **Jude** went to Cannes, I had to pay for my own flight and stay with my wife in this really, really cheap hotel, which was still very expensive because it was Cannes. But while I was there, I got introduced to Harvey Weinstein. Literally two days later, he flew me out on Concorde to meet him in New York to discuss doing stuff for Miramax. His idea was, "Come and work for me." I ended up doing it a couple of years later after **The Wings of the Dove**—it was an overall deal where I'd be writing stuff for Miramax exclusively. It was great in some ways, not great in others. They were making wonderful films, but what I didn't realize is that, as a writer, it's better to be freelance because then you have access to lots of places to take your ideas. The problem was I was slightly at the mercy of what Miramax wanted me to do and what they were →

02 Helena Bonham Carter as Kate Croy in **The Wings of the Dove** (1997)

AMINI ON HEAT

(03) Amini cites **Heat** (1995) as one of his favorite movies. "It has that theme that **Drive** has—these people who are trying to break out and be something else, but their background closes in on them and conspires against them," Amini says. "I constantly want to find a way to write a scene like the one where Al Pacino and Robert De Niro finally meet in **Heat**. That scene encapsulates so much of what I love about heroes and villains—there's no black and white." Amini appreciates writer-director Michael Mann's ability to keep the scene spare, but still very compelling. "There's a casualness in the way those two characters are talking. It seems undramatic, which is what I love about it—it becomes so much more emotional and powerful because of it. They're just talking over coffee, and then they suddenly digress and talk about recurring dreams they've each had. It's a perfect scene because it's the one time they talk in the whole movie—they're antagonists, but they find this shared bond. It's almost like a love scene."

Amini's favorite scene

(01–03) Asked to name a particular favorite scene of his, Amini picks a moment shortly before the death of Millie (Alison Elliott) in **The Wings of the Dove**. "I loved writing that scene where Merton"—played by Linus Roache—"goes to her and she forgives him," says Amini (01). Because the scene didn't exist in the original Henry James novel, Amini had to invent it. "But because his characters are so well-drawn, the dialogue just flowed really easily and the emotions flowed really easily. He's given you so much ammunition and so much energy to go and write those scenes." The scene was refined over a few drafts, but Amini says its essence was always there from the beginning. "The key was actually the line about the box of biscuits—there was something about the way that they weren't talking directly about what was going on. It was an easy scene to write because there was so much subtext happening—the scene begins so emotionally charged that they could talk about literally anything. Those are the scenes that I love—if you've set it up right, they could talk about the weather and it can be the most moving thing in the world. I'm more interested in what's *not* said rather than what is said. If the one thing they don't talk about is what the scene's about, then those scenes work really well. You can't do it all the time, but when you can, it's just a joy to write because there isn't the pressure of dialogue explaining anything or telling the story—you're just finding the emotions."

```
CONTINUED: (2)

                        MILLIE
            You should have seen him. He was so
            embarrassed. He kept trying to turn the tin
            on its side without me noticing-

                        MERTON
            Millie, please-

                        MILLIE
            Mark never does anything quite right. He
            came to hurt me and brought a box of
            biscuits.

                        MERTON
            What he told you isn't true.

Millie looks away. Merton can't see her eyes.

                        MILLIE
            I said that to him myself. That it wasn't
            true. And then I sent him away in the rain.

Merton still can't see her eyes.

                        MERTON
            But you believed him?

Millie looks up now, tears streaming down her face.

                        MERTON
            Millie, what can I do to persuade you?

                        MILLIE
            Don't.

Her eyes plead with him not to lie anymore.

                        MILLIE
            There's no need. We're past that, you and
            I.

Merton stares at her in silence. Millie gathers herself and
smiles softly, forgiving him.

                        MILLIE
            I love you. Both of you.

Merton can't help himself. He kneels at her feet, reaches
closer and kisses her.  She doesn't stop him, responding
gently.

Tears begin to fill Merton's eyes as he touches her face. He
kisses her eyes and her hair.

                                            (CONTINUED)
```

A painful ending

(04–06) When Amini was wrestling with how to adapt **The Wings of the Dove**, he latched onto the idea of ending the script with a sex scene that leads to the breakup of the scheming Kate (Helena Bonham Carter) and her lover Merton (Linus Roache) **(05–06)**. "In the book, it's not a sex scene," Amini says. "Henry James had this breakup scene, but my thought was that through the course of the movie, these two characters have destroyed their love by being careless about it and taking it for granted. By the end, it's become so corrupted that they break up." Amini based the ending of Kate and Merton's relationship partly on a breakup he'd experienced as a teenager, which he refers to "as that last desperate attempt to keep it alive—the awfulness of that feeling." But he was also inspired by Barbara Stanwyck's performance as the doomed *femme fatale* in **Double Indemnity** (1944). "I saw Kate as a *femme fatale*," Amini says. "There is a vulnerability to those types of characters—they wreak havoc, but destroy themselves in the process."

2.

CONTINUED:

She moves on top of his naked body and looks down at him.
Merton smiles gently and raises his arms to her shoulders. He
touches them lightly. Kate looks back into his eyes.

                    KATE
          What are you thinking about?

                    MERTON
          Millie.

                    KATE
          You are still in love with her.

                    MERTON
          I was never in love with her.

                    KATE
          Whilst she was alive, no.

Kate smiles sadly and helps him inside her, wincing slightly
from the pain. She lies down softly on his chest and starts to
move. They both look close to tears.

                    MERTON
          I'm sorry, Kate.

                    KATE
          It doesn't matter.

                    MERTON
          She wanted us to be together.

                    KATE
          We will be.

Kate wipes his tears away with tender fingers. She sways a
little faster now. They turn around together and move in slow,
perfect time. Neither looks at the other.

Kate groans softly as he finishes inside her. She moves quickly
to his breast. She doesn't want him to see her crying.

Merton breathes hard. He holds her for a moment in his arms.
His fingers gently explore her face. He feels her tears. For a
moment neither speaks.

                    MERTON
          I'm going to write that letter.

                    KATE
          Do whatever you want.

                                              (CONTINUED)

3.

CONTINUED: (2)

                    MERTON
          I want to marry you, Kate.
               (There's a long silence)
          Without her money.

                    KATE
          Is that your condition?

                    MERTON
          Yes.

                    KATE
          Am I allowed one too?

                    MERTON
          Of course you are.

Kate buries her face deeper into his chest. She kisses it
softly, her eyes wet.

                    KATE
          Give me your word of honour...Your word of
          honour that you're not in love with her
          memory.

Merton stares out. He doesn't reply. They stay there a moment
longer in each other's arms.

Kate rolls away from him and gets out of bed. She takes her
clothes and walks into the next room.

Merton doesn't follow her. He lies in bed and listens to her
put her clothes back on. He hears her walk out of the door and
close it behind her. He hears her footsteps on the stairs. He
makes no attempt to follow her.

He lies back and stares at the ceiling. There are tears in his
eyes. He rolls over on his front.

Writing an action scene

(01–04) One of **Drive**'s signature set pieces is its opening action sequence, an almost real-time heist that introduces the audience to the Driver's (Ryan Gosling) skill as a getaway man. "It was the one sequence that probably changed the least," says Amini. "It was there from the first draft, right to the finished thing. We had such specific research going into it. I spoke to the head of security at Universal, and he told me, 'There's no way you can get away from a helicopter in Los Angeles.' And I said, 'What if the Driver goes under a roof?' So, we devised the whole thing around that idea." Amini's scripted sequence contained almost no dialogue (02–03). "That was one of the first really big action sequences that I'd ever written," he recalls. As far as how the sequence played out on film in comparison to his script, Amini says, "It's maybe slightly longer on the page, but all the beats are there. But what made it special in the movie was Cliff Martinez's music and the angles that director Nicolas Winding Refn was shooting inside the car on Ryan's face. That's what a great director will do: The same sequence could have been shot by another director, written exactly as it was, and it wouldn't have worked nearly as well."

01

02

```
19   CONTINUED:                                          5.
                                                         19

                        POLICE SCANNER
                 ...1 David 11...suspect headed West on
                 Pico...

     Driver threads his way through the vehicles in front of him, so
     smooth and effortless it's hard to tell how fast he's going. He
     glances up as he hears the dull rumble of a police chopper
     overhead. The helicopter is almost directly above him, swinging
     its search-beam back and forth to get a lock on his position.

     Driver pushes the car as fast as it will go, but there's no way
     of outrunning the chopper. Blue light floods the asphalt around
     him as he guns down Figueroa.

                        POLICE SCANNER
                 All units...pursuit in progress...silver
                 Impala...Headed North on Figueroa...

     Even now Driver doesn't panic, turning his attention back to
     the basketball game.

                     BASKETBALL COMMENTARY
                 Thornton pulls up from behind the arc,
                 misses. Rebound New York. One eighteen to
                 play...

     Driver swerves sharply towards the sparkling lights of the
     Staples Centre.

20   INT/EXT. IMPALA/ STAPLES CENTRE/ PARKING LOT - NIGHT.    20

     The terraced parking lot looms up ahead. A sign above the
     barrier says 'Season Ticket Holders Only'. Driver punches in a
     ticket and roars into the parking lot.

21   INT. IMPALA/ STAPLES CENTRE PARKING LOT - NIGHT.         21

     The Impala screeches from one level to the next. With a game
     going on, the parking lot is almost full. Finally Driver pulls
     into a free parking space.

                     BASKETBALL COMMENTARY
                 ...Thirty seconds remaining and all the
                 Knicks have to do is run out the clock...

     Driver glances in his side mirror. Behind him, dozens of FANS
     are already streaming out into the parking lot before the game
     is over, hoping to avoid the inevitable traffic.

                     BASKETBALL COMMENTARY
                 ...Gordon back to Davis...Davis for
                 three...This is unbelievable!...

                                              (CONTINUED)
```

03

```
21   CONTINUED:                                          6.
                                                         21

     The jubilant commentary continues, but Driver isn't listening
     anymore. The game has served its purpose. More fans flood into
     the parking lot. Dozens of cars pull out of their places.

                     BASKETBALL COMMENTARY
                 ...What a remarkable comeback...Outplayed
                 for most of the game, the Clippers have
                 shown incredible resilience...

     Driver glances at the armed robbers and nods. It's time. They
     climb out of the car, merging in with the crowd. Driver watches
     them disappear, then slips on a Clippers cap, climbs out of the
     Impala himself and heads towards another car.

     EXT. STAPLES CENTRE/ DOWNTOWN L.A. - NIGHT.

     Outside the parking lot, the police are waiting, stopping
     anything that looks like an Impala, shining their flashlights
     into the windows. Wearing his Clippers cap and a Clippers
     sticker on his new car, Driver calmly drives past them, making
     his getaway.
```

Hossein Amini | Interview   21

"There's a struggle with integrity that I definitely feel as a writer, and I think every writer in Hollywood would probably say the same thing."

interested in. I ended up doing stuff that I wasn't particularly suited to.

Pretty quickly after I signed up with Miramax, there was an opportunity to work on **Gangs of New York**—that was the carrot. I thought, "If my career at Miramax is working with people like Martin Scorsese, why not?" I did one draft with Scorsese in New York before it got green-lit, and then I came in and did about three or four weeks' work in Rome just before they started shooting. It wasn't enough to get a credit, but it was an amazing experience. Unfortunately, I was rewriting **The Four Feathers** at the same time. **Gangs of New York** was the one I really wanted to be writing, and **The Four Feathers** was the one I was struggling with. But being the Miramax rewrite guy meant sometimes not necessarily working on the ones you wanted to work on, but instead the ones that they needed work on. It was an odd time: At one stage, I was flying between Rome for **Gangs of New York** and Morocco for **The Four Feathers**. **The Four Feathers** was very troubled from a very early stage—I felt caught between a director who had one vision and a studio who had a different vision. So I had this experience of going from the set of **Gangs of New York**—where everyone was really happy and there was real excitement—to this very troubled production where people were arguing the whole time.

I loved the way **Drive** was received in the sense of the reviews and the awards, but I think everyone else was disappointed with the US box office—it became about the fact that it didn't make the money that everyone was expecting. But I'm really proud of the film. With **Drive**, I was going back to **Jude** and **The Wings of the Dove** where I felt, "This is what I really want to write, and this is who I am, and this is what I should be writing." I'd done some big rewrites of things that haven't got made or were made badly—movies where I think back and wonder, "Did I feel passionately enough about it to do it?" There's a struggle with integrity that I definitely feel as a writer, and I think every writer in Hollywood would probably say the same thing. Sometimes

the movies you're drawn to and the ones that pay you the best are very, very different. With **Drive**, I was reclaiming some of that integrity. Before **Drive**, I'd never been offered one of those types of films—this dark, Western-type contemporary *film noir*. It was what I would have done if I had been offered them at the time of **The Wings of the Dove**—I just wasn't being offered those movies. But **Drive** was certainly where my cinematic passions lay, much more than in period films.

The moment I read James Sallis' book *Drive*, I was absolutely desperate to do it. **Le Samouraï** (1967) had been a huge influence on me, as had **Shane** (1953). I loved those "man with no name" Westerns—the idea of the silent hero. And I just loved that whole LA mood. I had gone back and forth from LA a lot for various studio assignments, but I don't drive. But you're more fascinated by LA if you don't drive—when you're on the street, you're so aware of the fact that you're the only person walking. I've always loved LA as a city, and I read a couple of books about

01 Snow White and the Huntsman (2012) starred Australian actor Chris Hemsworth as the Huntsman

SNOW WHITE AND THE HUNSTMAN

(02–03) Hossein Amini occasionally does rewrite work on big studio projects, such as **Snow White and the Huntsman**. "Universal approached me really late in the process," recalls Amini. "I worked on it for a little more than two months, but I don't know if there was enough time to be fully invested in it. I was doing what I could—character work, really. The shape of the film was there already, so it was one of those that feels like a job. It was one of those situations you get into as a writer where the studio is happy with something that you've done before and they need work on something else, and it's good money and you already have a relationship with them." As a studio rewriter, Amini notices he's often brought in for a specific reason. "They look at you as the guy who has done some artier-type things and that you're good with characters. I think the idea is to bring you on to reassure the actors and work with them on developing their part. I really enjoyed doing **Snow White and the Huntsman**, but honestly, it was such a rush in terms of needing to get the budget down and getting the page count down. I mean, they'd already started storyboarding it in places. At that point, the actors are already cast, and the director knows the scenes he wants. There's really not time to play around creatively—it's a race against time."

the city's downtown history, which I thought was just amazing. And **Chinatown** (1974) was a movie I'd always loved—there is something magnetic about LA as a film city. So as I didn't drive, the studio got someone to drive me around everywhere, and it was fantastic just going into all these places. I got this big map of LA, and I constantly thought about having the characters going from one place to another—I was always looking at maps trying to figure out getaways.

For a few years now, I've been putting together a film version of Patricia Highsmith's *The Two Faces of January*, which I'm going to direct. The character of Chester that Viggo Mortensen plays is a con man—everyone looks up to him and loves him. But gradually through the course of the movie, that's stripped away, and he ends up completely defeated. A movie like that, you have to do it on a smaller budget. It's like **Drive** or **The Wings of the Dove**—in a sense, they're not commercial movies. The things that I'm drawn to aren't commercial. I don't particularly like happy endings, and I like people who are ambiguous

and have contradictions and vulnerabilities— I like my heroes being slightly fucked-up. The period when I was growing up watching films, the blockbusters were **The French Connection** (1971), or **The Godfather** (1972), or **Chinatown**. I mean, **Chinatown** has the down-est ending. But those were the blockbusters, and those were the movies that were making lots and lots of money. And the problem is because I grew up on those movies, those are the big Hollywood movies that I'd love to make.

I think **Snow White and the Huntsman** made more money in its opening weekend than anything I've ever done put together. It's an interesting conundrum. As writers, we're desperate for everyone to love and go see what we write. But then I think, "Well, maybe I'm just not a very commercial writer." I mean, I'm intensely proud of **Jude**, and nobody went and saw that. So, sometimes I think, "Well, I can't have both—you can't get good reviews and get good box office." There are so few films that achieve both. "

Guillermo Arriaga

"I learned something from the very beginning: People buy what you sell. You shouldn't think, 'Oh, they're gonna shoot my script! Oh my, yes, oh, I'm so happy!' I was very clear from when I was 15: 'This is my work, you respect it. You don't want to respect it, I will not do it.'"

Babel (2006)

When screenwriter, novelist, and director Guillermo Arriaga was 10 years old, he practiced giving acceptance speeches with a Coke bottle. The reason, he explained to his parents, was because he was convinced he would win an Oscar, a Nobel Prize, or an award at the Cannes Film Festival. He's already achieved one of those goals—he was honored at Cannes with Best Screenplay for **The Three Burials of Melquiades Estrada** (2005), which also won Best Actor for director Tommy Lee Jones—and he's been nominated for the Academy Award for Best Original Screenplay for **Babel** (2006). Born in Mexico City, Arriaga is at the forefront of Mexican artists who have brought his country's cinema to the attention of worldwide audiences in the 21st century. With director Alejandro González Iñárritu, he wrote the screenplays for **Amores Perros** (2000), **21 Grams** (2003), and **Babel**, films that were praised for their unflinching view of humanity's darkness while at the same time offering hope in the form of community and individual compassion. Arriaga directed his first feature in 2008: **The Burning Plain**—which starred Charlize Theron, Kim Basinger, and Jennifer Lawrence—and continued his passion for nonlinear stories and complicated, compelling characters. Throughout his work, Arriaga has explored how different languages, cultures, and borders can divide people—but as well how those divisions can be broken down in unexpectedly moving or terrifying ways. A celebrated short-story writer and sports enthusiast, he is also the author of the novels *The Night Buffalo* and *A Sweet Scent of Death*.

Guillermo Arriaga

"I come from a tough middle-class neighborhood. It's not like I was in the slums, but I was drawn to trouble. I spent a lot of time on the streets. When I was a kid, I got into a lot of fights, and there was a lot of violence—extreme violence. That's where my inspiration comes from. There are people whose inspiration comes from books—mine comes from life. I had a discussion with Quentin Tarantino, who's a friend, and I told him, "What hurts sometimes about your movies is that you make fun of violence. And for me, it's real—a friend of mine can be decapitated. Violence here, it's real."

Writing came from my need to tell what was going on. I have severe ADD, and many teachers thought that I was just dumb. Expressing myself was difficult, but when I began writing I could put my thoughts in an orderly manner.

At the age of nine or 10, I began writing letters to girls—I was completely crazy for girls since I was, like, two years old. The letters didn't work so well with the girls. I was very shy. When you have ADD, your self-confidence is eroded. You don't feel you're intelligent—you feel you have no understanding of the world. I was flunking, and I was punished often. I was expelled from one school when I was 12, but I got into another school that really saved my confidence. You had to take theater, and I began writing theater pieces. The teachers were very encouraging about my writing—"Yeah, yeah, do it!"—and it helped me a lot.

Playing sports as a kid helped my confidence, too. With sports, I learned something very valuable. I was a very good basketball player, but when I was playing in championships, I felt so much pressure that I didn't play well. And I learned that you can't allow pressure to get into your system—there's no point. Players say, "Enjoy it just for the sake of playing. If you miss, you miss. If you fail, you fail. But enjoy it."

When I was 15, I wrote a play that we rehearsed for almost a year. We were two days before opening night, and the actors told me, "If you don't change the ending, we will not be in the play." They didn't give me any reason to

change it—they just said, "We don't like it." I said, "I'm not gonna change the ending." So they said, "We've been rehearsing for almost a year and you're gonna spoil everything just because you are stubborn?" I said, "Yes, I'm not gonna do that. All the work and the effort, I don't care—I'm not gonna change a word of it." It's not that I was stubborn. When you write, there's a logic to it—there's an organic need for everything that's in it. So if you don't like something I wrote, tell me why. If you tell me why, maybe I can consider it, but I don't just change something because people say, "Change it." →

01 Goya Toledo as Valeria, the model who loses her livelihood in the car crash that provides the unifying link of the three stories in **Amores Perros** (2000)

"I don't write any kind of outline. I don't want anything that constricts me—I don't want any kind of chains. And I don't develop any backstory or backgrounds for the characters—I have no idea."

03

AMORES PERROS

(02–03) The three jumbled storylines in **Amores Perros** are joined together by a devastating car accident. Guillermo Arriaga got the idea from a scary situation he was lucky to survive. "I was sleeping in the backseat of a truck without any safety belt—just laying on the seat," he recalls. The driver lost control, and they flew off a cliff. "We crashed and we began rolling, and I woke up in the middle of that. I had amnesia after that accident. I thought, 'What happened before the accident? What happened during the accident? And what happened after the accident?' That became the structure of **Amores Perros**."

"I put every effort in a screenplay to having beautiful language and a beauty of structure and a beauty in the construction of characters."

I've found there are many ways to protect your work. Everything is negotiable. You can say in your contract, "No one can change a line"—then it's in your contract. I learned something from the very beginning: People buy what you sell. You shouldn't think, "Oh, they're gonna shoot my script! Oh my, yes, oh, I'm so happy!" I was very clear from when I was 15: "This is my work, you respect it. You don't want to respect it, I will not do it."

ADD people, we don't think in a linear way—we jump all around. So the reason why my stories are nonlinear comes more from my ADD than anything. My first play, my first book, every short story—they all have time lapses. I just thought that was the organic way to tell a story. And then I read William Faulkner and Juan Rulfo—I remember reading *The Sound and the Fury*, and I thought, "Okay, it's possible."

I have a mild infection in my heart—it's in the membrane that covers the heart called the pericardium. It's nothing grave if you take care of it, but I was training to make the boxing team for the Olympics, and it got so swollen that I almost had a heart attack. That's when I decided I have to write every day, and I haven't stopped. I have lots of little skulls around my place, so when I am tired and don't want to write I see them and say, "Okay, man, you have to go and write." So I finish almost everything I begin.

I've written novels and screenplays, and with a screenplay you are writing something that's going to be filmed, and you have to understand that. But, for me, both are forms of literature. I hate when people say, "When are you going to go back to literature?" I say, "I never left." You never say that to a theater writer—I don't know why drama for the cinema is lesser than drama for the theater. So I feel that I'm always doing literature. I put every effort in a screenplay to having beautiful language and a beauty of structure and a beauty in the construction of characters. To make a film requires the interests of a lot of people—actors, directors, producers, financiers—and the way to draw them in is to write a beautiful piece. So this is literature. →

Quentin Tarantino's dialogue

(01) When Arriaga rewrites his screenplays, one of the first things he does is trim dialogue. "I don't like long dialogues," he says. "I hate them. I think that you need to be a genius like Quentin Tarantino to do it. I once told him, 'You know the great damage you're doing to cinema with your dialogue? You have a talent that no one has, and everyone wants to copy you. That talent for dialogue—it's basically you and Woody Allen, and that's it.' And Tarantino said, 'You know the huge amount of damage you've been doing with your twisted structures and twisted characters?'" Arriaga laughs while recounting this story, but he's very serious about the distinction between "good" dialogue and "colorful" dialogue. "Good dialogue is not writing only beautiful things," he insists. "It's making the story move forward. Many, many people think that the dialogue is only having a little bit of color, you know—they don't know that Tarantino's color is driving us some place." The "foot massage" conversation (01) in Tarantino's **Pulp Fiction** (1994) is a great example of his hardworking dialogue.

21 GRAMS

(02–05) "It takes a long time for me to write a first draft," says Arriaga. "Once I have the first draft, I begin questioning all my decisions." In the case of **21 Grams**, while Arriaga drew from his own heart condition for Sean Penn's mathematician, other characters changed radically. For example, the born-again convict played by Benicio Del Toro was at one point a wealthy businessman. "I question and question, and I change things," Arriaga says. "That's what I call rigor—you explore and question all your creative decisions."

THE THREE BURIALS OF MELQUIADES ESTRADA

(01–04) Because Arriaga draws from personal experiences in his work, it's understandable that he might have a deep emotional connection to his characters. But that's particularly true with **The Three Burials of Melquiades Estrada**, which tells the story of a Texas rancher (Tommy Lee Jones) who seeks an unusual vengeance for the death of his friend, illegal Mexican immigrant Melquiades Estrada (Julio César Cedillo), at the hands of a racist border cop (Barry Pepper). "Melquiades Estrada is the name of a friend of mine," he explains. "He's a poor farmer, he and his brothers—they are now living in the States. So, I know what it means to leave your family and to be heartbroken because you leave for 10 years without seeing your kids grow up. These are my friends—they are my compadres. I'm the godfather of their kids. We speak by phone every week, and we're still very close. I know that world. I'm not an illegal alien, but I have close, close friends from 30 years ago who are illegal aliens that have no idea how to read and write. They are making a living in the States, and they are honest people."

When I'm writing something I'm going to direct—like with **The Burning Plain**—my commitment is still to the story. I should not cut corners or compromise anything—I have to tell the story the way it has to be told. If I begin thinking as a producer or as a director while I'm writing, I am damaging the story. When I'm actually directing, then I will think how to make it work—I always have to think that the writer did it for some reason and I have to respect that. Charlize Theron was very intelligent on this point—I remember sometimes that things were turning difficult and I would say, "Let's just do this," but she would say, "No, I will never betray the great writer you are." That's a nice compliment, but she was also right—we needed to look back to the way it was on the page. →

"A mistake new writers make is over-exposition. I have a rule with my students: A scene can be no longer than one page, and the dialogue can be no longer than two lines. That forces you to concentrate."

05 The Three Burials of Melquiades Estrada (2005)

Different writers, different techniques

(01–02) Although Arriaga doesn't do research when he writes, he knows that's not everyone's approach. The year that he was nominated for the Best Original Screenplay Oscar for **Babel**, so was Peter Morgan for **The Queen** (2006). "He told me, 'Research is the basis for everything,'" Arriaga says. "And I was like, 'Come on, man—I don't research.' But we're different—he's writing about people he doesn't know personally, and so he's writing about things that you need to research about to make it credible. I'm writing about things that happened to me, so what's the point of researching? We had fun mocking each other: 'Oh yeah, research, research . . .'"

I'm obsessed with language. Once I have the first draft, I begin polishing it in terms of the beauty of the language. I don't know if it translates correctly in English because I write in Spanish, but I'm very careful not to repeat certain words through the whole screenplay, such as in the description of the action. I'm obsessed with the weight of every word.

I never do any kind of research—it's a waste of time for me. I always write about things I know and that have happened to me, so I don't need research. For instance, I had never been to Japan and Morocco when I wrote **Babel**. But

03 Amores Perros (2000)

> **"It's one thing to defend the integrity of your work, but it's dumb not to listen to other people's thoughts. I listen carefully to every note my friends give me—I'm humble enough to be quiet and listen."**

I was absolutely sure **Babel** was going to be believable—I had never been to Morocco, but I have been to the mountains in Mexico. I had been with goat keepers, and they behave exactly the same everywhere. I've been to extremely remote places, and I think they should be exactly the same. And it's funny, because many Moroccans and many Japanese ask me, "Wow, how many years did you live over there?" We have many more things in common than we think.

I don't write any kind of outline. I don't want anything that constricts me—I don't want any kind of chains. And I don't develop any backstory or backgrounds for the characters—I have no idea. And I have no idea of the ending—not a single idea of how this script is gonna end. That's how I work.

I always like to go against everything—no research, no outlines. And I hate this thing of writing "likable" characters. I always try to write the most horrible, hateful characters who do the meanest things. But even these people, you'll identify with them. For example, the character that Gael García Bernal plays in **Amores Perros**: This guy is trying to steal the pregnant wife of his brother. He fights his dog in order to get money. → **04** Babel (2006)

04

BABEL

(01–04) The multi-character, multi-locale **Babel** was inspired by one of Arriaga's enduring passions. "Hunting is my life," he explains. "If they outlaw hunting, I will be in serious trouble." One particular memory from childhood had stayed with him. "I was a kid, and my friends and I were in the desert with a .30-06 or some other high-caliber rifle." Arriaga and his friends were curious about the rifle's range, his pals particularly skeptical of the gun's claims that it could fire a bullet a distance of five miles. "So they said, 'Let's shoot the gun and see what happens.' I kept this idea in my mind for many, many years afterward: 'If I shoot, what happens to the people I shoot at?'" The incident gave birth to the harrowing journey of **Babel**'s Brad Pitt and Cate Blanchett. But there was also an underlying concept guiding the film. "I always work from a concept," Arriaga says. "If I didn't have a concept, it's difficult. Maybe I don't have an idea how it's gonna end, but I have a concept. And with **Babel**, the concept was, 'This should all happen in 24 hours—and it's something that will change the life of the characters forever.'"

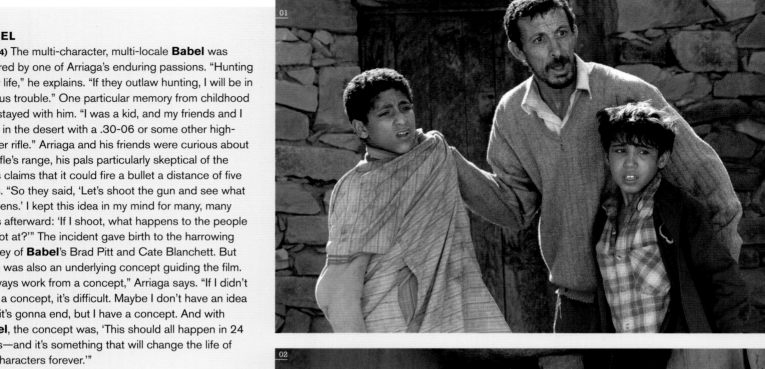

"I have to tell the story the way it has to be told.
If I begin thinking as a producer or as a director
while I'm writing, I am damaging the story."

He kills his best friend—and you still are with him. Or with **The Burning Plain**, Charlize Theron's character is disgusting, manipulative, cold, she fucks everything. And in the end, you say, "I'm with her." I love that. I don't ever consider this notion of "likable." I just write the story as creatively as I want. We all live in shades of gray, so it's not a problem if people will like a character. We are all like these characters—we're all more flawed than perfect.

Every Sunday from 7 to 12 p.m., I get a group together—my friends, my wife, and my kids—and we read 10 pages of what I'm working on.

I ask some of them to read it out loud, but I ask them not to lay any emotion on the words. Sometimes they want to act the scenes, but I say, "No, no, just read it plain. I want to see how it's working and how it sounds." And then when we're done, I ask a lot of questions, and I allow them to say anything they want, including "This is shit." If they know where the story's heading, though, I say, "No, this is heading in the wrong direction—it's too predictable. This is not the right way."

It's one thing to defend the integrity of your work, but it's dumb not to listen to other people's thoughts. I listen carefully to every note my →

05 **Babel** (2006)

05

"...with **The Burning Plain**, Charlize Theron's character is disgusting, manipulative, cold, she fucks everything. And in the end, you say, 'I'm with her.' I love that."

friends give me—I'm humble enough to be quiet and listen. Then I can say, "Okay, perfect, let me try your note." I always feel confident in my work, but I always feel it's a necessity to listen to other people's views. That doesn't make you an insecure person—instead, it's like, "I'm so confident that I can listen to anyone," you know? If you are very unsure about what you're writing, when someone criticizes you, you just die. Instead, I'll think, "I'm sure that I'm on the right track—I just need input to make it better." If you're confident, you can hear other people's criticisms and say, "Hmm, okay," and listen. It's like walking around naked—people are checking you out, and you think, "My body is looking bad, but I'll just do some exercise."

A mistake new writers make is over-exposition. I have a rule with my students: A scene can be no longer than one page, and the dialogue can be no longer than two lines. That forces you to concentrate. Another mistake they make is they don't have a voice—they are trying to copy someone else. I remember I was at the University of North Texas, and there were these kids I invited to lunch. They were writing stories about murderers and killers and blah, blah, blah, and I said, "Tell me about your life." And one of these kids says, "I come from artificial insemination—my mom went to a sperm bank— and I have all this mystery about who my dad is." I said, "That story is by far more interesting. Why the fuck are you telling these ridiculous stories? Write about yourselves—that's much more interesting."

No matter how harsh an environment you have and how violent it can be, there's always a way out. We have in ourselves a strength we never imagined. Really, I'm the most optimistic person in the world—I think the films I've written are feel-good movies. It's like, "If these people can get out of these extremely harsh situations they have, I can get out of my problems." I'm addicted to optimism. There was something that I loved that happened a lot with **21 Grams**: When it was over, people called their kids or their loved ones to say, "I love you." That's

optimistic, people watching a film and going, "I need to tell someone 'I love you.'"

Writing can be therapeutic, but I'm not exorcising demons. I'm just having a lot of fun. I love creating worlds. You know, it's funny: You are writing these scripts in the loneliness of your room, and then something comes out and it touches the lives of so many people, and it's overwhelming. How can you not enjoy that? **"**

01   The Burning Plain (2008)

THE BURNING PLAIN

(02–05) Arriaga made his feature directorial debut with **The Burning Plain**, which he also wrote. "I will always consider myself a writer," he says. "No matter what I do—produce, direct, anything—my heart is the heart of the writer. But, you know, this is lonely work and it can drive you crazy. Directing allows you to be outside with actors and other people, and I enjoy that a lot." But Arriaga rejects the notion of writers directing their own work just so they can retain control of their words. "It's not about control—it's about collaboration. I love collaboration and I love having people around who are all working in the same direction."

John August

"No matter the script . . . you're trying to make sure every moment can stand in for the whole movie. It needs to be fractal in a way. And yet, each of those moments has to be advancing the plot, too."

Charlie and the Chocolate Factory (2005)

John August wrote his first story, about a boy who gets trapped in a hole on Mars, at the age of seven on his mother's typewriter. From there, he's developed into one of Hollywood's most in-demand screenwriters, notably working on several projects with director Tim Burton. Their partnership began with **Big Fish** (2003), which earned August a BAFTA nomination for Best Adapted Screenplay. From there, he wrote the screenplay to **Charlie and the Chocolate Factory** (2005) and co-wrote the script for **Corpse Bride** (2005). More recently, August has collaborated with Burton on **Dark Shadows** (2012) and **Frankenweenie** (2012), the full-length adaptation of the director's cult 1984 animated short. August's first screen credit came from his original screenplay for the comedy-thriller **Go** (1999), a funny, vibrant examination of a collection of different characters on Christmas Eve. He co-wrote **Charlie's Angels** (2000) and **Charlie's Angels: Full Throttle** (2003), which combined have grossed more than $520 million worldwide, and **Titan A.E.** (2000), a multiple nominee at the Annie Awards, which recognize excellence in the field of animation. In 2007, he wrote and directed the provocative mind-twister **The Nines**. When he's not writing scripts, he devotes time to his website, johnaugust.com, where he discusses the business and art of screenwriting.

John August

" I was pretty sure early on that I'd be a writer, but I didn't know what kind of writer. I had no idea that screenwriting was a thing that existed.

I went to Drake University in Des Moines, Iowa, for their journalism and advertising program, which is a pretty good surrogate for screenwriting. Journalistic writing is very focused and structured, much like screenwriting. And advertising is a good blend of the creative instincts and the business instincts. Pitching an ad campaign is very much like pitching a movie:

"A lot of writers will play music while they're writing, or they'll have a scent that reminds them of the movie's world and smelling that gets them back into it. Anything's fair game as long as it works."

You're describing what it's going to be like when it's all done, but you're not describing every little step along the way.

A take on the book

(01–02) When August first met with Tim Burton about **Charlie and the Chocolate Factory**, the director had one question for him: "He asked me, 'Have you seen the Gene Wilder film?' I said, 'No, should I see it?' He's like, 'No, no, no, no—never see that movie.' He wanted me to come in clean and not have that in my head." But August was very familiar with the book, which was written by Roald Dahl. (In fact, August was such a fan of the author that he wrote to him in the third grade.) "What I remembered about the book from when I was a boy was thinking that Charlie Bucket was really, really lucky because he lives in this little house with a family who loves him so much," August remembers telling Burton. "Even if he never won the ticket, he's the luckiest kid in the world. Willy Wonka is this sad man who lives alone in a factory with these crazy Oompa-Loompas." Burton loved August's take, telling the writer, "I want everything from the book and then as much else as you need to add so that it all makes sense as a movie." August went back to the book, highlighting every passage he wanted to include in the film **(02)**. "I knew from the start that I would be flipping protagonists," August says. "Even though it says **Charlie and the Chocolate Factory**, Willy Wonka is really the protagonist—he's the one who changes. There's nothing for Charlie Bucket to really overcome—he's a good little kid who wins a ticket, and that's great. He's not a bad kid who learns a lesson. It's Wonka who has to make progress. So I filled out his backstory and gave him a father, which wasn't in the book at all. I made sure that the flashbacks were pushing his story forward and giving us more information about that character."

01

02 August's highlighted copy of *Charlie and the Chocolate Factory* (reproduced courtesy of Random House and David Higham Associates)

BIG FISH

(03–05) Big Fish is based on the novel by Daniel Wallace, which August was able to read before its publication in 1998. "My agency had sent it over," he recalls. "It was just a box of pages. I had overnight to read because they were going to take it out to try to sell it." He instantly gravitated to the story. "My father died six years before, so I very much knew what that experience was like—trying to deal with a dying guy in your house. But I also knew what would need to change for it to be a movie. The narrator of the book is the son, but the son really isn't a character. I needed to build that character out—I would make him my age so that the time-shifts between him and his father would be the same as between me and my father. I would make him a journalist because I was a journalism major. And I gave him a French wife because I needed there to be someone to be on the son's side that he could talk to about the situation." But once August got the idea for how to tackle the script, he then had to try to convince Sony that he was the right person for the job, even though he was still very early in his career. "I was not great at pitching at that point," he admits. "When I was pitching **Big Fish**, I described the two through-lines we were following. In one storyline, we're seeing the grown son and the father trying to come to terms with the truth behind his father's stories before his father dies. And in the other storyline, we're seeing the father's stories as he envisions them, so they're big and fantastical and larger than life. And the question kept coming back: 'Well, what is the tone?' And finally, in frustration, I said, 'Well, it's funny, and then it's funny, and then it's funny, and then it's funny, and then you're laughing through tears, and then it's over.'"

The first script I ever finished was a romantic tragedy set in Boulder, Colorado, my hometown. It had all of the classic first-script problems: I tried to wedge in everything I knew about everything into this one script because, well, maybe I'll never write another script. But it turned out pretty well, and it helped me get an agent, and the agent got me started. The script was called *Here and Now*, and it involved the atomic clock and was based very much on the scientific community that I grew up around. And it was weepy—it was my first weepy. In the script, you think you know what the tragedy will be, but then there's this surprise tragedy. It made people cry, which was great, and it started a precedent

of "John August makes people cry." I was writing for myself, and I had a sense that some people would like it.

I deliberately wrote something that wasn't like the other spec scripts that were selling at that time, which were much more high-concept. This was something small and personal and specific. I think specificity is where you recognize good writing: It feels like the writer actually knows what he or she's talking about and that the characters exist in a very clearly defined world. They're not in a generic movie world. You know, for the studios, it's important to write movies that make their concept clear—that you could make a poster for—but this wasn't going to be that. →

> "If I'm the second writer on a studio project, then I definitely want to make sure that the first writer understands that I'm not the enemy. If I'm being brought on the job, that other writer is going to be off the job. That decision has already been made."

When I was at USC's Peter Stark producing program, which was before I'd ever written a screenplay, we had an assignment to write the first 30 pages and the last 10 pages of our script—which is a genius trick because, by the time you've written all of that, you're going to want to finish the script. It very much set the way that I write screenplays today. I've never felt the burning need to write in order. I will write whatever moment in the script feels right for me at any given time. I may not have a physically written outline, but I'll have a good-enough sense of what all the scenes are in the movie before I start writing. If I sit down one day and I don't

really want to write that one scene, I can write any other scene. There are scenes that are really easy and there are scenes that are really hard, and sometimes it's better to just bang out the easy scenes so you can achieve a critical mass.

For **Big Fish**, the most difficult scenes were the opening 10 pages—which establish the two timelines and the nature of the conflict—to make sure it felt like one movie rather than two movies. I knew I had to crack the opening so I could figure out how to get the story started. The death scenes are the kind you push as far back in the process as you can because you know it's going to be hard when you get there.

THE NINES

(01–03) August made his feature directing debut with **The Nines**, a series of three vignettes whose connection becomes more apparent as the film unfolds. "That was a movie it wouldn't make sense for anyone else to direct," explains August. "I mean, the script was hugely autobiographical. It fit my brain very specifically, and so to try to explain to somebody else how to direct **The Nines** would be crazy. Plus, it was a chance to experiment with some things that I was just curious about. I'd restarted time before in **Go**, but my curiosity was whether you could have a movie in which the stories are stacked on top of each other. The three chapters of **The Nines** are not just nonlinear—they're nested in impossible ways." The actors (including Ryan Reynolds, Melissa McCarthy, and Hope Davis) play multiple characters, and the film bounces around between fantasy, drama, and satire, all the while touching on themes such as the nature of reality, the mystery of creativity, and the existence of a higher power. "There were a bunch of ideas that had sort of competed in my head for a number of years, each demanding to be written," August says. "Eventually, I realized they were all versions of the same idea: 'What is a creator's responsibility to its creations? At what point are you allowed to walk away from things you've done?' And I realized that these three stories could actually mesh together as one movie."

Being a craftsman

(04) As a Hollywood screenwriter, sometimes August will be hired for a short amount of time to fix a film that's trying to get into production. He won't do enough work to earn an onscreen credit, but he can help pull the script together. "I did two weeks of work on the first **Iron Man** (2008)," he says. "That was a really strong script, but then there was a section about midway through that had been rewritten fairly recently, and you could sort of smell the whiteboard markers. You could tell that these were great ideas—they just hadn't been fully implemented. So, I help implement them a little bit better. You're making small changes, and you're moving some stuff around in order to best utilize what you have. They had Robert Downey Jr., and they were trying to get Gwyneth Paltrow at that point, so in those cases, you're not the architect—you're just the craftsman. You're just the guy who's in there to build some cabinets and help it be better."

While working on **Big Fish**, I got very Method: I'd stare at a mirror until I could get myself crying, and then I would start writing. It was literally days of just staring at a mirror and crying, but it works—something about that process captures the right feeling. And by getting myself to the point of crying, it helped me get other people to that point. I had done it before with another project, a horror movie, so the process for that was to get myself terrified and then write. A lot of writers will play music while they're writing, or they'll have a scent that reminds them of the movie's world and smelling that gets them back into it. Anything's fair game as long as it works.

I haven't really done any acting, but I've read the books on acting. When I write, I'm playing all those characters until we assign it out to others. I'm a really good actor internally—I'm not a great actor externally. But screenwriting is essentially watching these scenes happen in your head and then figuring out words to describe it. I've always had a pretty good ear for dialogue. Dialogue is basically listening to how people talk and then optimizing it. It's saying, "If people had an extra five seconds while having a conversation, how would they optimize their words so it would sound best?"

You have to treat every script as if it's the first thing they've ever read of yours. Coming in with

a reputation doesn't give you any free passes. I've been frustrated by screenwriters who will get to an action sequence and just write, "Now comes a kick-ass action sequence that will blow you away." Sorry, but you actually have to write that.

A lot of the time when I'm coming in to help a project, I'm there to get the dialogue better and fix some story problems—but sometimes I'm just there to make it read better. Over the course of a project with different writers, the script gets messy, and it doesn't feel like a movie. And by going through and spending the time to make everything read better on the page, you give them a better sense of what this movie is that they're trying to make. Screenwriters are not just writing this for the director or the producer. A well-written script helps the costume designer know what the world feels like, and that's important, too.

If I'm the second writer on a studio project, then I definitely want to make sure that the first writer understands that I'm not the enemy. If I'm being brought on the job, that other writer is going to be off the job. That decision has already been made. If it wasn't me, some other writer would be doing the rewrite. But you want to know where all the bodies are buried, and I mean both in the script itself—what are the real challenges with the project?—and also what's really going →

> **"Go** was actually useful as a script because it showed people, 'Oh, you write comedy. You can write action stuff. You can write women.' However you wanted to look at **Go**, producers could use it to justify hiring me for something."

on and who do I need to be careful around? I've been rewritten on projects, too, and I always want to pass along that information, because you want things to be taken care of as best they can be. Screenwriters can be grownups and talk about this stuff calmly.

I met Tim Burton for the first time in Los Angeles right before he went to Alabama to make **Big Fish**. It was just a very general conversation about some of the things that we couldn't afford to shoot and how we could find less expensive alternatives. Considering how many movies share our names, I've spent very little time with him. Throughout all of **Big Fish**, I met with him for maybe two hours, and that includes when I was in Alabama for table readings and helping out where I needed to

help out. Most of my relationship with Tim has really been like that: I write something, he shoots it. I'm like a department head—I'm the guy that gives him the script, and then he goes off and does it. A screenwriter loves a director like that. Some directors want to walk through every line and every moment with you, and that's their process and that can be great. But some directors don't, and that's Tim—and that's worked out well.

When I'm writing, I have to have a sense of what the final movie should feel like. So with **Charlie's Angels**, it felt like your dorky kid sister who wins the Olympics—you're annoyed by her, but also proud of her. I wanted the movie to have a bright, sunny, Southern California feel to it. With **Go**, it's the experience of being 22 and picking yourself up, dusting yourself off, and everything

Writing the scene

(01–02) For August, writing a scene goes through three stages. "In my head, I'm figuring out what happens in the scene and I start hearing the characters talk." He quickly jots handwritten notes about the scene, which he calls the scribble version **(01)**. "I fold up the page four ways," he says, "so I can just put it in my back pocket." Then he handwrites the scene in screenplay form **(02)**, which his assistant then types up. Both **(01)** and **(02)** shown here are early versions of **Dark Shadows**. "In the scribble version, I get the rough idea of what the dialogue is and what the scene is. At this next stage, each page takes me about 20 minutes to write. I'm looking at it word-by-word and making it clear and clean. There'll be some times in here where I will make changes even as I'm doing stuff—I'll have little stars and asterisks for moving lines to different places after I've started." At this second stage, the dialogue that August crafts doesn't change too much when he goes to the final stage, the typed screenplay. "I try to get the scene really, really, really good the first time. I'm not one of those people who does the 'vomit draft' and then goes through and cleans up. I really try to get it the way I think the scene should be the first time. Sometimes I'm wrong, and I throw it out and have to start over again. But I try to get the scene right the first time."

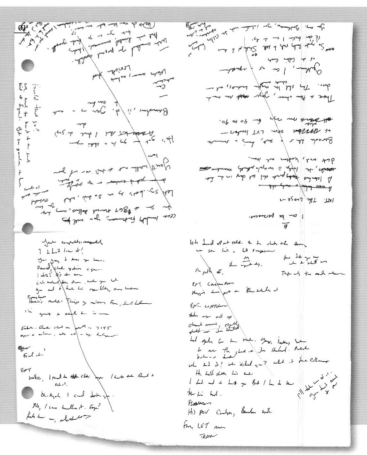

working out okay in the end. No matter the script, though, you're trying to make sure every moment can stand in for the whole movie. It needs to be fractal in a way. And yet, each of those moments has to be advancing the plot, too.

Even if **Go** hadn't been shot, that script was hugely helpful for me. When I wrote that script, I had already been hired to write the adaptation of the kids' book *How to Eat Fried Worms*, which was over at Imagine, and I'd done another kids' book adaptation over at Dimension of *A Wrinkle in Time*. Because of those, I was only being considered for kids' books or things involving gnomes, elves, dwarves, or Christmas. It can actually be really helpful to be typecast as a certain →

GO

(03) Go tells three interlocking stories that take place on one eventful Christmas Eve. It originated as a short that August wrote in graduate school about the Ronna character (played by Sarah Polley in the film). Encouraged by friends, he decided to develop the 30-page script into a feature, although he knew he didn't want to make it just about Ronna. "I always knew that I didn't want to just expand Ronna's story," he says, "because it worked in its tight little form. But all those other characters were in there already, and I knew exactly what they were doing the rest of the night." He was grateful for **Pulp Fiction**: "Thanks to that film, there was a precedent for restarting a movie and time-shifting. So I decided to restart **Go** and follow each of the three storylines. The great advantage of restarting something is you get to have three first acts and all the energy that goes along with coming up with new stuff to do." **Pulp Fiction** proved additionally helpful by showing others **Go**'s potential. "If that movie hadn't come out and been successful, no studio would have ever let us do it," says August. "And the audience wouldn't have been prepared for what we were. But because people liked **Pulp Fiction**, that made it okay and made it safe—it wasn't weird that we were doing this."

DRUGS 1 of 1

INT WYNDCLIFF SANITARIUM - DAY

Maggie sits center-frame, slouching in a patient's uniform. In a drugged stupor, she looks up as an orderly's HAND offers a paper cup filled with pills. She's slow to accept it.

Suddenly, another ORDERLY grabs her from behind, pinching her nose shut, while prying open her mouth. The pills go in, she's held until she swallows.

We move through days and weeks, in a continuous shot. Through it all, Maggie remains center-frame as the sanitarium swirls around her. She eats, sleeps, takes pills. Watches Tom and Jerry, plays checkers, stares at her OBESE PSYCHIATRIST. She's a passenger on this ride.

The sun goes up, down, up, up, up, down. She sits at Thanksgiving dinner. She watches as a Christmas tree is decorated. She stares at the blinking colored lights.

TRANSITION TO:

1

CHARLIE'S ANGELS

(01–03) When August came on board to rewrite the 2000 big-screen remake of **Charlie's Angels**, there was significant work to do. August recalls: "Ryan Rowe and Ed Solomon had written a script. Everyone loved the opening set piece—the same opening set piece that's in the final movie—where the Angels are parachuting out of the plane. But the rest of their script went in a very different direction. It was about cloned supermodels, and didn't feel like the same movie." So when he met with Drew Barrymore, who was also one of the producers, they spent their first four meetings simply talking about the tone and feel of the film. "I loved the show," he said, "and thought it was a unique opportunity to make an action movie where you were oddly proud of the girls. Also, it could be funny—the girls could be incredibly confident while they were on the job, but super-dorks when they were off the job. Comedy's never about cool people—comedy's about dorks." But despite the film's playful tone, August says writing the script was actually rather complicated. "**Charlie's Angels** is a surprisingly difficult movie, screenwriting-wise, because you have three protagonists, plus Bosley, plus a villain—and you needed to be surprised with the villain. So every scene had to do two or three things. You couldn't have a scene that was just a comedy moment for this one character. Everything had to be plot and comedy and character and advancing the romantic subplots."

kind of writer—at least then they can think of you for a certain kind of job—but I didn't want to only do those things. So I knew **Go** would be a chance to break out of that mold. Studios liked it, and producers liked it, but everyone thought, "Well, it's an R-rated comedy with teens and there's drugs in it—we can't make this movie." But it got me in a ton of meetings, and it got me hired to write stuff for other people, like **Blue Streak** (1999), the Martin Lawrence comedy. I got brought on to make things edgier—never mind that I was the same person who they were only hiring for little kids' things before that. So, **Go** was actually useful as a script because it showed people, "Oh, you write comedy. You can write action stuff. You can write women." However you wanted to look at **Go**, producers could use it to justify hiring me for something.

There are movies that are really yours, and you feel deeply connected to them. You've lived inside them for a long time, and they've become a part of you. And then there are other movies that are like friends you meet at camp: They're lovely, but you don't feel any deep, special connection to them. What's frustrating as a screenwriter is that there are a lot of those projects that I have deep, emotional connections to that aren't movies now. They're just frozen as 120 pages of typed Courier, and that's really maddening. For example, I have a script for a version of **Barbarella** (1968) that I wrote for Drew Barrymore. I would love to get that made. But I know that the rights will never be able to sort themselves out, and it's absolutely impossible to make that movie. But, other things, there might be potential. The challenge 10 or 20 years into your career is trying to decide at what point you give up on some projects.

The most frustrating time as a screenwriter is when you have to do another draft when you don't genuinely believe in the studio notes you've been given. It's sort of like the doctor's credo:

The limitations of animation

(04–05) August has worked on the scripts for **Titan A.E.** **(04)**, **Corpse Bride**, and **Frankenweenie (05)**, all animated films. And while the format allows for more inventiveness in some regards, August notes that there are also unexpected restrictions as well. "During the time I worked on **Titan A.E.**," he says, "it went from being all hand-drawn to all computer animation to the mix of things that it became. Every week, I would get a different set of instructions saying, like, 'Water's okay, but characters can't get wet.' Or even now with **Frankenweenie**, the puppets are amazing, but there are limitations: 'This character can't sit down—it's not built to sit down.' Or you can't have a scene with a lot of extras in it because, in stop-motion animation, each of those extras would take weeks to animate. So you have to be more mindful of that stuff. You write the script, and then that script, rather than going to the actors, goes to the story department, and the story department breaks it all down into storyboards and figures out which line of dialogue is going over which shot. In animation, you have to do it shot-by-shot so you can figure out the whole thing. And so sometimes, the story department will change things because of a different story idea or maybe because of some practical reason. You have to just accept that that is going to happen to some degree."

"First, do no harm." You can feel yourself violating that and trying to find the balance between what the movie is that you want to write versus the movie that they want to make. And sometimes, you can't always find a happy balance there. But if it's a scene the director doesn't like and doesn't understand, he will never be able to direct it well, so, therefore, you have to change it. That's just reality. If the actor can't make the line make sense, you have to change it. The real frustration is when the note comes from someone who's not really the person who's going to be executing the plan. Maybe the junior development exec has this one note that he feels has to be taken into account. You have to do that note because, otherwise, you're not going to make forward progress on getting the movie made. But it's not a good note, and it will not get the movie closer to being made in the way you want it to be made.

"The most frustrating time as a screenwriter is when you have to do another draft when you don't genuinely believe in the studio notes you've been given."

When you're a screenwriter, you're not the final artist. You're not directing these scenes. You can put your heart into it, but you have to know that your heart can get broken. That's tough, and you have to go through your little mourning process. But the good thing is that, unlike a lot of the other jobs in the film industry, you can always pick up your pen and write something new any time.

Woody Allen

Few film artists have been as prolific, talented, and utterly dismissive of their body of work as Woody Allen. "When I'm home lying on my bed and I'm writing something, I have these incredible ideas," he once said. "I think I'm going to write **Citizen Kane** every time out of the box, and it's going to be so great. And then I make the film, and I'm so humiliated by what I see afterward. I think: 'Where did I go wrong?'"

He is far too modest. Born in December 1935 in New York's Bronx, Allen has been steadily writing and directing (and often starring in) his own films since 1969, and he's proved equally capable at delivering hilarious comedies and thought-provoking dramas. Both have intrigued him since his childhood: In his teens, he was already selling jokes to local newspapers, but he was also intrigued by the great European films that were making their way to American cinemas. "Suddenly I saw that movies could actually be something substantially wonderful," he recalled. His journey to moviemaking began in earnest when he wrote the 1965 comedy **What's New Pussycat?**, but his unhappiness with how the film turned out convinced him that he needed to direct his screenplays in the future. Thus began a level of creative control that has been the envy of several generations of filmmakers.

After early success with comedic films like **Sleeper** (1973) and **Love and Death** (1975), Allen made a major creative breakthrough with **Annie Hall** (1977), a mature romantic comedy that went on to win four Academy Awards, including Best Picture and Best Original Screenplay (which Allen shared with co-writer Marshall Brickman). Determined to stretch himself, Allen spent the next several years making films that demonstrated the breadth of his ambitions, moving from the Bergman-esque drama of **Interiors** (1978) to the grand-canvas romantic melancholy of **Manhattan** (1979) to the 8½-inspired **Stardust Memories** (1980). The switching between serious and lighter fare has been a cornerstone of Allen's work ever since,

01

and indeed some of his very finest films are the ones that have merged the two: **Hannah and Her Sisters** (1986), **Crimes and Misdemeanors** (1989), and **Husbands and Wives** (1992).

Allen has received 23 Oscar nominations, winning four: three for writing and one for directing. Because of his self-effacing manner, he would probably diminish his own accolades. ("The whole concept of awards is silly," he said in 1974.) But perhaps he would be more receptive to the six Academy Awards that have gone to actors in his films, which explains in part why performers happily sign up for his projects, even if it means playing small roles for not much money. Indeed, few contemporary writers have crafted so many memorable parts, whether it's the movie-mad Depression-era wife (played by Mia Farrow) of **The Purple Rose of Cairo** (1985), the adulterous murderer (Martin Landau) of **Crimes and Misdemeanors**, the emotionally adrift philosophy professor (Gena Rowlands) of **Another Woman** (1988), or the lovable titular heroine (Diane Keaton) of **Annie Hall**.

As he is so prolific, Allen has experienced fallow periods in his career—it would be impossible not to have a few duds over the course of 45 films—but even his weakest efforts reveal an insight into eternal human concerns. Allen's writing grapples with how people struggle to find contentment: through love, through success, through a few laughs. But, as his characters discover repeatedly, those comforts don't last—a fact that supplies his films with their poignancy. At age 77, he remains as searching as his protagonists, and for audiences around the world, that tireless quest for meaning has been one of the greatest, most enduring rewards the cinema has offered over the last four decades. "I'm obeying nobody but my artistic muse," he once said about how he decides what project to write next. "The experience is doing the project; the critical and commercial responses are not terribly relevant. Doing the idea and expressing yourself, maintaining your own criteria, is."

02   Interiors (1978)

03   Hannah and Her Sisters (1986)

04   The Purple Rose of Cairo (1985)

05   Husbands and Wives (1992)

Mark Bomback

"I try my very best in every film I'm working on to try to make you fall in love with those characters. I feel like my number one job, regardless of the genre I'm working in, is to get you to care about the plight of the person whose story I'm telling."

Unstoppable (2010)

An English Literature and Film Studies major at Wesleyan University, Mark Bomback was inspired to pursue screenwriting by watching films like **La Dolce Vita** (1960) and Sam Fuller's **The Steel Helmet** (1951). And although his first produced credits were for unsuccessful projects, **The Night Caller** (1998) and **Godsend** (2004), he has more recently positioned himself as a respected event-movie writer. This process began with his script for **Live Free or Die Hard** (a.k.a. **Die Hard 4.0**) (2007), the highest-grossing **Die Hard** film worldwide and the one responsible for reviving the series after a 12-year absence from the big screen. Since then, he has worked on the screenplays for action films such as **Race to Witch Mountain** (2009) and **Total Recall** (2012). Additionally, he has done uncredited rewrites on projects like **Constantine** (2005) and **Rise of the Planet of the Apes** (2011). However, his finest script to date is 2010's **Unstoppable**, which was based loosely on an actual runaway-train incident that occurred in Ohio in 2001. He's modest about his status as an A-list action writer in Hollywood, saying, "I do feel like I've recently been added to a list that's really hard to get on—although I suspect I'm somewhere on the bottom half. The goal is to continue to slowly move up that list. But it's a very hard list to get on, because you have to be a true closer, and you're compensated accordingly."

Mark Bomback

I'm not sure I knew the term "screenwriter" until I was in my teens. I loved movies, but I rarely read the credits—I probably couldn't have told you the names of many of the people who directed the films I liked. Truthfully, when I was in high school and thinking a little bit about film as a career path, the filmmakers I liked were mostly writer-directors, so writing just seemed a function of getting your movie made. You know, "Spike Lee has to write a script, or else there's no movie." I probably falsely thought that Steven Spielberg wrote everything that Spielberg directed.

But when I got to college, I entered into a great film program. Wesleyan is so theory-heavy—film production was really secondary to understanding the language of cinema. The program was unconventional in that we didn't watch a lot of European films—we were exposed to the classics, but the focus was primarily on American directors like Capra, Hawks, Hitchcock, and Wilder; there was even a whole class just on *film noir*. It was around that time that I saw **In a Lonely Place** (1950) and **Barton Fink** (1991), two movies about screenwriters, and I realized, "Oh, there's this job, the screenwriter, a very particular job in which you're this mistreated, tortured intellectual." It wasn't totally accurate, I later discovered, but it depicted a tragically romantic vision of that job that intrigued me.

I had a very secure, safe childhood, and I suspect there was something about this slightly self-destructive artistic calling—which, at the same time, had some sort of institutional security to it—that was very appealing. I didn't read Kerouac and say, "Oh, I want to throw my life away!" It was more like, "I want to have a nice house and have a stable life, but I also want that tortured-artist feel." It sounds entirely pretentious, but I believe a part of me was drawn to that struggle to create something of value in the face of all the obstacles inherent in making a studio picture. The college-me thought there was something romantic about that struggle. But it's funny: I don't think the protagonists of **In a Lonely Place** and **Barton Fink** have inspired many people to become screenwriters.

After college, I moved to Los Angeles and found a job reading scripts and writing coverage. I must have read in that year, conservatively, 150 scripts, and most of it was frankly garbage. What was amazing to me, though, was how much of the crap was bound in script covers from top agencies like CAA and Endeavor and William Morris. There would occasionally be stuff I'd read that was so great that wouldn't get bought, and then there was this swathe of stuff in the middle—very good, not great, but separating itself from the crap mostly because of a really solid, cohesive idea at its core. The script might not be beautifully written, but it urged you to turn the page. And so early on I realized that was half the battle: You need to make a script very readable, and it has to have a truly strong idea as its engine.

Maybe this is just me, but I do feel that a lot of my friends who write experience a similar sensation where, deep down, they're a little bit worried that everyone's going to figure out that they really don't know what the hell they're doing. I remember searching for any interviews with writers I admired where they would admit that they ultimately feel a bit fraudulent. I think it was a big thing for me to make peace with the feeling that I was somehow faking people out. Most people feel that way when they're doing something creative. Confidence is such a massive part of being a screenwriter. Only in the last five or six years do I feel my confidence has risen to the level where it's become an asset. Sometimes if I have a really important meeting, I will actually say to myself, "Be the person that they want you to be when you walk in that room. Give them that sense of security so they feel like, 'Okay, we hired the right guy.' Save your anxieties for when you're home at midnight at your laptop." And it does become something of a self-fulfilling prophecy—you sit down to write and you think, "They wouldn't have hired me if they didn't think

". . . early on I realized that was half the battle: You need to make a script very readable, and it has to have a truly strong idea as its engine."

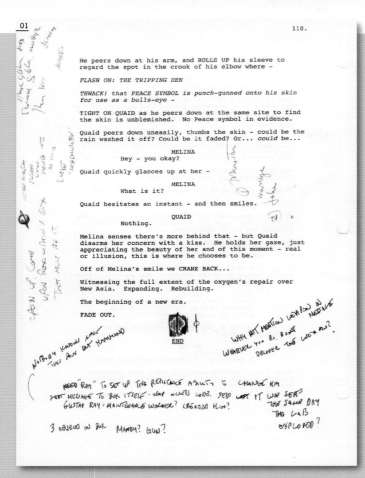

01 Handwritten revisions to the
final scene of **Total Recall** (2012)

He peers down at his arm, and ROLLS UP his sleeve to
regard the spot in the crook of his elbow where -

FLASH ON: THE TRIPPING DEN

THWACK! that PEACE SYMBOL is punch-gunned onto his skin
for use as a bulls-eye -

TIGHT ON QUAID as he peers down at the same site to find
the skin is unblemished. No Peace symbol in evidence.

Quaid peers down uneasily, thumbs the skin - could be the
rain washed it off? Could be it faded? Or... could be...

                    MELINA
            Hey - you okay?

Quaid quickly glances up at her -

                    MELINA
            What is it?

Quaid hesitates an instant - and then smiles.

                    QUAID
            Nothing.

Melina senses there's more behind that - but Quaid
disarms her concern with a kiss. He holds her gaze, just
appreciating the beauty of her and of this moment - real
or illusion, this is where he chooses to be.

Off of Melina's smile we CRANE BACK...

Witnessing the full extent of the oxygen's repair over
New Asia. Expanding. Rebuilding.

The beginning of a new era.

FADE OUT.

                    END

A new take on a classic: find your own angle

(01–02) Bomback experienced the challenge of remaking a popular film when he signed on for the remake of **Total Recall**, starring Colin Farrell in the role that was originated by Arnold Schwarzenegger. "When they approached me about it, I said I hadn't seen the original since it was in the theaters," recalls Bomback. "I watched it again, and my response was, 'Honestly, I just think it's a really good film. I don't really have any insight into how to make it significantly fresh or better. I'm probably not the right guy.'" Much later, Len Wiseman, the director of **Live Free or Die Hard**, approached Bomback after coming on board **Total Recall**. "They had a script by Kurt Wimmer that needed to be rewritten, and I looked at it. Kurt had come up with a fresh take that really worked. I thought, 'Oh my God, how did I not see this? You take out going to Mars and keep it on Earth, and it suddenly becomes like a futuristic **Bourne Identity** (2002).' He'd found a new way to tell the story. Plus, what's great about the original Philip K. Dick short story is that core idea of once you've given your mind over to something, you'll never really get it back. You'll never be 100 percent sure of what's real and what's not. It's like this acid trip that won't end. It's almost ludicrous to suggest that a movie shouldn't have been remade when it contains such a strong hook that could be taken in another direction." As to the comparisons audiences will make between the two films, Bomback admits, "It will bum me out if people who have seen the original film go in with two strikes against our version simply because it's a remake of a film they remember fondly. I do believe that if you were to watch the two films back to back, you'd probably find some things you'd like about the older one better; you'd probably like that you laugh more and that some of the action is so ridiculously over-the-top. But my hope is that you'll find that the new film is a more successfully told story. We certainly closed off a lot of the logic gaps, and it has a different kind of energy and pacing."

I was the right person for this job. I wouldn't be sitting here doing this for a living if I wasn't meant to do it. I would have wiped out by now.''

Live Free or Die Hard was a movie I really had no business writing. Prior to that, I had been working on a rewrite of a movie Bruce Willis was attached to star in, and although that movie fell apart, Bruce and his producing partner at the time, Arnold Rifkin, liked the work that I had done on that. They were looking for a writer to write

a new **Die Hard** movie. My only produced credits at that time were **Godsend** and **The Night Caller**, and so I desperately wanted to make a move toward films that would have a higher profile. More importantly, I just really loved the first **Die Hard** film—I like the second two a lot, but the first one I loved. Also, this was right around the time that this franchise fever kicked in at the studios, and I realized it was probably smart career-wise to work on a →

Script doctor on call

(01–02) After **Live Free or Die Hard**, Bomback was asked to rewrite several other Fox projects, such as **Rise of the Planet of the Apes**. Asked what Fox looks for from him as a writer, Bomback replies, "In terms of rewrites, Fox probably comes to me because I'm fairly adept at making every element feel organic to the story as a whole, and when I'm done with my pass, the film makes more sense both on a narrative level and on a character level. I've gotten pretty good at diagnosing what's not working in a script, isolating certain things: 'What is this character's path to repair or destruction? What's broken about this character that you want to see fixed?' Having that concern threaded consistently through the whole story, really getting involved with what a character's situation is, seeing that dilemma in some way mirrored in the larger theme of the story, keeping those things working in tandem—with some of these big-budget films, that aspect of the storytelling can get lost in the shuffle as the studio and the director near production. I'm brought in to really make sure the script results in a movie about a character's journey, and that the larger ideas in the movie stay serviced throughout."

franchise because, if you succeed, more opportunities may follow. And what better franchise than **Die Hard**? It just seemed so ideal to me. And so I killed myself pitching the best take I could. I sensed immediately that the execs at Fox in the back of their heads were like, "We're doing a favor to Bruce and Arnold, we'll hear this guy's pitch, but there is no way on Earth we're hiring the **Godsend** guy." But fortunately I'd come up with a couple of ideas that they were genuinely thrilled by. I got very specific about how John McClane's character would evolve over the course of the film. I was really into the analog/digital thing. My angle was, "The fun of this movie is that a **Die Hard** movie itself seems like a relic of another era, and so we're going to play with that and have McClane himself seem like a man out of time." I was very into the idea of this character reclaiming his genre. So they hired me. But I was positive the Fox execs were thinking, "We'll just fire him after the first draft and bring in someone who really knows how to do this kind of writing." And because of that insecurity, I wrote that first draft almost out of spite, but also with a desperate certainty that everything was on the line career-wise. And my first draft of that film

wound up being the best first draft I'd ever written at that point. It was coherent—you could see what the movie could be. Most important for a **Die Hard** film, I managed to capture McClane's voice in the humor. So I wasn't fired, and that movie opened the door for every other I've worked on since.

I did a rewrite of the upcoming sequel to **X Men Origins: Wolverine** (2009), and when I came on board, the existing script wasn't really about "enough." In other words, it was a little too beholden to some ideas within the Wolverine universe that didn't actually expand outward to anything fundamentally relatable. I just saw **The Avengers** (2012) last night, and to me it's a perfect example of how to execute a comic-book movie. You want people who are in the know to feel really satisfied, but at the same time you don't want to isolate people who just decided to finally try one of these films. First off, it's shortsighted. Thirty years from now, it's unlikely your audience will demand an insane amount of fidelity to the source material—they're just going to want to watch a well-written movie. Do you want them to enjoy your movie or not? So the **Wolverine** script they had was just a little too insular, and what I tried to do was find some things about Wolverine's

> "At any one time, I'll have about five or six things floating around in my head, story-wise, that I can devote varying amounts of energy to."

character that were more relatable and universal, particularly the notion of Wolverine's potential immortality. Is that a blessing or a curse? How does one go about living their life when everyone around them will eventually die and they don't? It may not be the newest idea under the sun, but it's an interesting way for an audience to engage with his character.

A big misconception that people have about these franchise movies is that all the studios care about is the action. It's very cynical and untrue to believe that studio heads don't care whether the movie has a solid story and real characters. When the studio execs are talking with the cinematographer, say, or with the publicity department, then sure, they don't need to worry about the characters. But when they speak with the writer, they are focused almost exclusively on issues of character and narrative to make sure that the story really is working as best it can. It would be easy for me to sit back and blame the studio system and say, "Well, how could you make a great movie in this system? All they care about is the explosions." They do want movies to be big and spectacular, but they desperately want their movies to have stories populated by characters with which people can relate. They're hiring a screenwriter to make sure that happens. I try my very best in every film I'm working on to try to make you fall in love with those characters. I feel like my number one job, regardless of the genre I'm working in, is to get you to care about the plight of the person whose story I'm telling. I want my audience to be able to answer the question "Why did this movie have to happen to this person?" And so when I'm writing, I'm constantly answering that question for myself. The wonky development term for this is, of course, the character's "arc," but it is, for me, a crucial component to a successful film.

Take **Unstoppable**. There were two big ideas going on in terms of who the characters were and how they might grow. One was that these are two people who have lost the ability to value themselves. They no longer have any self-worth. And coupled with that was this runaway-train →

Action, but with an arc

(03) Before scripting **Live Free or Die Hard**, Bomback hadn't written many action sequences in his career, although he was a big fan of the genre. But he got some insight from an executive at Fox. "A then-studio exec who's now a producer, Alex Young, was smart enough to help me compartmentalize," Bomback recalls. "He assured me, 'The action is going to take care of itself when we bring a director on. Just write the action in the most fun way you can and don't get too hung up on the particulars. Really make sure the story works and the character stuff is clicking—at the script stage, the action is the least of our concerns.' Of course once you get closer to production, then the action becomes the most of everyone's concerns. But, ideally, you've done your development right so that the other elements have all been taken care of and you're focused solely on the action. Len Wiseman, who directed that movie, loves working on set pieces, so it would have been foolish of me to go crazy and try to get too specific in terms of beat-by-beat action. I would come up with ideas for set pieces—I'd say to him, 'Here's the big-idea thumbnail sketch for this action sequence'—and Len would then say, 'Well, here's some ideas I have for that.' And then we'd just go back and forth. My job was to take his ideas and make sure they flowed well in terms of how the scene worked, incorporating the dialogue as best I could into the sequence's structure, and, most important, trying to make sure the characters had some sort of journey over the course of that set piece. The best set pieces are where the characters have made a move forward in terms of their arc, whether it's that their relationships have changed slightly or they've learned something through the ordeal of the action. The writer's job on an action film for the most part is coming up with just the big idea for each of the set pieces—and keeping everything else alive within it."

03

DECEPTION

(01) The 2008 thriller **Deception** was sold as a pitch called **The Tourist** several years earlier by Bomback. "I was into this idea of a secret world where people who had very high-powered jobs could blow off steam at night by having anonymous sex with each other and then go back to work," he recalls. "It was called **The Tourist** because it was about what it means to live your life in hotel rooms. The protagonist was periodically getting mistaken for a tourist, and on a character-level he was a tourist in his own life." Excited about the idea, he attempted something he'd never done before. "I started writing without coming up with a true plot at all—I just was writing. I had these particularly strong 30 pages of a first act, which I would give to my friends to read, and they would be like, 'Oh my God, this movie's going to be great. I can't wait to read the rest.' Little did they know I didn't have much more road in front of me. I kept circling back through the first act—I wasn't able to move forward." Nonetheless, he sold the idea, although he admits the rest of the story "wasn't really well thought-

out." When he tried to complete the script, he discovered that finishing it was as difficult as he'd feared. "The first half of the script was so much stronger than the second half, and I realized the hard way that it was a mistake to have thought of writing a film without at least conceiving of the broadest strokes of what the second half of the film should be." Eventually renamed **Deception**, the film went through a few other writers before finally opening to bad reviews and mediocre box office. "It's hard to talk about that movie without blaming a lot of other people," Bomback says. "I hate sounding that way, so I'd rather just not get into it. But if I'd written a better script, it would have been a better film. When I think about it now, what strikes me is that it forecasts its punches so early that I can't imagine anyone is really fooled by much of the plot. There's just so much blame to go around in every different direction when a movie doesn't work, but a large part of the blame does fall to myself. If there'd been a great script from the outset, there wouldn't have been as many problems."

01

RACE TO WITCH MOUNTAIN

(02–03) One of the first projects Bomback worked on after the success of **Live Free or Die Hard** was **Race to Witch Mountain**, a family action film starring Dwayne Johnson. "It was really geared for kids," he recalls. "The action was almost nonexistent—it just had a very PG or G tone to it. But Disney felt there was an opportunity to make an action movie for kids, and they were fans of **Live Free or Die Hard**, so they said, 'Couldn't you **Die Hard**-ize this script that we have?'" Bomback took the job, but he soon realized it wouldn't be that easy. "Once you start changing the tone and the style of the action, the characters need to then behave accordingly. It became a pretty decent-sized overhaul. The films they were using as models were **T2** (1991), **Die Hard** (1988), **Lethal Weapon** (1987)—they really wanted it to have that kind of energy. I wouldn't have written **Race to Witch Mountain** in the other direction, like if they had said, 'The movie's too hard-edged—we need to make it cuter and softer.' That's not where my strengths lie." Asked his opinion of the final film, Bomback admits, "I don't know what I would think of **Race to Witch Mountain** if I hadn't worked on it. I don't know if I would have liked it or not—I really have no perspective on it. But I know my kids genuinely liked it, and their friends really liked it. I got a lot of enjoyment out of watching them watch it. And to this day, if I ever meet a kid and they ask me what I've worked on, they always think that's the coolest movie." Bomback laughs. "So I'd qualify it as a success."

> " ... when [the studio representatives] speak with the writer, they are focused almost exclusively on issues of character and narrative to make sure that the story really is working as best it can."

motif—sometimes events contain no rhyme or reason, and life will just kick you in the ass out of nowhere. Those are the moments when your mettle is tested. And so that script was me finding a way that two characters, who on the surface don't seem to really have very much in common, discover over the course of this one crazy day that they are indeed valuable people.

At any one time, I'll have about five or six things floating around in my head, story-wise, that I can devote varying amounts of energy to. Usually one or two of them are really a priority that need to be focused on today. That juggling is as stressful as you allow yourself to make it. Personally, I think it's stressful working on the cure for cancer—I think it's stressful being a cop. I don't think it's really that stressful being a screenwriter. To me, the stresses aren't so much about the work. Maybe they used to be more so, but I feel like I've gotten good enough at my job that I wouldn't have taken on these projects if I

didn't believe I could write them well. So I don't really lose too much sleep worrying about "Oh, I'm not going to be able to deliver what they've asked for." However, I do sometimes lose sleep thinking "If this doesn't turn out as well as I think it has, what will that mean for future jobs?" Or put another way, I guess my stresses have more to do with the inevitable career highs and lows: "Is this the high? It feels like it's going pretty well, but if this is as good as it gets, does that mean that things are going to go south soon?" I feel like every job I have, I'm at the free-throw line. You have to sink every shot. But I feel that kind of internalized stress is a useful motivator, and pales →

An antagonist without rationality

(01–03) When writing **Unstoppable**, Bomback had two different inspirations for the film, which stars Denzel Washington and Chris Pine. "I was very into **The West Wing**," says Bomback. "So my thought process was 'I'm going to borrow stylistically from **The West Wing** when I write this.' And so it had that Sorkin-esque bouncing-from-person-to-person-to-person thing—everybody just talking, talking, talking while they're moving." The other reference point was **Jaws** (1975). "You have an antagonist that you cannot rationalize with," he explains. "I was so burnt out on trying to write good villains, which I'd never been really that great at, so it was a pleasure to take the villain out of the equation. I structured the movie like **Jaws**: Every 10 minutes, the shark will appear. And the movie was paced like **Jaws**, where it's going to be more leisurely at the start and then get faster and faster."

02 Handwritten notes made to a draft of the script for **Unstoppable** (2010)

03 Notes from interviews Bomback conducted with train engineers

01

02

8-25-09 White 9.

15 CONTINUED: 15

FRANK
I got only one rule: you do something, do it right. If you don't know how to do it, ask. ~~See that guy over there with nine fingers? He didn't ask.~~ *
*

Will smiles at this. ← Frank knew * you gonna set me up w/your daughter?

FRANK
Likewise, you need something from me, you gotta speak up. You're the conductor - once we've got our freight, it's your train, I'm just the guy driving it. How long you been out of training? *

When you gonna set me up w/ your mother.

WILL
About 4 months. How long have you been ~~railroading~~?

FRANK
About 28 years. What'd you do before this?

WILL
Bunch of different jobs. *

FRANK
~~Anything but~~ railroading, huh? *
No

WILL *
No. I was just looking to do something-different. *

FRANK *
you mean Better? *

WILL *
Different. *

FRANK *
~~So what I've been doing all my life is your last resort.~~ *
*

Will looks self-conscious, but Frank takes it in stride. *

FRANK *
I get it. You said 1206, right? that's the one *

Will nods as they arrive at locomotive 1206: a tough engine with lots of miles.

FRANK
Let's run our checks.

CUT TO:

03

can ease them on gradually, but when you release them, they come off completely. If you're trying to stop a train in a precise position, you use minimum throttle to pull it up exactly where you want it.

CAN'T EASE OFF A TRAIN BRAKE, USE THE THROTTLE.

How could the brakes slip off?

There's a separate brake handle, separate throttle.

The engineer also has locomotive brakes - these are called "independent brakes."

The whole train brakes, including for the locomotive, are called "automatic air brakes."

The engineer has the option of "bailing off the brakes" (slang), which means you have the automatic air brakes on for the whole train, but you take off the locomotive brakes.

On older locomotives, the controls are on the left side of the engineer in the following positions:

The handle on top: the automatic air brakes

The handle on the bottom: the independent brakes

The throttle: 45 degrees forward left-hand position

Also: many locomotives have a third set of brakes, the "dynamic brakes," which are underneath the throttle, they take the electric motors on the locomotives and use them as generators that feed electricity into a resistor grid, and in that way they brake the train electrically

On newer locomotives: have a "control stand" where the engineer sits. It's like a desktop control, with T-handle levers

T-HANDLE LEVERS

6. How do you stop a runaway train? YOU DON'T.

You generally can't. The train usually wrecks before you can do anything, so generally railway companies don't have procedures for stopping runaway trains.

There were two runaway freight train incidents in Cajon Pass, California (1995 and 1996, both have NTSB accident reports - Lauby was involved in the

BOMBACK ON MYSTIC RIVER

(04–05) "It's no secret: We all know the best writing is on TV right now," says Bomback. "**Mad Men**, **Breaking Bad**, **Sherlock**—to my mind these are the best-written programs right now. But I'd say the one thing that TV lacks is a sense of closure, and I think sometimes you desire a really interesting, engaging narrative that also will end. I feel that movies took a weird right turn somewhere in the late 1980s or early 1990s. This notion of an 'indie film' emerged, and the bigger budget movies stopped having the burden of being really great dramas. And then TV took over the indie film space, so there's even less room for movies that are not necessarily beholden to the genre they're in." But happily for Bomback, there are exceptions. "To me, the last really great studio movie of that medium-big size that I was just super-excited about was **Mystic River** (2003). I just thought, 'Wow, this is a stunning example of what movies do well.' I think the writing in **Mystic River** is just as good as what you see on TV. It doesn't hurt that it's based on a fantastic book [by Dennis Lehane]. But there's no TV version of **Mystic River**—it was meant to be a movie. I think in some ways it's as good if not better a movie than it is a book, because it benefits from spot-on casting and excellent directing. And it's a really well-written screenplay by Brian Helgeland. I think he is so gifted at taking source material that seems on the surface pretty readily adaptable, like **LA Confidential** (1997) and **Mystic River**, and finding the absolutely perfect way to re-tell the story cinematically."

in comparison to the stresses of many other jobs.

I now live outside of New York City. The reason we moved from LA was simply for family—my wife and I wanted our kids to be raised near my brothers and their children and my parents. I didn't really think through what it would mean to be a screenwriter here—I knew it would require a lot of travel back to LA, but the unexpected discovery has been that it's actually easier to do my job from here. For one thing, if I go out to LA for meetings, people tend not to cancel on me because they know I'm only in town for a couple of days, so they actually bend over backwards to make meetings productive. When I work with directors or producers, we hunker down and get a lot done quickly because they know I'm going to go back to New York. Another advantage of living here is that when I was living in LA, I had stopped thinking that being a screenwriter was cool. In LA, so many people, even if they're not screenwriters themselves, they know

screenwriters, or they work in another part of the business. Not only does screenwriting become just a job, it becomes a job where you're competing with your neighbors. You're at Starbucks, and everyone has a laptop open. The people I know here in New York don't work in the film industry—they work in finance or they're doctors or teachers or photographers. Because of that—this is going to sound a bit precious—but I do believe there's simply more creative energy to go around out here in suburban New York. It belongs to me more. I have come to appreciate what I do for a living in a way that I'm not sure I ever would have if I'd remained in LA. I should add that I'd hoped that my kids would think my job was cooler here in New York than they might have if we'd raised them in LA. But that's actually proved to be the complete opposite. They tell me that if I was really cool, we would have stayed in LA. But you can't have everything.

Jean-Claude Carrière

"The world is changing all the time, and so is the movie language—it's impossible to stop it. You must be in the flow of the river, not looking at the river passing by—you must be inside, you must dive."

Belle de Jour (1967)

French writer Jean-Claude Carrière's creative life has encompassed novels, plays, cartoons, poems, and short films. But it is his screenplays that have most assuredly cemented his position as one of the century's great writers. Receiving his start in cinema in the mid-1950s by writing book adaptations of director Jacques Tati's **Mr. Hulot's Holiday** (1953) and **Mon Oncle** (1958), Carrière eventually teamed up with comic filmmaker Pierre Étaix on two short films, including the Oscar-winning **Happy Anniversary** (1962). From there, he began a long and fruitful collaboration with director Luis Buñuel, a 13-year partnership that resulted in six films: **Diary of a Chambermaid** (1964), **Belle de Jour** (1967), **The Milky Way** (1969), **The Discreet Charm of the Bourgeoisie** (1972), **The Phantom of Liberty** (1974), and **That Obscure Object of Desire** (1977). He has proved equally confident with original screenplays and adapted works, and he has received three Academy Award nominations for his scripts. Highlights of his filmography include **The Tin Drum** (1979), which won the Best Foreign Language Film Oscar, **The Return of Martin Guerre** (1982), which earned him and co-writer Daniel Vigne a César for Best Original Screenplay, his adaptation of **The Unbearable Lightness of Being** (1988), and his acclaimed **Cyrano de Bergerac** (1990) with Gérard Depardieu. A recipient of the Laurel Award for Achievement from the Writers Guild Of America, Carrière remains a prolific writer, contributing to the screenplays of both **Birth** (2004) and **The White Ribbon** (2009), which won the Palme d'Or at the Cannes Film Festival. "I'm writing every day," he says at age 80. "When I'm not working on a script or on a play or on a book, I'm writing notes in the subway or in taxis. I'm working constantly."

Jean-Claude Carrière

I was born in a house in the country in a village where there was not one book and not one image. I spent the rest of my life in books and images. My family were all peasants—they were farmers. I didn't despise them at all, but I was like a strange animal in the family because I was a very good student when I was young. When I started writing, nobody in my family could appreciate what I was doing, and that was the case all my life long.

When I was 10 or 11, I was already beginning to write, but I was writing cartoons—stories with cowboys and pirates and things like this—and starting to write poems. When I was 15 or 16, I was beginning to be extremely attracted to the movies. During the War, we couldn't see American films in France—they weren't permitted, and we could only see French and German films. So at the end of the War, it was like an orgy of cinema to me. I was discovering the whole history of cinema.

When I made the decision to become a screenwriter, I realize now that I did it for two reasons. The first was that I wasn't really attracted by the work of a director. I mean, being responsible for a film for four, five, or six years seemed to me too long a time. The second reason was that I wanted to write in other fields than movies. The moment you are a film director, you cannot be a novelist because you need to be the king of your little kingdom, which is the film. But if you are a screenwriter, you can very well keep writing novels, plays, songs, librettos— everything I did all my life. I never felt sorry about that decision. Never—not even today.

I direct a lot of writing workshops all over the world, and I tell students on the very first day that a screenwriter is not a writer. A screenwriter is a filmmaker, and he must know absolutely from the very beginning that what he's writing is going to be made into a film. If he considers himself a writer—that he must write a very elegant script

DIARY OF A CHAMBERMAID

(01–03) Carrière's first collaboration with director Luis Buñuel was on 1964's **Diary of a Chambermaid**. "At the beginning it was quite difficult for me," Carrière admits. "I was a beginner, and it was quite difficult for me to say no to Buñuel when he was proposing ideas." But their relationship changed after one of the film's producers, Serge Silberman, invited Carrière to dinner. "He told me, 'You know, Luis is very, very happy with you,'" Carrière recalls. "'He thinks you are bright and you work well together, but you should say no to him from time to time.'" Silberman's comment boosted Carrière's confidence, but only later did the screenwriter learn the whole truth. "I found out that Buñuel had asked Silberman to come and tell me that," Carrière says. "In a way, Buñuel needed an opponent. He didn't need a secretary—he needed someone to contradict him and to oppose him and to make suggestions, which I began to try. And at the end of the first film, it went all right, and that's why he worked with me for the second film and all the others."

01

> **"The moment you are a film director, you cannot be a novelist because you need to be the king of your little kingdom, which is the film. But if you are a screenwriter, you can very well keep writing novels, plays, songs, librettos—everything I did all my life."**

with very good literary effects—he's lost, and he's going to fail.

If you are looking for fame, don't be a screenwriter. The screenwriter goes behind the director and sometimes even behind the actors—the screenwriter is hidden in a way. The playwright is much more famous than a screenwriter, and so is the novelist if he's successful. But a screenwriter has to be humble and know that his name is going to more or less disappear. So, if he wants to get famous, he must do something else.

All the great filmmakers from all over the world have developed the language of cinema. They have refined it—sometimes they have perverted it—but our main task is not only to know the language we are going to use, but also to try to make it better, if possible. The reason why so many novelist friends fail when they try to make a film is that they're using a language they don't know anything about. The language of film is very

complex. It is made up not only of images and sounds, but it also includes acting. The actors and the actresses—they are part of this language. You must absolutely know if what you are writing can be transmitted by actors. The main question you are asking all the time when you're working with the director is, "Is it possible to act this or not?"

Film language is in perpetual evolution—it changes every day. I remember when Jean-Luc Godard and I went one day to see a film by Abbas Kiarostami, the Iranian director. We were extremely surprised because this guy, coming from another country, was showing us new ways of using our language that we thought we knew. But we didn't know everything—he had invented some new methods. That's extremely exciting for me when that happens. It's impossible to say, "Now we know how to make films. We know exactly how long each scene should last. We know how long we can stay on one shot and then on the other one." No, that's absurd, because the →

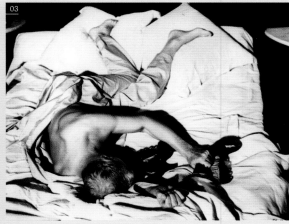

Constructing the finale

(01–03) The finale of **Belle de Jour** is one of the film's strongest, most enigmatic segments, suggesting a happy ending that, more than likely, exists entirely in Séverine's (Catherine Deneuve) mind. It did not come to Carrière and Buñuel easily. "We were looking for an ending that would join the two dimensions of the film: reality and unreality," Carrière says. "That was quite difficult and we looked for a long time—we had different endings. One night, it was very late, around two, and I was sleeping already. My telephone rang and it was Buñuel. He said, 'Jean-Claude, come, I think I have an idea for the ending.' I put on some clothing, and I went to his room. He was so moved that he was almost crying. And he told me something, which is not exactly the ending that we have in the film now, but something which was going in that direction. And I said, 'Yes,' and I was myself moved. The following day, we wrote the scene. Usually, he would go to bed quite early and sleep very well—he would go to bed at ten o'clock. The fact that he was still awake at two in the morning means that he was really torn by this idea of not finding the right ending." In the final sequence of the film Monsieur Husson (played by Michel Piccoli) reveals everything he knows about Séverine's exploits to her wheelchair-bound husband. The fallout is both real and unreal, with a close-up of Pierre's face, tear-stained, and then a movement into an almost fantastical ending where Séverine and Pierre speak tenderly, as if nothing has happened, and Pierre appears physically uninjured. **(02)** Michel Piccoli (left) and director Luis Buñuel (right) on the set with Catherine Deneuve during the shooting of the scene.

moment you establish that, a new genius appears and turns everything upside down. The world is changing all the time, and so is the movie language—it's impossible to stop it. You must be in the flow of the river, not looking at the river passing by—you must be inside, you must dive.

You have to be totally with the film—you have to be all the characters of the film yourself. Very often when I'm beginning to have an idea for a film or I'm offered a film, I tell the story to my friends, my wife, or my daughters. In the case of **The Return of Martin Guerre**, I remember telling the story to my mother one day. And I saw that she was so interested—I said to myself, "There might be a good story here." If you are too far away, too detached from the story—if you write a film just because you need some money and you're offered a good deal—that leads nowhere.

I work closely with the director, even during the editing. I was an editor myself, and I think it's absolutely essential for a writer to spend a lot of time in the editing room because that's where

"You must absolutely know if what you are writing can be transmitted by actors. The main question you are asking all the time when you're working with the director is, 'Is it possible to act this or not?'"

you see if you lost the script, what happened, or whether the film is worse or if it is better. The moment you see the first screening, that's the first copy of the film, and you always have something that surprises you. But the surprise is not always a bad one—sometimes it could be a good one. I remember **Cyrano de Bergerac**, for instance, was a good surprise for all of us when we saw the film for the first time. We had all done our best possible job, but the result, which was a mixture of all our efforts, went beyond what we hoped. We knew that it was difficult to make a film in classical verse, but we were absolutely surprised to see how it worked out. But in some cases, the result is disappointing, →

BELLE DE JOUR

(04) While working on the script for **Belle de Jour**, Carrière says that he and director Luis Buñuel would act out the parts. But where Carrière played the brothel owner and the clients, Buñuel would handle the lead role of Séverine. "Why was Buñuel choosing to be Séverine?" Carrière asks. "Probably because it was the most remote character from himself. He knew very well that one day he would have to direct an actress playing Séverine, and so he wanted to put himself—being 65 years old and Spanish—in the mental condition and physical condition of Séverine. He wanted to get as near as possible to the character." But even then, the two men needed help tapping into the female psyche. "All the fantasies in **Belle de Jour** were told to us by women," says Carrière. "It was impossible for two men to describe feminine eroticism, so that's why we asked many women to tell us what they were dreaming of." He pauses and laughs. "I won't tell you which ones were which, because my wife was one of them."

04

"With Buñuel, we had the right of veto: When somebody proposes an idea, the other one has three seconds to say 'yes' or 'no.' If he says 'no,' the other one has no right to insist."

01 The Discreet Charm of the Bourgeoisie (1972)

and sometimes it's because of us. And we must admit it.

It's almost impossible to describe how I collaborate with a director on a script. You are facing each other for hours every day, improvising, trying to convince the other of the excellence of your ideas and then renouncing them if the other is not seduced. It's a way of working which only belongs to the film business. You know, I don't see two novelists working that way—that that be impossible.

With the script for **The Discreet Charm of the Bourgeoisie**, Luis Buñuel and I were working on an original screenplay, so the work is slightly different than with an adaptation. When it comes from a novel, at least you have a starting point— you know what the story's about and which are the main characters. But when you start from nothing, from scratch, then you are lost—you do not know where to go. Of course, you are more free, but you have nothing to refer to as a model. With **The Discreet Charm of the Bourgeoisie**, I remember we didn't even know which film we could compare it to. So you have to try to figure

out how the film is going to be, and the only person who can help you is the one who's facing you.

Collaborating with a director is like a negotiation. Sometimes you fight. Sometimes you propose something, and the other shrugs and makes a face and doesn't like it at all, and you don't understand, because it pleases you. So you want to defend your idea at any price—sometimes you are acute, sometimes you are clever, sometimes you are stupid. You try everything possible. But, there comes a moment where you have to give up. If you cannot convince the director that what you have in mind is a good solution for his film, you'd better give up and find something else.

With Buñuel, we had the right of veto: When somebody proposes an idea, the other one has three seconds to say "yes" or "no." If he says "no," the other one has no right to insist. We have to forget about it and go to another idea. If he says "yes," we keep working on the idea and developing it. And why three seconds? Because it was to prevent our mind from finding some secret reasons to defend or reject the idea. We →

THE DISCREET CHARM OF THE BOURGEOISIE

(02–03) "For **The Discreet Charm of the Bourgeoisie**, Luis Buñuel and I wrote five different versions of the film, and it took us two years," says Carrière. But throughout the arduous process, the guiding principle behind the film remained the same: "The idea was an action that repeats itself without getting to a conclusion. The characters just want to have a nice dinner together, and they cannot." The film went on to win the Best Foreign Language Film Oscar, and Carrière and Buñuel shared a nomination for original screenplay. But during the process of making **The Discreet Charm of the Bourgeoisie**, Carrière wanted to ensure that he and his director saw eye to eye on the film they were making. And he developed an interesting way to check. "At the end of the day, I would draw some sketches of the scenes we had been working on," Carrière explains. "The following morning, without showing the drawings to Buñuel, I would ask Luis, 'In the scene of the paratroopers, where is the main entrance of the room?' If he says 'to the left' and the entrance is on the left in my drawing, we are in the same space. If he says 'on the right,' we are not and we have more work to do—we see a different film. Of course, I will never be him and he will never be me, but we have to get as deeply close together as we can to get the right result, which is going to be the film."

CYRANO DE BERGERAC

(01–02) "When I have an actual actor in mind when I'm writing, so much the better," says Carrière, "because the actor is going to be one of our main collaborators." This proved especially true while working on **Cyrano de Bergerac**, which was nominated for five Oscars, including Best Actor for Gérard Depardieu. "Before beginning to write the script with director Jean-Paul Rappeneau, we asked Gérard to record the entire play—playing all the roles, including the women—and to make a CD." Listening to Depardieu's voice while working on the script had a unique effect on the screenplay. "It was extremely interesting to see how he would approach this scene or that scene," Carrière says. "And one thing that appeared immediately is that Gérard Depardieu was a fantastic contrast between an enormous body and a very weak and delicate voice. His voice was and still is very vulnerable. And that's exactly what we wanted: We had the voice of Cyrano next to us while writing."

had very clever brains, but we wanted just to get a spontaneous reaction to the idea from the other person. Buñuel wanted the reaction of the other to come from the deepest part of his personality.

I have never written less than four versions of a script and sometimes up to 11. But everything we do is not constantly conscious. Psychiatrists say we all have inside ourselves what we call "the invisible worker." There in our subconscious there is a worker—a very nice man or woman. You don't have to pay him, and you don't have to feed him—he's there. And he works even when

you are sleeping. Even when you work on something else, he keeps working on that script. So, when Buñuel and I would take some time apart and then meet again after two or three months, all of a sudden some scenes that we liked before would seem dull to us. On the other hand, some solution that we were looking for to fix something in the script, all of a sudden it appears. That's all the work of the invisible worker. I've witnessed this strange process happen very often—not only with Buñuel, but with other directors as well. We must give way

BIRTH

(03–04) When Carrière began working with director Jonathan Glazer on the dark romantic drama **Birth**, Glazer had only a general notion of a story. "He had just the idea of reincarnation," Carrière says. "So I said, 'Why not? He's a very charming guy, very bright, very talented.'" Glazer moved from London to live at Carrière's home in Paris, and together they developed the idea of a young widow (played by Nicole Kidman) who is confronted by a boy (Cameron Bright) claiming to be her deceased husband. For the actual writing, though, Carrière suggested an unusual strategy. "The two of us would talk a lot—I would propose a lot of different solutions, scenes, characters—but I never wrote a line. When the moment came to write the film, I gave Jonathan the pen and told him, 'You write,' since the film was going to be in English. And it was quite interesting because he had never written anything. I was there next to him, but he was very anxious to write himself." But while others might look at **Birth** as a romantic triangle between Kidman, the boy, and her fiancé (Danny Huston), Carrière sees the narrative differently. "It's a love story between the woman, the boy and time," he says. "She knows very well that nobody has ever loved her the way the boy loves her. But on the other hand, he's 10 and she's 35. Time is a very tough barrier between the two of them—it's a real character in the film. I worked with time in **Birth** almost as if it were an actor in the film."

to this invisible worker. Of course, sometimes my conscious mind and my unconscious mind working together can't reach the solution. I have right now behind me a pile of unfinished scripts—they will be there forever, most probably. From time to time, I hear the voices of the characters. They are crying up to me: "Oh, don't forget us! Think about us! Here we are, give us a chance!" But I can't find the solution sometimes.

The advice I would give to all screenwriters would be not to be obsessed about one

script. Always have three or four or five ideas going at the same time. Like we say in France, have several irons in the fire. Considering the problems in finding financing or actors, you never know which film is going to be made. So you'd better have three or four ideas all the time.

Once you begin to adapt a novel, the question is not how you adapt the novel—the question is how you make a good film. You have to close the novel and go your own way. Of course, I have memories of adaptations that I haven't done well. For instance, I wrote **Les Possédés** (1988), based →

> **"The advice I would give to all screenwriters would be not to be obsessed about one script. Always have three or four or five ideas going at the same time. Like we say in France, have several irons in the fire."**

on *The Demons* by Dostoyevsky. It's a book that I love. I knew from the very beginning it was impossible, but since I liked the director, Andrzej Wajda, very much, I decided to try to help him. The result was not what it should have been. And I wonder if we should have given up making the film. You know, the book is so extraordinary that it was just impossible to go through with making a film. Sometimes, there is pressure to adapt a work that's well-known. I have been offered to adapt some very famous novels and plays into films. For instance, twice I've been asked to adapt *Under the Volcano* by Malcolm Lowry, which is a book that I like very much. But I couldn't see the film. That's quite important—a film is made of scenes, which go one after the other, and the scenes are played by actors. If you don't have these elements in the novel or in the play, forget about a film. There is no film.

At my age, it happens sometimes that I'm watching some film that I wrote 30, 40, even 50 years ago. I have always one of two reactions. One is to say, "Oh my God, that scene doesn't work. I shouldn't have written it that way." But sometimes I go, "Oh my God, that scene is well-written—would I be able to write that today?" I'll think that, because maybe I'm declining. Maybe I'm an old man and I haven't kept following carefully enough the evolution of film. Maybe I haven't seen enough films. It's hard work to keep following the big river. If you stay on the banks, then forget about it— the water will go away, and so will the boats and the fish.

01 The White Ribbon (2009)

01

Knowing what to cut

(02–04) Sometimes the secret to a successful rewrite is knowing what to remove, as opposed to what to add. Such was the case with **The White Ribbon**, a disturbing drama set in pre-World War I Germany where ominous, unexplained violence is occurring in a small village. "Director Michael Haneke had a script for a miniseries," explains Carrière. "The script was four-and-a-half hours long, and he couldn't find the money to produce the film. So he came to me and said, 'Listen, read this, and tell me if you find it interesting.'" Carrière did, and the two set about winnowing the script down to feature length. The writer's chief suggestion was to cut scenes where the village's children were alone. By doing this, the audience would not immediately begin to suspect that the children were behind the random acts of violence that were happening on-screen. "In his script, it was obvious after 20 minutes that the children were doing everything bad in the village," Carrière says. "I proposed to postpone that until the very end—and maybe not even ever to say clearly who had done it." Haneke agreed, and the resulting film is an uneasy study of inexplicable, menacing behavior. "A huge part of the original script was thrown away," he says. "I didn't have to invent the story. I didn't have to invent characters. They were all there. What I had to do was almost the work of an editor—to take three scenes and make one."

Lee Chang-dong

"One thing I learned as a novelist is asking questions about life and the world we live in. A novel is not only telling a story, but also asking questions about life, like other forms of art. That attitude did not change when I made movies—I ask audiences questions through movies, and I hope that audiences find the answers on their own."

Secret Sunshine (2007)

A celebrated international writer-director, Lee Chang-dong was born in South Korea in 1954. First working as a novelist, he transitioned to film in the early 1990s, scripting two movies for director Park Kwang-su: **To the Starry Island** (1993), which he co-wrote, and **A Single Spark** (1995). In 1997, he made his directorial debut with **Green Fish**, a noir-ish thriller that won prizes at the Vancouver International Film Festival and the International Film Festival Rotterdam. His second film, **Peppermint Candy** (1999), told its story in reverse chronological order, looking back at the last two decades in the life of a man who has committed suicide. Lee followed it up with **Oasis** (2002), an unlikely love story between an intellectually disabled man and a woman with cerebral palsy that won the FIPRESCI award at the Venice Film Festival. In 2003, Lee put aside filmmaking to serve as South Korea's Minister of Culture and Tourism, but he returned to the cinema with **Secret Sunshine** (2007), a drama about a young mother whose husband and son die, which won Jeon Do-yeon the Best Actress prize at the Cannes Film Festival. His most recent film is **Poetry** (2010), a prize-winner at Cannes for Best Screenplay. Throughout his career, Lee's films have embraced ordinary characters, often residing on the margins of existence, who reflect the realities of contemporary South Korea. In 2011, he told a journalist that he had two possible ideas for his next film: "One is about the apocalypse, and one is a film where the lead character is a samurai."

Lee Chang-dong

My mother made me write initially. My family lived in urban poverty after we left our rural hometown, and my mother forced me to sit down and write a letter back to my grandmother in the town. In the first or second grade, I just started writing letters with my poor handwriting. At that time, all I needed to do was to take down what my mom said. Thanks to that, I was praised by adults and was known as a good letter-writer. My mother was very familiar with what kind of children's writing makes adults feel good—in this sense, my mother was a very creative person. I learned then that writing could move people and make them happy. Although I technically wrote the letters, they were not mine, so consequently I decided to write a letter on my own. Fortunately, I could write successfully without my mom's help.

Writing is such lonely work. I can say that I became accustomed to the loneliness as an older teen when I was working to be a writer. Whenever I wrote novels in the middle of the night after waking up alone, I felt lonely, as if I was the only one who was awake in the world. Nevertheless, I always wrote while thinking that somebody might feel the same way as me about the one line and the one word I was writing at that time and empathize with them. In this sense, writing novels is the same as writing love letters. I write only for a person whose face and name I do not know. The person is connected to me with a piece of string—although the string is weak, the feeling that a writer is directly connected to a reader one-on-one is the power that made me write novels. Compared to this, I cannot make a movie for only one person—I have to make a movie that a number of people can watch together in theaters. In this respect, writing scripts is the same as writing love letters for an invisible group. That makes me feel even lonelier, as if I am isolated. Sometimes it is pretty hard to tolerate. How do I overcome it? There is no special way other than taking the loneliness as it is. I just need to get used to being lonely.

I was a novelist before I became a movie director. To be honest, I had never imagined that I could be a film director, let alone want to be a

"I always wrote while thinking that somebody might feel the same way as me about the one line and the one word I was writing at that time and empathize with them."

film director, until I wrote my first script. I got to write my first film script because both the film director and the writer of the original novel were my friends, and I told them a few ideas in a meeting. Consequently, while writing the script I was able to study and understand movies, and it was the most precious experience. My opinions were sometimes very different from the director's, and my pride as a writer was hurt when the director revised my script to his liking. However, there was no denying that I got to understand movies from different points of view and learn about them in my own way through these experiences. These experiences, afterwards, became my basis for directing movies.

One thing I learned as a novelist is asking questions about life and the world we live in. A novel is not only telling a story, but also asking questions about life, like other forms of art. That attitude did not change when I made movies—I ask audiences questions through movies, and I hope that audiences find the answers on their own. This is my basic attitude when it comes to making movies. In fact, I do not believe movies should have much of a message. I think art or the act of creation is asking questions rather than delivering any answers, and then people need to seek the answers to the questions. Giving definite answers, or believing there are answers, is not my way. We can say that a movie, made mainly for amusement, has an obvious message such as "Justice prevails in the end." However, do audiences take home the message after the movie ends? Of course, audiences are uncomfortable with movies that do not give answers but ask questions—nevertheless, I think that we should not stop asking questions.

I wanted to tell a story about communication breakdown in **Oasis**. I think Korean society and →

POETRY

(01) The plot for **Poetry** was inspired by true events. "A few years ago, in a small city in South Korea, a group of teenage boys raped some middle school girls," recalls Lee. "I do not know why, but I kept remembering the incident. However, I could not find a way to deal with it in a movie. I could have created a trite story commonly found in movies, and it could have been more interesting commercially, but this was not my way of making a movie. One day during a trip to Japan, while I was reading a book with the TV on in my hotel room, I came up with a word: 'poetry.' I must have been watching a TV channel for travelers who could not fall asleep—it was a very typical scene, which had a peaceful river, birds flying away, and fishermen throwing nets and catching fish, with meditative music in the background. All at once, I realized how I could deal with the atrocious incident in a movie. It needed dealing with through poetry. In other words, I had to deal with the violence not through violence, but through 'beauty.' The main characters would be a woman in her mid-sixties who learns how to write poetry for the first time in her life, and her grandson who has committed a violent crime. These characters, a basic plot, and the title 'Poetry' simultaneously came into my mind."

The search for beauty

(02) Mija, the main character of **Poetry**, is a woman suffering from Alzheimer's. To combat the malady—and to cope with the fact that her grandson took part in the brutal rape of a classmate—she takes up an interest in poetry. "When she goes about entering the world of poetry, it looks similar to the world of ordinary people," Lee says. "She does her best to find and express invisible beauties, and she slowly realizes that beauty is inseparable from filthiness, ugliness, sorrow, and pain. She also realizes real beauty is not a visible thing, and beauty is not only 'mine,' but is also connected to the relationship with other people. While realizing these things, she keeps entering a sort of mysterious region with which she becomes more and more familiar. At the same time, she has been losing memories and words—she has been getting closer to her death. Forgetting is one form of death. I thought this forgetting could make her adventure in completing a poem for the first time in her life more tragic and reveal a cruel paradox and irony in life."

Grief as a theme in **Secret Sunshine**

(01) The searing drama **Secret Sunshine**, which examines the role of faith in people's lives, features a young widow named Shin-ae (played by Jeon Do-yeon) who experiences further misery when her son is murdered. "Pain is unavoidable in our lives," writer-director Lee Chang-dong explains. "Although we feel that today life is happy and peaceful without any problems, nobody knows what kind of accident we will meet with tomorrow. Or perhaps it will come to us very slowly in the form of disease and death. No one can avoid it. This is why religion is necessary for people, because there is no logical and reasonable way to explain why human beings have to undergo pain. Art tells us about inexplicable things in a different way than religion does. Of course, what I want to tell audiences is not about the pain itself, but about finding regeneration after overcoming the pain. A secret of regeneration is hidden in the cycle of every life. Every epic is essentially an adventure story that describes a struggle toward regeneration. Everyone has a finite life, and art asks people the meaning of this finite life. Trying to get through the finitude of life is the will of regeneration."

SECRET SUNSHINE

(02–04) **Secret Sunshine** premiered in 2007, but its origins trace back several decades. "The film is based on 'A Story of a Worm,' a short story written by the Korean writer Lee Cheong-jun," says Lee. "I added a number of new settings to the very basic plot, but the topic about forgiveness came from the original story. I read the story for the first time almost 20 years ago, when I never thought about becoming a film director. However, it seemed that the shock I got the first time I read the story must have stayed in my mind and been growing on its own. One day, I made up my mind to film the story. It occurred to me, very naturally, that the setting of the movie should be the city Milyang. Milyang is a small city, an hour away from the town where I was born and grew up. I guess the name Milyang has been attractive to me since I was young. It means 'secret sunshine' in Chinese characters. I was wondering why this old and normal city, which does not have anything to show off, got such a poetic and figurative name. I regarded it as a metaphor for life itself. Though the city is humble and ordinary, it has a certain meaning. In other words, the original story is about forgiveness, but I wanted to ask about the meaning of life itself beyond that."

"... I do not believe movies should have much of a message. I think art or the act of creation is asking questions rather than delivering any answers, and then people need to seek the answers to the questions."

today's world have a serious problem with communication. I tried to put the issue of communication into a love story. The two main characters in **Oasis** have a communication problem. They are abandoned people on the margins of society who are not recognized by anybody. They are characters who make us wonder, "Can they even fall in love with someone, like other people do?"

In regards to the main male character in **Oasis**, the first image I came up with was the scene of a winter day when it was freezing cold. It was a man with short hair wearing a short-sleeved summer shirt with a palm tree pattern— usually worn on summer vacation—getting a cigarette from a person next to him at a bus stop on the outskirts of the city. I do not know why the image occurred to me—I may have seen that kind of man in person before. Anyway, this was the starting point of my imagining of the character. I created the main female character as a person with cerebral palsy because cerebral palsy is a disability that limits not only physical activities, but also communication. Once women with cerebral palsy reach puberty, which is when people tend to be very sensitive, they become self-conscious and hide inside their homes in order to avoid people. The main female character in **Oasis** is that kind of person. I am very accustomed to people with cerebral palsy because my older sister has it. If there is a person with this kind of disability in a family, all family members should share the burden, big or small. The whole family is overshadowed by the disability—as long as they live together, nobody can be free from it. In **Oasis**, she comforts herself only through fantasy in her own imagination. For instance, she imagines a beam of light as

butterflies or birds while playing with a mirror. After I created these two characters, I thought in the end their love story had no choice but to have the structure of a romantic adventure, where a knight rescues a princess who is cursed and locked inside a tower. This is the archetype of every love story, but I wanted to show the structure more explicitly. Accordingly, I named the lead actress Gongju (which means "princess"), and nicknamed the lead actor General.

It seems that I always write my scripts after I decide the ending. As Aristotle says, a story should have a beginning and an ending. An excellent and meaningful story has an excellent ending. Even though a story has an exciting beginning, if a writer cannot end the story properly, the story will have a problem. On the other hand, if a writer comes up with a splendid ending, the writer has solved the biggest problem in writing the story. If there →

05 Moon So-ri's performance in **Oasis** (2002) won her a Blue Dragon Award for Best New Actress, while actor Sol Kyung-gu has worked with Lee Chang-dong on several occasions. He played the lead role in Lee's 1999 film **Peppermint Candy**

Commenting on South Korean society

(01–03) Lee's films, for all their other accolades, have also been praised for their depiction of and commentary on South Korean life. "I do not actually intend to make comments on Korean society in my movies," Lee says. "I only want to talk about humans and their lives. However, it is not possible to talk about one human exclusive of the reality surrounding him—such as the environment, politics, and history—since no one can live without being related to the reality of society. I think, in movies, separating humans from reality and describing them as if they have no relation to everyday reality distorts existence. On the other hand, when I describe reality, I pay careful attention to avoid the description being considered an intentional and exaggerated criticism of society. This kind of criticism is not a natural and honest way of reflecting reality." Lee's **Peppermint Candy** explores how decisions made during life have far-reaching consequences unimaginable to those living through the events at the time.

03 The movie poster for **Peppermint Candy** (1999)

> **"It seems that I always write my scripts after I decide the ending. As Aristotle says, a story should have a beginning and an ending. An excellent and meaningful story has an excellent ending."**

is a beginning, there might not be an end, but if there is an end, there must be a beginning. When I write novels, I sometimes change the ending, depending on the flow of the story. However, I never change the ending when I write scripts—I can start writing after the ending is decided, and the story will naturally flow to the ending.

In **Secret Sunshine**, the main character, Shin-ae, loses her son and was obsessed with God because of her unbearable pain. One day, she realizes that God has already forgiven the criminal who killed her son before she has forgiven him, and she is seized with a sense of hopeless betrayal. She starts fighting against God, like the main character of a Greek tragedy. However, unlike the hero of a Greek tragedy, how

can the young lady, running a piano school in a rural city in Korea, fight against God? She cannot even receive any message from God. She decided to struggle against God by violating God's commandments—she steals and even commits adultery. I believed that such an extreme psychological condition might be hard for audiences to accept, but at least it could be understood because her behavior asks underlying questions about God, religion, and the human condition that everyone can empathize with. The important thing is that although she keeps trying to fight against God, she does not deny the existence of God. Fighting against God also means she admits the existence of God. We say that believing and →

LORD JIM

(04) "I have liked movies since I was young," says Lee, "but I did not have many opportunities to watch them and never dreamed of becoming a movie director. The most memorable movie from the ones I watched in my youth was **Lord Jim** (1965). When I was about 10 years old, the first animated movie in South Korea was showing in theaters—it was highly popular among children and making a big splash. My cousin, who realized that I wanted to see the movie, gave me the money for the ticket. I elatedly ran to the theater. However, by the time I went into the theater, strangely, I felt that the movie would not be worth my money. Instead of the animated movie, I wanted to watch an adult movie. That movie was **Lord Jim**, which was showing in the next theater. Maybe I suddenly wanted to get out of the children's world. **Lord Jim** was too difficult for me to understand, and yet the story was as intense as a nightmare. It was a world of stormy oceans and jungles as well as unknown people. A few years later, I read Joseph Conrad's original novel, and a few more years later I watched the movie again. I was able to confirm the fact that my early memories were a lot more different than the actual movie. However, I still have the intense and bizarre images and impression **Lord Jim** gave me in my early memory. Since then, for me movies have become journeys that approach the core of mysterious and unknown darkness, which is life."

"Once an idea comes into my mind, I keep it in my head for a long time before I write a script. I, so to speak, let it ripen a while."

following God is faith, and that fighting against God is madness. In other words, faith is a matter of humans, not God. Therefore, this movie is not about God or religion, but humans. While writing this script and creating the character Shin-ae, what I really cared about was how I could persuade audiences about these things.

It is not always possible to write a script with a specific actor or actress in mind because I am not sure whether I can cast him or her. In my case, I have written scripts without thinking of any actor or actress, and I have also written scripts with a specific actor or actress in mind, but he or she rejected my movie and I had to cast a different actor or actress. Then there has been a lucky case when I wrote a script after I got a specific actor or actress to agree. **Oasis** and **Poetry** are the cases when actors and actresses were already decided during the writing of the scripts. The actress Yun Jung-hee, who plays the main character in **Poetry**, is a legendary Korean actress who appeared in more than 300 movies in the 1960s and 1970s. When I was young, she was like a star shining in the sky. One day, however, she disappeared from the screen—she left for Paris after marrying a pianist. After I became a movie director, I met her briefly twice at film festivals and I did not know her very well. However, she almost automatically came into my mind as the main character, Mija, when I was sketching out my first ideas for **Poetry**. There was no alternative. Strangely, I never thought that she might not want to play this role. Even though I did not know her very well personally, I instinctively felt she would take to Mija, who has a timeless beauty, like a dried flower. Mija has an unrealistic personality in that she still feels and talks like an immature girl although she is old, which is very similar to Yun Jung-hee. I named the character Mija because I could not come up with any other name—Mija is an old-fashioned name that means "a beautiful girl." I found out that Jung-hee's real name is Mija—I thought it not a coincidence, but destiny. One day, before I wrote the script, I told her the plot of the movie while having dinner together. No need to persuade her, since she

really wanted to play this role. What if she had not taken the role? There would not have been any other alternatives. Nonetheless, another actress would have been cast and the movie would have turned out differently.

After I made **Secret Sunshine** and **Poetry**, I was often asked, "Why do you choose a woman as a main character? How can you understand a woman's mentality?" I answer that I have heard that as men grow older, their bodies start producing female hormones, and I thought that might be the reason. Of course, that was a joke, but actually, part of it is true. When I was young, I always thought of women as different from me. However, as I get older, I often think of a woman as not a woman, but a human. The ability to distinguish gender inside me is getting weaker. In retrospect, I had trouble in describing main female characters when I was a young novelist. However, now there is no difference between a woman and a man in describing characters, and I even feel more comfortable describing the

<u>01</u>   1. 도로(외부/낮)

화면은 구름이 드문드문 있는 푸른 하늘에서부터 시작한다. 카메라가 눈에 띄지 않게 천천히 돌아나면, 누군가의 시점으로 차 안에서 바라보는 하늘임을 알게 된다. 약간 양각.

승용차의 실내 유리창으로 보이는 굴의 얼굴. 머리를 예쁘게 염색한 일곱 살 남짓한 남자 아이. 때문에 바로 약간 지적 보인다. 그 얼굴 뒤로 구름이 흩어진 푸른 하늘이 반사되어 있다. 아이는 눈살을 찌푸린 채 약간 화가 난 것처럼 하늘을 쳐다보고 있다. 아까부터 신예에게 전화하는 소리 들린다.

신예(O.S)   여기가 어딘지 모르겠어요. 아까 밀양 5키로라고 쓰인 표지판을 지나오긴 했는데…….

밀양시 외곽의 어느 한적한 국도변. 승용차 한 대가 길가에 멈춰져 있고, 신예(33세)가 차에서 내려 전화를 하고 있다. 통화 내용으로 봐서 차가 고장이 나서 카센타에 전화하고 있는 듯하다. 일곱 살 난 아이의 엄마라고는 아주 앳된 느낌을 주는 얼굴이다. 어떻게 보면 그녀 자신이 고집 세고 결없는 어린아이 같기도 하고, 한편으로는 이미 세상살이의 어려움을 다 터득한 듯한 느낌을 주기도 하는, 묘하게도 이중적인 인상을 가졌다.

신예   어디서 왔나구요? 글쎄요, 어디서 왔나? (스스로도 우습다는 듯 소리내어 웃는다.) 잘 안 봤어요. 골란만요…….

그녀가 골을 요란하게 흔든다. 달려오던 트럭 한 대가 그녀를 지나쳐가 섰더니, 직진해서 가서 선다. 달려가는 신예.

트럭기사가 신예의 핸드폰으로 통화하면서 그녀 대신 위치를 설명해주고 있다. 신예는 기사에 심한 경상도 사투리가 배어있다는 표정이다.

기사   어, 여기 어디로 카아, 밀양서 다리 건너가 정도로 빠지는 20번 도로로 들어와갖고 큰 8키로 지킴을 되꼈삤네. 예, 작가 비상 깜빡이 키고 있으께 내…… 금방 보입니다. (신예에게 전화기를 건넨다.)

신예   감사합니다. (출발하는 트럭을 보며 다시 통화한다) 위치 아셨어요? 빨리 와주세요…….

그녀는 자기 차를 향해 걸어간다.

신예   (차창을 두드리며)준! 차 안에만 있지 말고 내려서 맑은 공기 좀 쐐!

준은 뭔지 심통이 난 것처럼 꿈쩍도 않는다. 차문을 열고 아이를 안아 내리는 신예. 아이는 내리기 싫다는 듯 몸부림을 흔드리고 다리를 달랑 들고 있다.

<u>01</u> The first page of Lee's script for **Secret Sunshine** (2007)

delicate feelings of main female characters.

Once an idea comes into my mind, I keep it in my head for a long time before I write a script. I, so to speak, let it ripen a while. How long do I keep it in my head? It depends. It might take a few years. I often forget about some ideas—I just wait until the ideas knock, saying, "It is time to get out of here. We are grown up, so please open the door." However, I do not write right after I hear them—I keep thinking and making notes until the story has a much clearer skeleton and more details. The most necessary thing for me to do at this stage is to tell other people about the brief story. This is a way of gathering feedback. People react in various ways and, mostly, I can judge what the story is like by their reactions. One more necessary thing to do is to research to find the details that I can never imagine in my head. After these are ready, I finally start writing the script. It does not take me a long time to finish the script once I start writing it.

The main character in **Poetry**, Mija, asks "How can I find genuine beauty?" to a poetry teacher. Her question somewhat represents my question and my attitude of making movies. The camera lens makes the subject in front of us look different and often makes reality look "nice and beautiful." However, I want my movie not to make our reality, lives, and living spaces look different. I want my movie to show them as they are and to let audiences feel and accept "invisible" beauty. If I have my own style and sensibility, they must come from my attitude toward movies.

In my writings I want to describe how all humans have their own dignity. Even though the protagonists in my work look weak, they struggle for their own self-respect. They do not give in to political and social violence, to problematic institutions, or even to God, or to the finitude of life. They struggle while trying not to yield to the meaninglessness of life. By the same token, I write novels and scripts and make movies.

02 Yun Jung-hee won several Best Actress awards for her role as Mija in **Poetry** (2010), including the Los Angeles Film Critics Association and the South Korean Grand Bell Awards

Bergman spent more than 60 years passionately funneling life into his art. As a result, he taught several generations of filmmakers about the power and possibility of autobiographical cinema.

Born in Sweden in 1918, Bergman attended Stockholm University, developing an interest in theater and film. (Indeed, an entirely separate appreciation could be written about Bergman's lifelong contributions to the stage, where his legacy also looms large.) By the early 1940s, he was already writing screenplays, notably **Torment** (1944), which was directed by Alf Sjöberg. Soon after, he was directing his own films, but it wasn't until the mid-1950s that he started to establish himself as a filmmaker of the first order. Two early successes were with films he wrote and directed: the comedy **Smiles of a**

to those who only know Bergman from his later reputation as a brooding chronicler of existential angst. As for **The Seventh Seal**, film history has reduced it to two indelible images: one of Death (portrayed by Bengt Ekerot) playing chess with a beleaguered knight (Max von Sydow); and the other of Death leading a procession of souls into the afterlife. But a careful viewing of the film reveals a playful, impish comic tone amidst the dire Crusades-era setting and stench of death.

From there, Bergman continued to demonstrate his versatility. He crafted a series of elegant fantasy and flashback scenes to dramatize the regrets of an aging professor in **Wild Strawberries** (1957). He mixed comedy and horror in **The Magician** (1958). He then delivered his so-called "Silence of God" trilogy:

01 Bergman with Norwegian actress Liv Ullmann on the set of **Autumn Sonata** (1978).

For Bergman, writing and directing were tied together, and the finished film was a collaboration between his vision and what his actors brought to the material."

Through a Glass Darkly (1961), **Winter Light** (1963), and **The Silence** (1963). By this point, Bergman had already received two Academy Award nominations for his screenplays for **Wild Strawberries** and **Through a Glass Darkly**—before he was done, he would be nominated nine times, five for his writing, three for directing, and one for Best Picture. (He would be given the Irving G. Thalberg Memorial Award in 1971.)

But awards are not how one should measure Bergman's impact. Rather, it's the sheer heft of his *oeuvre* that impresses. Whether examining his childhood in **Fanny and Alexander** (1982) or exploring family crisis in **Cries and Whispers** (1972), **Autumn Sonata** (1978), **Scenes From a Marriage** (1973) and its sequel **Saraband** (2003), his best work seemed pulled from personal anguish and the unconscious, which in part explains why his work has spoken to so many people despite language or cultural barriers. It also explains why his stories have inspired so many other filmmakers: Robert Altman's **3 Women** (1977) is unimaginable without Bergman's **Persona** (1966), while

Bergman-devotee Woody Allen has repeatedly cribbed from his idol, most notably **Wild Strawberries** for **Deconstructing Harry** (1997) and **Smiles of a Summer Night** for **A Midsummer Night's Sex Comedy** (1982). Taken as a collection, Bergman's films are a journal of a man working through his preoccupations.

"When I write I must try to capture something in words which for all useful purposes, you might say, can't be expressed in words," Bergman said in 1968. "Later it is necessary to translate the words again so that in quite another context they'll come alive." For Bergman, writing and directing were tied together, and the finished film was a collaboration between his vision and what his actors brought to the material. "While that original conception must always be in the background, I must not let it become too dictatorial," he explained. "The whole process is essentially creative. You write down a melodic line and after that, with the orchestra, you work out the instrumentation."

Bergman died in July 2007 at the age of 89. He was credited as a writer on over 45 films

02 Smiles of a Summer Night (1955)

03 Wild Strawberries (1957)

04 The Seventh Seal (1957)

Stephen Gaghan

"...when I was seven and told my mom, 'I'm gonna be a writer,' she said, 'Oh, that's a terrible idea. You'll live in misery and die teaching other people's children badly.' My parents wanted the safer path for me, and I think they failed miserably achieving that."

Syriana (2005)

Stephen Gaghan's writing career started quite promisingly, publishing a short story in *The Iowa Review* before he was even 26. He also impressed the writing staff of **The Simpsons** with a spec episode entitled "Family Wheel of Jeopardy," as well as producer and talent agent Bernie Brillstein with a collection of **Saturday Night Live** sketches he'd written. But a career in television writing in the 1990s—including stints at **New York Undercover**, **The Practice**, **American Gothic**, and **NYPD Blue** (where he shared an Emmy for Outstanding Writing for a Drama Series)—soon gave way to screenwriting. His first produced film credit was **Rules of Engagement** (2000), which starred Samuel L. Jackson and Tommy Lee Jones, but he received much acclaim for his next film, **Traffic** (2000), which was based on the 1989 British miniseries **Traffik**. **Traffic** went on to win four Academy Awards, including a Best Adapted Screenplay Oscar for Gaghan. Around the same time as **Traffic**'s release, Gaghan revealed that he had himself been a longtime drug addict, finally getting clean in 1997. Subsequently, he made his feature directing debut with **Abandon** (2002) and was one of three credited writers on the historical drama **The Alamo** (2004). His next great triumph occurred in 2005 with the release of **Syriana**, a multi-character drama he wrote and directed that examined the danger of the world's addiction to oil. The film earned Gaghan his second Academy Award nomination, this time for Best Original Screenplay, and George Clooney won the Oscar for Best Supporting Actor. More recently, he's one of the writers (uncredited) on the 2013 big-budget sci-fi film **After Earth**, which stars Will Smith and his son Jaden. "I'm in the adult-serious ghetto," Gaghan says about his niche in Hollywood. "That's my pigeonhole. I made it, I dug it out, I climbed in the hole—it's dark and airless. But I dug it, you know? And no other hole exists."

Stephen Gaghan

" My father's father wrote for a Philadelphia newspaper and aspired to be a playwright. We had in our house a couple of crazy unproduced plays that he had written. For the one creative writing class I took in my life, I didn't do any writing—I decided that I would plagiarize his terrible play to not fail the class. That didn't work out very well. Later, when I won the Oscar, there was a federal judge who contacted me to say, "I went to school with your grandfather, and he was a smart guy, got the classics prize in Greek, was voted most likely to succeed, that kind of thing." My grandfather thought he was gonna take over the world, but he didn't—I think he got drunk for 50 years, and then he was a nightclub columnist and reviewed plays. He was a charming guy—you know, the hard-drinking, chain-smoking newspaperman. He was married to my grandmother, who was a painter, and his father had been a concert pianist, so there was this thread of drunk, failed artists that went back on my dad's side. The thing I wrote in **Syriana** where Jeffrey Wright's dad carries a card in his wallet that says, "If you find me, call my son"? That's based 100 percent on my grandfather, who carried that same card. I try to imagine what that was like for my dad—he's working and suddenly gets a call: "There's this guy here, can you come get him?" So when I was seven and told my mom, "I'm gonna be a writer," she said, "Oh, that's a terrible idea. You'll live in misery and die teaching other people's children badly." My parents wanted the safer path for me, and I think they failed miserably achieving that.

I didn't mention anything about writing again until I was about 20. It was a secret that I kept inside of me. I didn't know anyone who was a writer—I didn't even know what it meant to be a writer. I just loved books. But there was nothing on the surface that said I would be a writer. I didn't work at it. I didn't write. I didn't even know how to type. But I just had this sense in a totally mystical, strange way—I would get in trouble, and there would be a voice in my head that would say, "Well, you'll be able to write your way out of this one." I don't know where it came from.

And as I got into my teens, I started reading better books, beginning with the Beats and then the hippie writers, people like Wallace Stegner up in Northern California, and all the political New Journalism stuff, the *Boys on the Bus* dudes and Ken Kesey. I loved those guys, and I loved the lifestyle—take tons of drugs and you too can write *One Flew Over the Cuckoo's Nest*. I think I had the chronology of Kesey's achievements a little cockeyed, but by then I loved the trio of great drunk Americans: Faulkner, Hemingway, and Fitzgerald. Not so much for the writing yet—I just really liked the drinking and smoking and all that stuff.

When I moved to Los Angeles, I wrote spec screenplays. I was really poor, and I thought I was just gonna do this for a while to make a little money so I could write novels. I thought movies were a second-class art form. I condescended to it—I didn't know enough to know it was really gonna be hard.

Things changed around the time I met Michael Tolkin. When I saw **The Player** (1992), when I was still living in New York, I had thought, "I wonder if I could do that." A couple of years later I had become friends with an executive who was working with him on a project for HBO about Microsoft, and she put the two of us together. When he and I first met, we talked about Proust, and we both loved Tolstoy, and we had a lot of similar references. So we ended up spending the whole meeting talking about *The Death of Ivan Ilyich* and *The Kreutzer Sonata*. And I was just so happy. I didn't care what happened after that—it was just the greatest afternoon. I thought, "I love this guy. He's so funny and so cool, and just an absolutely first-rate artist in all of his thinking."

We teamed up on the HBO project, which was a satire about Bill Gates and Microsoft, a sort of **Dr. Strangelove** piece about technology, called **20 Billion**. We'd break up the scenes, we'd write our scenes, we'd get back together, and his scenes were just so much better than mine that I couldn't believe it. I'm lucky I could see how much better his were—I mean, that's the first real break, realizing how not-good you actually are,

Empire as a notion

(01–02) When Gaghan was hired to rewrite the courtroom thriller **Rules of Engagement** early in his career, he dived into the project. "I read all the great Vietnam novels," he recalls, "like Tim O'Brien's *The Things They Carried* and *Going After Cacciato*. And I watched **Paths of Glory** (1957), like, 900,000 times. So that's the kind of stuff I was throwing in the hopper, and I squirreled away and wrote this 154-page draft." Richard Zanuck was so impressed with Gaghan's draft that the producer was convinced they would soon be ready to shoot the film. But director William Friedkin had other thoughts. "It was the most unbelievable meeting of my whole life," Gaghan says. "To this day, I've never experienced anything like it. He was a few minutes late, and he sat down and he said, 'Dick thinks we're on the 20-yard line'—pause—'I don't even think we've gotten on the field.' Then his voice starts to rise. 'War on trial? War's always on trial! You think that's a story? War on trial? That's nothing! You want to make a 60-million-dollar movie in Hollywood, you better have a fucking antagonist! And in the third act, the fucking antagonist goes down, and the fucking audience comes out of their seat like monkeys and they clap! What is it about this dynamic you don't understand?' He continued for two hours at that volume." Gaghan eventually made changes to the script, but he admits that Friedkin had been right in his assessment about Gaghan's take on the material. "For me, it was putting war on trial—it was putting our presence in Vietnam on trial. It was putting killing innocent people on trial and the whole notion of empire. I really wanted to put empire on trial, and I've tried to do that again and again ever since."

and cutting through all the nonsense smoke that's usually being blown at you in the zip codes around Beverly and La Cienega boulevards. But I knew—I knew he was great and I was terrible, so I started literally sitting behind him and watching him type when he would write his scenes. We'd keep reworking the story, and this went on for a long time. And then one day, I riffed out a subplot involving two characters who were sort of like the girl I was living with at the time and myself. I wrote the scenes, maybe 15 pages, in a few hours. I showed Michael the scenes, and I saw it in his face: "Hey, this is actually pretty good. That's gonna be in the movie." And he was happy for me, too. And when it was over, I was at the point where I felt like, "Wow, I'm writing

"I thought movies were a second-class art form. I condescended to it—I didn't know enough to know this is really gonna be hard."

scenes that should be shot." Three years of my writing career had gone by—I used to think, "I'll just dash off some **Simpsons** episode and make some money and come back to fiction"—and in that time, I had written volumes of terrible stuff. But watching Michael changed my approach to everything. I realized that this was a real art form and that I didn't understand it. I had to prostrate myself before it and study it if I wanted to be good. I had some other friends around this time, too, who were doing very interesting →

Filling your well

(01–05) "The screenwriter Frank Pierson once told me, 'Steve, I know how good dialogue works. It's just good lines somebody else said that I had the good sense to write down.' There's a lot of truth in that. I'm the beneficiary of having the time and the will to go out and talk to these people who say things that are incredible and are born out of world expertise in some particular situation. I always say I'm an amateur journalist—I hope for the good fortune to have awesome research. So much of what I'm doing is casting around for somebody who's lived something and knows what it is and can tell you what it is." For **Syriana**, Gaghan did extensive interviews, "meeting with spooks and criminals and arms dealers and oil men and heads of state and royalty." The reason he does such legwork, he says, is because he wants to have the authentic voice of that experience. "Growing up, I was a suburban fuckup. I got kicked out of a prep school in Kentucky. I was a high achiever who didn't live up to my potential. I was a National Merit Semifinalist and on the high-IQ team, and I was all-state in two sports. And I got kicked out in my senior year without any fallback plan. How does that happen? Well, I'm an expert on that. I can tell you what it's like to score weed in the suburbs—I know all about that. I know about being arrested in New York. Certain things I know about really well, but I used those up pretty quickly. I think you've got to replenish that well, or find a new well, and I'm always looking for a new well. Always. I love looking at systems and seeing how they really work." **(05)** Shown here are interview notes showing some of the exhaustive research Gaghan did for **Syriana**.

scripts: Charlie Kaufman and Owen Wilson and Wes Anderson. We traded our stuff back and forth. I saw early drafts of **Being John Malkovich** (1999) and **Rushmore** (1998). I saw fully formed film artists who were my peers and I wanted to do what they were doing—get my own voice or vision of the world out into that world. I had no clue how this was going to happen, but suddenly I just really loved this fucking art form. It's like haiku repeated 10,000 times in one document. The bar was set way higher than I thought.

My first produced credit was on **Rules of Engagement**. I did a major rewrite on it, and I was on the set. And I learned that a film is like this great circus that's been brought together.

They create a circus, and the circus travels around together, and then the circus disappears, and you're left with a commemorative watch. And then it's time to make a new circus. I loved that—I was not sentimental, and the process is not sentimental. It's a business, and you fling your script into this machine. The machine is very powerful, and it can destroy the material very easily, and the fight never ends to get it out the way you see it. You can't ever give up, even at the end—you just have to keep fighting. But the great thing about that machine is that it's also an accelerator, and it puts your work out into the world with such volume that it is seen in little villages in countries that barely have

03

04

05

DINNER WITH "SON OF SALIM" IN CANNES

Carlton in Cannes. Rich people everywhere. Always rich people everywhere.

"You present a Syrian passport and it's a hundred questions. You give your Canadian passport, it's 'hello, Sir, welcome." "Present your Iranian passport, it's fingerprints."

Bob tells story, "they were trying to set me up with a woman named Dominique in Paris. I ran a check on her. She's known as the Black Widow. She had five Palestinian boyfriends meet violent ends. I find pictures of her from Beirut where she's running across the street, bandoliers over her chest, firing an AK-47. This is my kind of woman. I meet her for dinner in London, then she takes me to an EST meeting."
King Fahd spent 100 million U.S. on his summer trip to Geneva. He was spending 2.5 million a week at the Intercontinental. His son took 280 rooms at the Hilton. They leased 600 Mercedes limos to drive everyone around. And when they left they leased 350 trucks to take their purchases to Marbella.

DINNER WITH XXX IN GENEVA

The moment the lawsuit was filed against the Saudis, they took 210 billion in investment in the U.S. out and put it into the Euro and gold.
XXX talking about how his father hired ex CIA chiefs back in the eighties, "one hundred, one twenty, I think that was the going rate. Ah, we had them by the dozen, Crutchfield, Stolz, Turner, Helms, Waller, Fees. Jim Fees went into business for himself, helped trigger Kuwaiti property investment in Spain. Billions of dollars."

Abdul Azis, King Fahd's son, is surrounded by sharks, guys who have something on him, have him locked up tight. He's Richie Rich, surrounded by leeches, wondering who are his friends?
There is "easy come, easy go," and "hard come, easy go," and then there are the survivors.

---

electricity. And that's a really awesome thing to be a part of.

When I started writing what would become **Traffic**, I wasn't aware of the miniseries **Traffik**. I just wanted to write a story about the War on Drugs. I quit my television jobs because I wanted to do this movie really badly. I mean, on some level I'd been training all my life to write this movie. So I did all this research, and I read a bunch of books, and I met all these people. I conducted a bunch of interviews, and I found that tape-recorders make people in power very nervous. But thankfully I'm not a real journalist—I'm just a screenwriter. So if you don't record them, and you just write stuff down subtly, they'll

"Every time I do a script, I go completely insane: 'Why isn't this working?' I get lost."

talk so honestly about everything. And so I started developing this interview methodology that worked really well. When I met all these people, I'd get Stockholm Syndrome—even if my point of view is quite different, I tend to like almost everybody I talk to. And so I think it gets people to really talk to me in a way that they don't always talk. But after all that research, I didn't know where to start. I knew I wanted to have a drug czar, I wanted to have Colombia, I wanted to have Mexico, I wanted to have the consumer →

"If I'm lucky, it's like some fucking other thing happens, and voices start popping from nowhere and I'm just transcribing, really."

side—I knew I wanted to have all these things. But I couldn't make it work because the hero basically had to time travel. He couldn't be in enough places plausibly to get all the story I wanted. So I literally had a nervous breakdown. Nothing happened for six months—I couldn't write. I was reading more, researching more, writing notes, but I didn't know what I was doing—I'm not writing anything. A professor friend of mine said this great thing to me once: "At a certain point, research becomes a form of cowardice."

Out of the blue Steven Soderbergh contacted me, because he was trying to do a War on Drugs film, too. So he came to lunch and gave me this miniseries from England. **Traffik** with a "K" it was called. I looked at that miniseries, and there was a very melodramatic quality to the stories. I thought it was really well done—the scenes are very well-written—but at its core, it was like the melodramatic TV stuff that I didn't really like, that I was trying to get away from. But I realized my script had the same types of stories, and I saw the brilliance of the way **Traffik** had strung this all together, and the necessity for clarity when you are crosscutting like that on a bigger canvas. It's funny: I had written a lot of TV very fast by that point, and TV was typically an A-B-C-D story, but for some reason I hadn't seen that I could do that in film, too. It didn't occur to me to do multiple narratives in the movies.

The process of figuring out how the stories wove together in **Traffic** was a learning process in understanding the value of a narrative spine that starts *here* and ends *there*. When I'm writing scenes, I fall down a well and time stops. I'm not thinking about the plot. If I'm lucky, it's like some other thing happens, and voices start popping from nowhere and I'm just transcribing, really. It may not have anything to do with what I'm

ABANDON

(01) Gaghan made his directorial debut on **Abandon**, which he also wrote. "I wanted to do a psychological thriller," says Gaghan. "I wanted to do **Repulsion** (1965). I went up to Harvard and did a lot of research and talked to a bunch of kids there. I met this very compelling girl whose brother had become a schizophrenic at 18, and she was the smartest one of all these smart people. She was really special—beautiful, talented, and just enigmatic. She was terrified she was gonna lose her mind like her brother, who was in a mental institution. Guys were attracted to her like bugs to a lamp. And I thought, 'I can do a modern version of **Repulsion**.' In that movie, Catherine Deneuve is so beautiful that nobody can see past her looks to realize she's psychotic. Also, I wanted to shoot college the way college really feels, which is that it's scary. There was pressure at these really high-end institutions that was crippling. You're not there for knowledge's sake—you're there to meet the person to get a job. Over 50 percent of Harvard's graduating class applies for the same jobs on Wall Street. So college is this weird pressure cooker—and it can make you crazy."

THE ALAMO

(02) Gaghan shared screenplay credit on **The Alamo**, but he worked on the project rather early in the process, back when it was still going to star Russell Crowe and be directed by Ron Howard. "I read every book about the Alamo and it was quickly apparent these are the most amazing characters you ever heard of," says Gaghan. "All the famous guys who died in the Alamo— Davy Crockett, Jim Bowie—they were all drunks. They're bad guys—I mean, they were good guys, but they were bad guys. Maybe 'human' is the word. They were such dual-purpose characters. They had drinking problems, they cheated on women, they knocked up women and wouldn't honor their paternity . . . They were slave traders. And that's who was in the Alamo—those were Americans. That's what an American is. These flawed dudes are riding off to build this country. And they all die. That's just a helluva story."

supposed to be writing, but it will have real energy and feel very vital, like it has to be in a movie. The scene is declaring itself, and it's coming from some pure place of inspiration—it's disconnected from anything. I can't take credit for it—nobody can take credit for it. It's just appeared, and it has to be in a movie, but the terrifying question is: What movie?

I was working with Will Smith on **After Earth**, and he broke this down brilliantly. He said, "Oh yeah, you can start with character—you start with character all you want. You'll get lost for years. It'll be great, but no one will know it's a movie. Or you can start with structure, and that will be a device that you can present to a financing entity and say, 'Here is your movie.' But it'll suck, and you'll have to find the character. You can start with character and take forever—all that will make it into the movie once you finally submit and focus on structure. Or you can start with structure, and you're still gonna spend all that time trying to find the character stuff later. Your choice."

Every time I do a script, I go completely insane: "Why isn't this working?" I get lost. The process for me is somehow stealing the time to be lost for a very long time and to not know what I'm doing at all. I need to have a complete crippling loss of confidence where I think, "Why am I doing this? This is too ambitious. This makes no sense." And then I'm bumbling, bumbling,

giving up completely—three, four, five times— coming back to it, changing it entirely, restructuring it, throwing it in a different way. And then I've got 50 pages that work, and I wonder what the movie's about. Plus, there's always this sense of, "I don't want to do something that's been done before." I want the scenes to come from a magical place that I don't understand. I don't want it to be, "That scene worked great in **Mission: Impossible** (1996)—let's do that scene." →

03 The Alamo (2004)

> "When you look at **Traffic**, what does it mean? Well, I guess it's saying that love and patience and good parenting can help an individual with a pernicious and often deadly problem."

I just don't want to work like that. It's what I love best and fear most about the process. Screenwriters face the void. There's nothing, and then there's going to be something. It's the something-from-nothing business. Like magic. But all too often, the stakes are very high and what feels familiar feels safe. And you have to fight the derivative urge, the urge to safety, at every step in the process.

With **After Earth**, they're swinging for the fence—they created an entire world that is as full and as rich as the world of **Star Wars** (1977). But at its heart, it's a father-son story, and that's the story I've been writing my whole life. My dad died when I was 15. He was released from a lot of suffering, and there was something noble about it, and I learned a lot from him. A lot of the stories I've written have a father-son element. Some of them are father-daughter—often, I make it a girl because it's just easier, but it's the same stuff. The Clooney character in **Syriana** had a son who ultimately wasn't in the movie that much, but it was a big deal. Matt Damon's trying to figure out how to be a father and a husband in the middle of a tragedy. In my draft of **The Alamo**, they're all terrible fathers. **Havoc** (2005) is about this daughter whose parents are absent and is trying to parent herself, but has no role models. I adapted Malcolm Gladwell's book *Blink* into a coming-of-age story about the son of a corporate raider. When you look at **Traffic**, what does it mean? Well, I guess it's saying that love and patience and good parenting can help an individual with a pernicious and often deadly →

The influence of Z

(01–03) While Gaghan has written movies like **Traffic** and **Syriana** that tackle societal issues, he's not convinced that a film can necessarily change the world. "I'm suspicious of film as propaganda or as a political tool," he says. "Obviously, used by someone like Leni Riefenstahl it can be a powerful tool. And there are extremely effective documentaries that have come out on all sorts of issues, but I think politics is also the last refuge of scoundrels. I mean you really gotta hide the strings. I grew up loving those big-boy fiction writers like Faulkner, Tolstoy, Nabokov, and Hemingway. There were people writing nonfiction books about all the things those people wrote their novels about, but to me I find that non-journalistic recreations are just this other thing entirely—you've made something new." To illustrate his point, he mentions a personal favorite, Costa-Gavras' 1969 thriller **Z**. "It's a staggering work of art," says Gaghan. "It's like a speech of Martin Luther King. I've watched it 50 times, and every time I get to the end, I want to run into the street and burn shit down and change the world. How? I don't know. Why? I don't know. Do I understand fascism in mid-1960s Greece? Maybe. How does it relate to my life? Every way. **Z** couldn't be anything else. It's not a novel, it's not a **Frontline** piece, it's not **60 Minutes**, and it's not a documentary. It's not anything except **Z**."

HAVOC

(04–06) Havoc, a drama about spoiled Los Angeles teens, was originally written by Jessica Kaplan, an Angeleno who died before the film was made. Gaghan came on to rewrite the project, and he had a deep affinity for the material. "It was a story about rich kids partying on the Westside," he says, "and I understood that from my suburban upbringing in Kentucky. I had really written an original script, truthfully—I started over, and I wrote a whole new movie based on my own life and transposed it to the Palisades, a place I'd never been. I just imagined what it would be like. At that time, I lived in Hollywood, and I'd never seen it." **Havoc**, which starred Anne Hathaway and Bijou Phillips, didn't receive great reviews, but the script opened an unexpected door for Gaghan. "I had a reference to **sex, lies, and videotape** (1989) in it—there was a scene where I said the light is like **sex, lies, and videotape**—and the script got to Steven Soderbergh, and he called me up and said, 'Do you want to have lunch?'" When the two had lunch, Soderbergh asked him if he'd be interested in writing what would eventually become **Traffic**.

Traffic and addiction

(01–03) Although Gaghan deftly balances **Traffic**'s multiple storylines, he admits that some of the narrative threads are closer to his heart. "The Michael Douglas story—the guy being told by his wife, 'Why don't you see if your daughter will pencil you in for a little face time?'—that's my mom trying to talk to me as a teenager, who was just going wild. That storyline mattered to me—how a suburban family can break down, despite everyone's best intentions. I tried to imagine what it was like to watch me go off the rails if I was my mother, and put that into that storyline." Asked how therapeutic it was to write about drug addiction as a recovering addict, Gaghan responds, "I had a seizure writing the overdose scene—I fell out of my chair at my desk and everything just short-circuited. I was writhing on the floor like an epileptic. I was just starting the process of trying to get my act together during that time. Some people call it growing up—people call it all sorts of things—but it got started for me around then and continues to this day. Believe me, I didn't just wake up one day and say, 'Oh, fortune, I've been struck sober, and now I'm happy, joyous, and free forever.'"

The ending of Traffic

(04–05) In **Traffic**, Gaghan initially concluded the storyline concerning Caroline Wakefield (played by Erika Christensen) in a darker way. "I felt very, very strongly that she should sneak out of her house and go out to get more drugs at the end of the movie," says Gaghan. "She's too young, shit's coming too easy, and she's just not going to get religion at this point. I had a knock-down, drag-out argument with Steven Soderbergh about it that lasted quite a while. I wrote specifically that there was a window in her parents' house where her room jutted out over the garage. The window slides up, her leg appears, and she sneaks off into the night, and that's the end—her disappearing into the woods. It was dark and ominous and scary—their little girl is gone. Roll credits. But I think from Steven's perspective he felt, 'Wow, we have this 45-million-dollar movie, and at the end of the day, that's really not what we want to say—that it's hopeless on every level. People need a little shred of hope.' We argued and argued and argued about it, and he said, finally, 'Look, you're probably right that she wouldn't get religion. But is it possible that on any given day, there would be a day that she's trying to change her life in this other way?' I'm like, 'Absolutely. That is absolutely possible. She would be trying, and you could end on that.' I got my mind around that, and I realized it's true. You can kick drugs. It happens every day. Usually not all at once, with little slips here and there, but that's how you do it— slow accrual—and it works. So that's possible. And so I came around on that."

problem. With **Syriana**, it's that foreign policy driven by greed will end in disaster, but it's also saying that with family, love, and forgiveness, you can make a go of it in an almost absolutely overwhelming and uncontrollable world. It's the same story again and again and again. I don't have any other story—that's the story. My friend Adam Gopnik once read a bunch of my stuff and he said, "You have a story, Gaghan, and it's the same one every time." I was really offended, and he said, "You should be happy—most people don't have one at all."

I've been working on a project that took three years, and it sucked every day—except where I had like three hours where I just went, "Hey, wait, we have a movie." It's so preposterous to be lost for so long and yet to have faith you're gonna

have those three hours. Anybody working like this, they would quit. I've been screenwriting for quite a while, and I've had maybe a handful of really good moments. But one of those was when I saw the first cut of **Traffic** at this little screening room at Warner Bros. When the film ended, Soderbergh was in the back of the theater. I was in the very front, and I got up and I ran back toward him, and I can see in his face that he's thinking, "Holy shit, he's gonna attack me." I hugged him—and he's not a hugger—and I just said, "You're gonna win the Oscar for Best Director. This is the happiest day of my life." And it was—it was one of the happiest days of my life. And that sustains you for a really, really long time.

Christopher Hampton

"I write about things that really intrigue me or nag at me, but I generally don't know when I start writing what conclusions I'm going to make and what directions these pieces are going to go in."

Atonement (2007)

A writer celebrated equally for his work on the stage and the screen, Christopher Hampton was born in the Archipalego of the Azores, living as a child for a time in Egypt and Zanzibar because of his father's job with the communications company Cable & Wireless. Studying French and German at university in England, Hampton knew from a young age that he wanted to be a writer, but after an unsuccessful stab at a novel, he turned his attention to playwriting. He wrote the play *When Did You Last See My Mother?* when he was only 18—it was produced at The Royal Court Theater two years later, to much acclaim. From there, Hampton enjoyed a flourishing theatrical career with works such as *Total Eclipse* and *The Philanthropist*. His success as a screenwriter began with **Carrington** (1995), which he wrote in the mid-1970s after being moved by Michael Holroyd's extensive biography of writer Lytton Strachey. **Carrington** took 20 years to reach cinemas, but Hampton had a much quicker turnaround with his screenplay for **Dangerous Liaisons** (1988), which was based on his hit play and adapted from the 18th-century novel by Pierre Choderlos de Laclos. Written in three weeks in the late fall of 1987, the film landed in theaters a little over a year later, winning Hampton an Oscar for Best Adapted Screenplay. Hampton's career has encompassed translations of the plays *God of Carnage* and *Hedda Gabler*, and he has also co-written the book and lyrics for the 1990s musical based on Billy Wilder's **Sunset Boulevard** (1950). Hampton adapted his own play for the film **Total Eclipse** (1995) and received a second Academy Award nomination for his screenplay for **Atonement** (2007). In 2011, he turned his play *The Talking Cure* into the script for director David Cronenberg's **A Dangerous Method**. Other notable screenplay adaptations include **Mary Reilly** (1996), **The Quiet American** (2002), and **Chéri** (2009). Hampton has also directed three of his scripts: **Carrington, The Secret Agent** (1996), and **Imagining Argentina** (2003).

Christopher Hampton

"Growing up, there were hardly any books in the house. In fact, I came from a very sporty family. My parents played tennis a lot. My father played rugby for Egypt at one point, and my older brother was very keen on sport. I was the geek in the corner with the thick glasses, reading a book. They were very tolerant about it, but my bookishness was certainly unusual in my family. I boxed when I was young—you had to do sport at my boarding school—and I was quite good at it, but I didn't really enjoy it. Once, I was matched against a boy who went on to be Junior Amateur Boxing Association champion, and he knocked me unconscious in 45 seconds—after that, I rethought the whole idea of boxing.

After my father's older brother died, it was discovered that he had written short stories for women's magazines under a pseudonym. I knew him quite well, and he had always been very encouraging. He gave me *The Complete Works of Shakespeare* for my ninth birthday, but he never let on that he was interested in writing. By that point, I was writing little plays, and I guess that he thought that it was an appropriate gift. It was in one volume, with tiny print, and I was fascinated by it. It was hard to read for a child—it was hard to understand and hard to get through. But I loved it—I was sure that when I couldn't understand it, it was my fault, rather than the playwright's.

I've done many adaptations in my career, and I first got into it through translation. The Royal Court put on my first play, *When Did You Last See My Mother?*, while I was still at college. Because of that, I was asked by The Royal Court to translate a Soviet play called *Maria* by Isaac Babel—just to rework the dialogue to make it more speakable. I enjoyed that, and then when I graduated in 1968, I went to work at The Royal Court, and I got assigned to do a new translation of *Uncle Vanya* with Paul Scofield. I really enjoyed doing those translations—I realized that two or three months working on a masterpiece could only help your own work and nourish it.

I sold the film rights of my first play and was hired to write a screenplay. That first screenplay

"David Lean had several principles, which he repeated more than once. Lesson One was that the most important thing in any screenplay is the final image of one scene and the first image of the next scene and how they flow into one another."

was not very good—everyone was quite charitable about it, but I didn't feel it was very good as I was writing it. And, indeed, for some unknown reason, whereas writing for the theater had come quite naturally to me, the business of writing movies took me about 10 years to figure out. My father loved the cinema, so we'd see two or three movies a week—I reckon I saw just about every American movie of the 1950s. By contrast, I'd hardly ever been to a theater. I mean, the first play I ever saw at The Royal Court was mine. In school, we got taken to see theater, but it was always a special occasion, never a casual habit like going to the cinema. So, I think I was very unanalytical about the movies—I thought movies were quite easy. That was a mistake.

I spent 10 years in and around The Royal Court Theater, and I had written five plays and a number of translations, and all of them had been done there. And in 1976, they said, "Well, what's your next play?" And I said, "Look, I always thought that The Royal Court was supposed to be for new writers—I'm no longer a new writer. I'm going to go off and try to do something else." And the "something else" that I wanted to try was to really think out how to write a screenplay in a more effective way than I had been doing.

And so, over the course of a year, I wrote **Carrington**, which took about 20 years to reach the screen, although I didn't know that then. That script was the beginning of an enormous learning process for me. I wrote a huge rough draft, which probably would've run about four hours long, and then I started to try and shave it down. Warner Bros. had commissioned the screenplay, and I took nine months before I gave them the first draft, by which time the executive who'd commissioned me had long disappeared →

Limitations foster creativity

(01–03) Beyond its tragic love story, the film **Atonement** is perhaps best known for its sweeping Steadicam shot of the beach at Dunkirk. "That was a very good example of necessity being the mother of invention," Hampton says. "I think the budget was something like 35 million dollars for the film, and at a certain point they got nervous and said they didn't want to spend more than 30 on it." Before the film was shot, director Joe Wright elected to remove several scenes that led to the battle and instead combine them on the scene at the beach. "So you had the soldiers shooting their horses, the mayhem, the anarchy of the soldiers, and so on. We made it into something that was more interesting than what we would have made if we'd had the extra five million dollars and spent it on the script as written." (02–03) Shown are two pages of the extended beach scene as written by Hampton.

57.

Harnessed but riderless horses gallop across the sand. A whaler with ragged black sails lies fifty yards from the sea. A football game is in progress. A small group of men throw off their clothes and splash into the sea for a swim. Another larger group huddles in a bandstand, singing a hymn.

A chaplain and his clerk are throwing prayer books and bibles into a bonfire; the thin pages catch and float into the air like black snowflakes. A YOUNG SOLDIER of no more than 17 sits quietly looking out to sea with tears streaming down his face.

ROBBIE approaches a group of NAVAL OFFICERS, as they stride down the beach with a clipboard, trying to do a head-count. They keep moving briskly throughout the conversation.

                    ROBBIE
          We've just arrived, Sir. Can you tell
          us what we're supposed to do?

                    NAVAL OFFICER
          Nothing. Just wait.

                    ROBBIE
          Where are the ships?

                    NAVAL OFFICER
          A few made it in yesterday but the
          Luftwaffe blew them to buggery. We
          lost five hundred men when they sank
          the Endurance. And high command in its
          infinite wisdom is denying us air
          cover. It's a disgrace, it's a fucking
          disaster.

                    ROBBIE
          The thing is, I'm expected back, you
          see.

                    NAVAL OFFICER
          There's over three hundred thousand
          men on this beach, private. So you'll
          have to wait your turn. Just be
          grateful that you're not wounded,
          we've had orders to leave the wounded
          behind.

NETTLE pulls ROBBIE away, as the NAVAL OFFICER continues up the beach.

                    NETTLE
          Come on, guv, never trust a sailor on
          dry land. Best off out of it.

58.

ROBBIE moves on, dazed, through crowds streaming across the beach in opposite directions, past gutted and blazing vehicles.

From up ahead, the SOUND of a gunshot.

                    MACE
          That's not right.

To one side is a detachment of French cavalry, each man dismounted and standing to attention beside his horse. A FRENCH OFFICER with a pistol moves slowly, almost ceremoniously, down the line, shooting each horse in the head.

ROBBIE moves on, as another horse goes down in the background. He rounds the back of the beached whaler where a deranged SOLDIER is perched up on the mast, furiously waving and shouting at the top of his voice.

                    SOLDIER
          Can you hear me, laddies? I'm coming
          home.

The seafront, or what's left of it was once a cheerful resort with cafes and little shops. ROBBIE, MACE and NETTLE pass a bandstand and merry-go-round decorated in red, white and blue. Soldiers have opened up the cafes and a good portion of them are raucously drunk. Some lark about on bikes. A solitary sunbather in his underpants lies on a towel. A brawling couple rolls down the bank on to the beach.

MACE climbs up on to the gazebo-shaped bandstand where a tight knot of SOLDIERS is singing "Dear Lord and Father of Mankind". Then he catches up with ROBBIE and NETTLE as they plunge on ahead.

                    ROBBIE
          Come on. I have to get something to
          drink.

                    NETTLE
          You need one. You're grey.

He turns to MACE.

                    NETTLE
          He's gone all grey, look.

They move on past another group of SOLDIERS, disabling vehicles with their rifle-butts. Then ROBBIE points ahead to where a cinema sits, perched unexpectedly at the top of the beach.

Translating a script is an art in itself

(01–02) "Everybody has different reasons for translating works," says Hampton. "Mine would always be to try to reproduce as exactly and as accurately and as fairly as possible whatever was the original author's intention. But even if you do that, there's an enormous variation within those parameters." To illustrate his point, he cites his translation of the plays of celebrated French playwright Yasmina Reza, specifically *Art* and *God of Carnage*. "With *God of Carnage*, I did an English translation for the English actors and then sat around the table with the American cast and did an American translation, which differs in several significant ways. Then, when they came to do the movie—for reasons you'd have to ask them about, but to do with Roman Polanski's comfort level or something—they got a completely different translation. I watched the movie **Carnage** with the greatest of interest, and one of the things I noticed was that it was totally unamusing. I'm not saying it doesn't have laughs in it, but there's no conscious wit in the language at all. And that's a choice—that's a naturalistic choice. In other words, that's a writer saying, 'I want these people to say what they probably would have said without prettying it up—without changing it in some witty way.' Whereas when I do those plays, I'm very aware of how to make them work with an audience and make the audience laugh. I think that enhances them and I think that makes them more serious as well as everything else. Anyway, this is a long way around to saying what seems to be a very circumscribed exercise—translating a play—actually leaves you with an enormous amount of leeway as the writer. You still have an enormous number of decisions to make creatively."

into the mist. Next, I was hired to write a movie for Fred Zinnemann—I spent a year working with him, and that film didn't get made either. But I was working with a man who was obsessed about narrative and how to tell a story and wasn't really interested in anything else—he just wanted an awesome juggernaut of narrative, and that was a very, very useful lesson for me. Then I got hired by David Lean to write a script of *Nostromo* from the book by Joseph Conrad for a movie that was ultimately never released. It's a very difficult book to adapt, although it's a masterpiece. I spent a full year working with him, doing several drafts, and he taught me an absolutely enormous

amount. It's no coincidence that the next screenplay I wrote was for the movie of **Dangerous Liaisons**—if you looked at the screenplays I'd written in the 1970s and compared them with **Dangerous Liaisons**, you would see that this writer has made progress.

David Lean had several principles, that he repeated more than once. Lesson One was that the most important thing in any screenplay is the final image of one scene and the first image of the next scene and how they flow into one another. If you do that right, you will have something that is not a disparate set of 250 scenes—you will have about six to 10 chapters

CARRINGTON

(03–05) Ask Hampton where the idea for **Carrington** originated, and he responds, "It had to do with chance, which is often the way things go." Hampton had been reading Michael Holroyd's biography on Lytton Strachey, the writer and Bloomsbury Group member. "It's an enormous biography. I mean, it's 2,000 pages or something. It came out in two volumes, a couple of years apart. It was one of the first really candid biographies where you discovered everything about Strachey's life—Holroyd had been able to distill a really interesting story from it. When I started to read it, I knew very little about Lytton Strachey, but when I came to the end of the second volume, I became interested in his relationship with Dora Carrington, which didn't start until the middle of the second volume. The biography ends with Lytton's sudden illness and death and Dora's suicide—I was more moved by it than anything I'd read for years. I couldn't get it out of my head." Hampton wrote the first draft of the screenplay in the mid-1970s—the film, which he directed and which starred Jonathan Pryce (as Strachey) and Emma Thompson (as Carrington), made its premiere at the 1995 Cannes Film Festival, where Pryce won Best Actor and the film took home a Special Jury Prize.

within which everything flows from one scene to the next in the most effortless way. You can shock the audience—you can do all sorts of things—but you have to do it in a way that maintains the narrative integrity of the piece. There was a montage sequence in the middle of **Nostromo** at a rather crucial point where the exhausted rebel army finally conquers the town that they've been besieging. As they march into the town, the sexton starts to ring the church bells to indicate that the rebel army has arrived, and there are six or seven characters in different parts of the town, all at different stages of their story, and all of whom will be affected. And the question was, "What order should we put this montage in? Which characters' reactions should we see first?" It was three days' work, but finally we had it in the right order. Earlier in my career, I would have just whizzed by that—I would have put the characters in any random order. But those small choices make a difference.

Theater and film are such different media. Often, you see a film that's from a stage play and it doesn't seem to work. It smells of the theater—

> **"Whenever I think, 'Well, why wasn't that as good as I thought it was going to be?', it generally turns out to be something to do with the structure and the fact that it isn't properly organized. The foundation and the organization are something that should be invisible, but they've got to be there."**

it hasn't been re-imagined for cinema. Obviously, I have nothing against adapting plays for the screen, but you really have to rethink it in cinematic terms. Before writing the film version of **Dangerous Liaisons**, I had adapted a couple of my plays to screenplays before and been unsatisfied with them because they had been too slavishly like the plays. So, I was determined with the play of *Dangerous Liaisons* to re-conceive it as a film, and in a curious way, it's a film that is traveling toward the play all the way through. It becomes more and more like the play, but in its first halfhour, it's opened up a great deal—there are a number of things in →

"I'm not sure I've ever written a film with a traditional structure—I don't believe in any of those rules for writing screenplays. What that gives you is a formula, and inevitably the result will be formulaic."

the movie that aren't in the play. It tells the story in a different way.

When I first had the idea of adapting *Les Liaisons Dangereuses* for the stage in the mid-1970s, I told the literary manager of the National Theater, and he said, "We think it's not a good idea—the two main characters never meet each other. They just write letters." I said, "Well, I'm going to make them meet." When I finally decided to sit down and write the play, there was a geographical problem. The characters were always in inconvenient places—one would be in Paris, the other would be in the country. So, the first thing I had to do writing the play was actually do a big chart and start moving people around: "What happens if Valmont was not there, but here? What if Merteuil was over there?" Eventually, you shape this down into a plot where the same things happened as happened in the book, but the characters are with each other—the

dialogue takes place between the characters on the spot rather than by letter. But when we made the film, director Stephen Frears intuited very quickly that the idea of letters, which is not helpful on the stage, was very helpful in the movie. So we went back to having people sending letters to one another in the movie, which hadn't happened at all in the stage version. In the film, you can see somebody writing and then you do a cut, and you could see the effect of Michelle Pfeiffer reading the letter and weeping.

I'm not sure I've ever written a film with a traditional structure—I don't believe in any of those rules for writing screenplays. What that gives you is a formula, and inevitably the result will be formulaic. I've always refused to do treatments, but I can do outlines: "This happens in this scene, then this happens, then this happens, then this happens." That way, you're liberated within the scene, but you have your

DANGEROUS LIAISONS

(01) When Hampton set about writing the film version of his play *Dangerous Liaisons* **(01)**, time was of the essence because of a competing project. "We knew that Milos Forman was doing **Valmont** (1989)," he recalls. "Most studios would've backed away, but Lorimar said, 'We'll do **Dangerous Liaisons** if you can guarantee to get yours in first.' I wrote the screenplay in three weeks with blood coming out of my ears. All I thought was, 'I've got to get this done.' Milos had made his announcement, already had his script, was swinging into production— his previous two films were **Amadeus** (1984) and **One Flew Over the Cuckoo's Nest** (1975), both of which won Best Picture Oscars. So, I just got going as fast as I possibly could. I was frightened—I thought, probably rightly, that some sort of sense would prevail with Lorimar or somebody would say to them, 'Are you crazy?' Fortunately, when I finished the first draft, we didn't need to change it all that much afterward." **Dangerous Liaisons** was nominated for seven Academy Awards, including Best Picture, and won three Oscars, including Best Adapted Screenplay for Hampton. How did the Oscar change Hampton's life? "Well, your price goes up enormously," he responds with a chuckle, "which is very satisfactory."

01

A DANGEROUS METHOD

(02–03) A Dangerous Method, which Hampton adapted from his play *The Talking Cure*, was directed by David Cronenberg. "David doesn't like to make films that are very long," Hampton says. "When we had our very first meeting, he said he'd like the script to be 87 pages. The first draft I sent him was, I think, 101." Because the play was two-and-a-half-hours long, how was Hampton able to condense the work, which focuses on the tense relationship between Sigmund Freud (Viggo Mortensen in the film), Carl Jung (Michael Fassbender), and Jung's patient Sabina (Keira Knightley)? "I just felt that we could cut certain speeches and arguments that an audience will sit still for in a theater, but not in a movie. **A Dangerous Method** is certainly a talky film, and it's quite close to the edge of what an audience would put up with in the cinema. So I thought in advance where we needed to scale some of that stuff down." When Hampton presented Cronenberg with the 101-page draft, the director went away to make further trims. "He sent me a final draft edited by him with another 10 pages cut out. I was prepared to be horrified, but he'd done it so elegantly that I hardly missed anything. If you work with good people, you learn things, and I really did with David—I learned how to think about what was truly essential in the screenplay."

milestones along the way. If you do it right, the audience doesn't feel the presence of a structure—if you've done it subtly enough, it won't impose itself on them. But if you don't have some kind of structure, they'll feel there's something lacking—I mean, I do as an audience. Whenever I think, "Well, why wasn't that as good as I thought it was going to be?", it generally turns out to be something to do with the structure and the fact that it isn't properly organized. The foundation and the organization are something that should be invisible, but they've got to be there.

I'd always liked Ian McEwan's books, but when I read *Atonement*, I felt sure it could make a really good film. It reminded me of **The Go-Between** (1970), which is a film I absolutely adore, but it also reminded me of, surprisingly enough, **The Deer Hunter** (1978), because in **Atonement** you get more than a third of the way

through and then suddenly you cut to the Second World War—you're in the middle of Dunkirk. I thought it had a very original structure—it's not those "three acts" that they always tell you a film script has to have. It's two acts, the second of which breaks in half and contradicts itself at the end.

I love the collaborative process of working with a director on the set. But I'm also perfectly happy to work for directors like Joe Wright, who go off and make a film and then call you up and show it to you. I was introduced to Joe on **Atonement**, and at the first meeting, he said, "I like the script very much, but if you don't mind, I'd like to go back and start from scratch," which is a phrase that strikes terror into a screenwriter's heart. But he had a very clear idea of what he wanted, and as we worked on it and developed it, it seemed to me that his idea was clearer and better than what we had started with. In the first →

> **"Theater and film are such different media. Often, you see a film that's from a stage play and it doesn't seem to work. It smells of the theater—it hasn't been re-imagined for cinema."**

draft I wrote for **Atonement**, there was a framework—it started with Briony as an adult woman going back to the house, which was now a hotel, for the party that they were throwing for her birthday. She punctuated the film—every now and then, you'd see this old woman watching. And it was Joe who said, "You know, the great thing in the novel is it's a big surprise when the final reveal happens. Shouldn't we keep that? Shouldn't we give them a big surprise?" And, of course, he was absolutely right. We did shoot the final scene of the novel, which was also the final scene in my screenplay, which was her watching the play that they put on at the beginning of the film—she's standing up to say, "Thank you," and seeing Robbie and Cecilia sitting at the back. Joe shot that, and it was very powerful. But Joe is very ruthless with his own work, which is often a sign of a very good director, and although we all said, "That scene is very, very good," he said, "No, there's something wrong with it." Ultimately he changed it for the ending of them together on the beach.

I have written a lot about relationships between colleagues and artists that are close, but rivalrous at the same time, such as in **Total Eclipse** and **A Dangerous Method**. If you look at these divisions in several of my plays and films, you'll find that the argument is going on between a liberal and a radical. This is one of the main dialogues of the 20th century, the dialogue between the liberal left and the radical left. Sometimes I come down on the side of the radical, and sometimes I come down on the side of the liberal. In **Total Eclipse**, I come down on the side of Verlaine, who was the weak liberal, as opposed to the tough-minded radical. In **A Dangerous Method**, Freud is far, far more radical than Jung, and I really felt myself on his side a lot of the time. Now, I have to resist these temptations to take one side or the other and instead try to present each character's argument as strongly as I can. But I had a real problem with Jung: His books are very woolly and difficult to digest, while Freud's books are very lucid and well-argued and fascinating. And by and large, I

01

share Freud's antireligious bias. But Jung is the central character, and so I had to submerge myself further and further in Jung. Eventually, I did identify with him, but it was much more of a struggle than it was with Freud.

I write about things that really intrigue me or nag at me, but I generally don't know when I start writing what conclusions I'm going to make and what directions these pieces are going to go in. Not to sound mystical about it, but at some point, the piece of work starts to tell you what to do and starts to clarify to you what it's about. You think somehow you are imposing what you wanted to write about on a piece of paper. But in some mysterious way, it's the other way around. **"**

01 The final scene of **Atonement** (2007)

MARY REILLY

(02) Mary Reilly (1996), which tells the story of Dr. Jekyll and Mr. Hyde from the perspective of the titular servant (Julia Roberts), was a critical and box office disappointment at the time, but Hampton still quite likes the film. "That book was sent to me," Hampton recalls. "I loved the book. It was such a clever idea, and it was very well-written by Valerie Martin. I wrote the script in a week. It's the only time I've done that—I thought, 'I know how to do this,' and I sat down and did it in a week. After I sent it in, there was this modest feeding frenzy—it's the only script that I've ever sent in which was unanimously praised by the studio and everybody who read it. There were directors fighting for it and actresses ringing up and saying, 'I want to do this.' We started on a wave of euphoria." Stephen Frears directed the film, which was embroiled in a lengthy post-production that involved several different editors. According to Hampton, Frears and the studio, TriStar, were at odds about the final cut, and as a result the film's release suffered. "**Mary Reilly** ended up being the film that Stephen wanted released, but the studio was so furious by this time that they kind of threw it away, and they conveyed to the critical establishment that this was a film they really didn't like." But Hampton remains proud of his work. "My inspiration in writing Jekyll"—who was played by John Malkovich— "was Baudelaire, who is one of my favorite poets. In fact, a lot of Jekyll's lines come from Baudelaire. Later, I said to Stephen, 'Well, maybe the movie didn't work out, but how many big studio projects contain seven or eight lines from Baudelaire?'"

Working with Stephen Frears

(03) Hampton has collaborated with director Stephen Frears on several occasions, starting in 1977 for the BBC television film **Able's Will**. "That was my first original play for television," Hampton recalls. "It was assigned to Stephen, and I just liked the way he worked very much. I, of course, particularly liked the way he is extremely consultative—he wants the writer there all the time. In fact, the only trouble we've ever really had was when I was shooting **Carrington** at the same time as he was shooting **Mary Reilly** (03)—he was very annoyed with me for not being on the set. He likes you to be on the set so that if some change to the script needs to be made, it can be made by the writer and at once." It was Hampton who helped sell the producers of **Dangerous Liaisons** on Frears as its director. "They said, 'He just does television—he's never done anything like this before. We need somebody who is used to this sort of scale of project and can do period pictures.' And I said, 'No, no, you don't understand—that's precisely why he's exactly the right man for the job. He can do a sort of anti-period picture, which is what I have in mind.'"

David Hare

"When I talk to the young I say, 'Things are always worth trying.' I don't think there's anything more exciting in life than discovering a gift you didn't know you had. And it might have gone undiscovered."

The Hours (2002)

Heralded as a playwright, screenwriter, and director, Sir David Hare has enjoyed a professional career that has stretched across more than 40 years. His time in the theater has been marked by several triumphs, including *Plenty*, *The Blue Room*, and *Stuff Happens*, and in 2011 he was awarded the PEN Pinter Prize for his thought-provoking and politically engaging *oeuvre*. Hare's transition to film began in earnest in the 1980s when he wrote and directed **Wetherby** (1985), which won the Golden Bear at the Berlin Film Festival, **Paris by Night** (1988), and **Strapless** (1989). But a growing dissatisfaction with his films inspired him to refocus on theater, where he wrote his celebrated trilogy of plays about British life—*Racing Demon*, *Murmuring Judges*, and *The Absence of War*—in the early 1990s. Thankfully, Hare returned to screenplays with his terrific script for Louis Malle's **Damage** (1992), a portrait of obsessive, doomed love based on Josephine Hart's novel. More recently, he has received Academy Award nominations for his adapted screenplays for **The Hours** (2002) and **The Reader** (2008), which won, respectively, Nicole Kidman and Kate Winslet the Oscar for Best Actress. He also worked to adapt author Jonathan Franzen's 2001 novel, *The Corrections*, into a feature film. His plays *Plenty* and *The Secret Rapture* have been adapted into films, and in 2011 he wrote and directed the conspiracy thriller **Page Eight**, which starred Bill Nighy, Rachel Weisz, and Michael Gambon.

David Hare

"I only went into the theater because it was impossible to go into the cinema. Cinema in the 1960s, particularly in Europe, was the most exciting art form, but British cinema was going through one of its many collapses. And so I started a traveling theater company, and I was the director of it. One day, somebody failed to deliver a play—it was a Wednesday, and we had nothing to rehearse for the following Monday—so I sat down and wrote a one-act play, *How Brophy Made Good*, which we then started rehearsing. But I didn't think of myself as a writer. For many years, I just thought of myself as a director who wrote.

That first play wasn't very good—I was 22, it was terrible. But then the most famous producer on the West End—Michael Codron, who had produced Joe Orton and Peter Nichols and Harold Pinter—commissioned me to write a full-length play. I stumbled into an ability I didn't know I had. It was just chance. When I talk to the young I say, "Things are always worth trying." I don't think there's anything more exciting in life than discovering a gift you didn't know you had. And it might have gone undiscovered. It might be for tending a garden beautifully. Or it might be for making a nice pair of curtains. But you don't know until you've tried, and it's always worth trying.

Even though my first play was no good, when I handed it to the actors they looked at the dialogue, and I knew they were thinking, "Oh, this is fine, I can say this." I'd been a literary manager, so I'd read a lot of plays. It's like a chef in a restaurant—when the plate is put before you, you know whether it's edible or not. And it was exactly the same thing when I wrote a page of dialogue—it looked like a page of dialogue. That's harder than it seems. And actors immediately went, "Oh great, if I say this, I can

DAMAGE

(01) Although Hare rightly considers **Damage** a complete success, he notes that it wasn't a commercial hit—and it wasn't a particularly delightful production. "It was a famously unhappy shoot," recalls Hare with a laugh. "Juliette Binoche and Jeremy Irons did not exactly see eye-to-eye. I think that part of that was because they were being confronted with a script which just presented them with a *fait accompli*: 'You two fall passionately and madly in love, and one of you walks away and the other is destroyed. And yet for both of you, it's just a fact.'" But despite the actors' struggles to find motivations for their characters' ambiguous actions, Hare believes that their mysterious attraction was entirely the point. "**Damage** is about the arbitrariness of passion," he says. "We all know periods in our lives in which we would have killed—simply thrown people off bridges—in order to be with the object of our love. And when this magnetic pull happens, which makes your whole life seem completely meaningless apart from the passion that is consuming you, it's very hard to say what it is in the other person that is making this feeling happen. It just happens for no apparent reason."

> **"If my life in the cinema has been about anything, it's been about introducing subject matter that is not normally seen in mainstream films."**

do that," and it fired up their imagination. Of course, I didn't know anything about writing plays, but it's like an artist being able to do hands and feet—you've got to be able to do those or you can't draw.

I wrote and directed feature films in the 1980s, and each one was worse than the last. Like a lot of directors, my life as a director was U-shaped. It's a familiar pattern: Your first film is very good, and then your second film is really bad, and then you bump along the bottom for a while. Some people never go back up the other side of the U. I've only climbed up the far side recently by making **Page Eight**. But after my films in the 1980s, I realized that I was facing a choice. I could either bump along and become a film director and commit my life to that, or I could be a playwright. There was no time to be both. And I was being asked to write a trilogy of plays for the National Theater, so I really threw my lot

in with the British theater and gave it all my energy. But then my life was changed by Louis Malle, who asked me to do **Damage**, which I really, really didn't want to do. I said, "You know, I'm finished with the cinema, I'm just getting worse at it." And Louis said, "Well, you won't have to make this one—I'll make it. All you have to do is write it." I said no. Later, I was on a holiday, lying on a beach in the south of France. The phone rang and it was Louis. He said, "I'm coming down to join you." I said no, but he came down and said, "I know you're not going to write it, but, on the other hand, why don't we just imagine you were going to write it? Let's talk about how you would write it."

He had this incredible method which taught me everything about writing movies. Louis would start every day at 8:30 with a cup of coffee, and I would have a croissant. And he would say, "Tell me the story of the film." And I would say, "Well, →

02

The French New Wave

(02) When Hare and director Louis Malle were developing the story for **Damage** and exploring its flawed, human characters, they drew inspiration from French New Wave classics like **Breathless** (1960). "The *Nouvelle Vague* is very much about human behavior," says Hare. "The reason that everybody woke up to French cinema at the end of the 1950s and the beginning of the 1960s is that suddenly people were behaving like human beings. They were not behaving as if they were puppets to the storyline. In a classic Hollywood film, people move along the tracks that are determined by the narrative, and they fulfill the story and that's their job. But French cinema wants people to be people, and they want them to be contradictory and ambiguous—sometimes likable, sometimes unlikable, sometimes warm and sometimes cold, presenting one facet of themselves to one character and another facet of themselves to someone else. Just like you and me—not like people who are controlled by an author. The whole effect of the *Nouvelle Vague* is to make it seem that Jean-Paul Belmondo **(02)** or Jean Seberg are thinking up their own lines. They aren't, of course. But it looks as if they are."

"...I'm all for good entertainment—I wish there were some in the mainstream cinema. But so much of the stuff that's presented to us I don't find very entertaining. Do I want my films to have some content? Yes, I would prefer that."

there's this conservative politician . . ." And within about two sentences he'd say, "What sort of person is he? Why is he doing that?" He'd just ask questions. And so maybe by lunchtime we had got through about six scenes, and it would be really solid. Then the next day, he'd get up and say, "Tell me the story of the film." And I'd try and pick up where I left off the day before, and he'd say, "No, no, you've got to go back to the beginning." And this went on for about 10 days. By the end of that process, I could tell the story of **Damage** in about 20 minutes. He said, "Well, you've done the hard work now—you've written the film. Just go and hang some dialogue on it." It was an incredible way to write. And writing the dialogue only took me a few weeks, because the story was already completely laid out. It was the most severe way that I've ever worked on structure, but it was also the best way ever of writing a film. It does drive you absolutely mad—you just think, "Oh, I'm going insane." But that's when I began to realize why my own films were so bad: I'd never subjected them to this narrative test and created such a

taut string on which you could just hang the pearls.

If my life in the cinema has been about anything, it's been about introducing subject matter that is not normally seen in mainstream films. During **The Hours**, director Stephen Daldry and I did our very best not to use the word "lesbianism" or "suicide," but ultimately, that's what that film is about. And if you start thinking about movies about lesbianism or suicide that have played in multiplexes, there are actually very few. I've written plays about aid to the Third World, the Chinese Revolution, the privatization of the railways, the diplomatic process leading up to the Iraq War. These are not regular mainstream subjects, but what I want to do is get this kind of subject matter into the mainstream. That's the first thing that draws me to a movie.

People who disdain my movies tend to complain about them having "messages," and implicitly say how much they prefer what they call "pure" entertainment. Well, I'm all for good entertainment—I wish there were some in the →

THE READER

(01–03) Because **The Reader** won Kate Winslet a Best Actress Oscar, it might be easy to presume that she's the film's protagonist. But Hare knew that Michael Berg (played by David Kross as a youth and Ralph Fiennes as an adult) was the story's central character. "After the film was made and it became apparent that Kate Winslet had given this completely wonderful performance and was going to draw all the praise," Hare recalls, "Ralph would say to me, 'You and I know this is a film about Michael, don't we?' Hanna is a brilliant part and it's a showy part, and Kate played it better than anyone in the world could play it, but actually, it's not the heart of the film. The heart of the film is Michael's story. But because it's a reactive story and an essentially passive story, he's not an active hero. Everyone is drawn, of course, to the more showy side, which is the story of her—and properly so. But Ralph and I know how that film works."

01

Stylistic dialogue

(04–05) "Dialogue's a form of stylization," says David Hare. "The question is, is the audience going to accept that stylization? In **Sweet Smell of Success** (1957) (04), the dialogue is as mannered as Jacobean or Elizabethan tragedy. Clifford Odets"—who co-wrote the screenplay with Ernest Lehman—"consciously modeled it on Jacobean plays. In real life who ever said 'Match me, Sidney'—I mean, who ever talked like that? But it works perfectly." Hare also pointed to the dialogue in **The Godfather** (05). "If you actually analyze the lines in **The Godfather**," he says, "the level of literacy is way beyond anything you'll hear from a mafia hood. But you accept it. And why? Because it has a great stylistic consistency. Just as a painting doesn't look like a photograph, verisimilitude is not always the point in dialogue."

mainstream cinema. But so much of the stuff that's presented to us, I don't find very entertaining. Do I want my films to have some content? Yes, I would prefer that. But this idea that my films have "messages"? To me, it's just a nonsensical line of argument. You know, who are these tender flowers, these sort of overprotected people, who just feel that they're going to wither if anybody brings content to them? I'm bewildered by this line of argument. So many great American films are full of content. But now there's this extraordinary delicacy that everybody has developed lately, as if they're not hardy enough to be able to withstand a plot with something urgent to say.

After Nicole Kidman won an Oscar for **The Hours** and Kate Winslet won an Oscar for **The Reader**, I got a lot of telephone calls from actresses saying, "Oh, I understand you're the man who writes films that win actresses Oscars." And I had to explain to them, "You know, Nicole Kidman won the Oscar for **The Hours**." If she hadn't played it, the actress playing it would not have won. Same with Kate Winslet. It's not the

Invisible exposition

(01) "What you're trying to do as a screenwriter," Hare says, "is bring out the best in everybody else. You're meant to be providing an opportunity for the director and an opportunity for the actors to do the thing they can do." To illustrate his point, he cites **Moneyball** (2011), which was written by Steven Zaillian and Aaron Sorkin from a story by Stan Chervin. "They created this fantastic structure that was so secure and so in place that it allowed Brad Pitt to be Brad Pitt," Hare says. "Brad Pitt could be that relaxed and that charming and that mellow because he's sitting there thinking, 'This script is holding me up. I'm just in such safe hands here that I can be this incredibly relaxed figure at the center of the film.' And it's no coincidence that it's one of Brad Pitt's greatest performances—he's incredible in it. He's not having to work, he's not having to sweat—the effort is not showing. He's not appearing to have to characterize, but actually he's characterizing brilliantly. You can't see him do anything because it's all being done for him. And then he comes along and does the extra thing he can do. The actor isn't thinking, 'Oh, I've got this bloody long speech where I'm going to have to sweat like a pig to do the exposition.' The actor doesn't have to do the exposition because the screenwriters have hidden the exposition away, which, if you look at the book [written by Michael Lewis], my God, they've hidden it away so beautifully. It's almost Zen-like when Zaillian and Sorkin are on form like that. You don't see them, and yet they're doing everything. I so admire that."

01

> **"The whole notion that an actor saying the first thing that comes into his or her head somehow delivers authenticity is a complete misunderstanding of what art is."**

part, it's the actor. The idea that I write these parts that are a free pass to winning an Oscar is nonsense. I just happen to have worked with two very great actresses.

I don't have any insights into how to write Oscar-winning roles—I only know how to write good parts, but that's completely different. That's something I developed. My first play I had in the West End was called *Knuckle*, and there was a part of a barman in it. The barman had to say, "Do you want a drink?"—that sort of thing. The actor was sitting around in the dressing room all evening just to say that. And I thought, "I'm never going to do that again—I'm never going to get people along for something that isn't worth playing." And so now, I look at every character and think of it from the actor's way around: "Is this worth it? Is there going to be something in this to play?" I mean, everybody in **Page Eight** remarked to me how incredible that cast was. They all came because the parts were worth playing. And that's because I thought about the structure of their parts—even if they only last three scenes. Gary Oldman did a film of mine, and he said, "I did it for this one line that I just knew I wanted to say." And so what you're trying to do is give actors something that they go, "Oh yeah, I'd really want to do this—this gives me something extra."

Lately I've seen some absolutely appalling films where actors have obviously been allowed to improvise their own dialogue. You know, when Mike Leigh improvises, it takes him three months. When John Cassavetes improvised, it took him six months. And yet, now I regularly go to the cinema and see films where the actors have plainly improvised on the spot. You can feel the whole film sag when it happens. Last month I saw the dramatic climax of a film where the actor's line in response to the film's principal revelation was, "Wow, hey, that's a real slap in the face." Now, no writer has written that line—you can tell the actor has improvised it. And this foolish director imagines the line is more authentic for the fact that it's the first line an actor can think of on the day. You can only say

in response, "Get a professional," because a writer will spend a week working on what that line should be. And they will know as much about writing as the actor knows about acting. The whole notion that an actor saying the first thing that comes into his or her head somehow delivers authenticity is a complete misunderstanding of what art is.

I was asked during previews of the musical of *The Lion King* to rewrite it. They said to me, "The dialogue is very bad, and you're very good at dialogue, right?" And I said, "Nobody is listening to the dialogue in this thing. That's not what it's about." I saw the musical, and it was dazzling, but the dialogue is not important—it's only there to express what's going on. If a lion cub wants to go back to its dad, then "I must return to my father" is a perfectly reasonable line. I can't come up with a better line than that. I can't make something happen between those lines that's not happening anyway. The audience will be perfectly satisfied with that line. It may not be the greatest line ever written, but it's doing the job you want it to do. Good dialogue is not something that you slap arbitrarily on top of a narrative: Good dialogue is the expression of good ideas and complex feelings. It grows out of ideas, it isn't decoration you add at the last minute.

I'm very pleased with **Page Eight**, but my only regret is that it's genre. I've been trying to avoid genre all my life. I think it's the death of cinema. Nearly all the interesting work these days is from people defying genre. I've tried hard to avoid genre because the audience know the game so well. They know more about Joseph Campbell's writings than the screenwriters do—they've read all that stuff about character arcs and journeys and all that mythic nonsense. They know the hero's setting out to find the holy fucking ring or grail or goat's foot or whatever it is. They can see the strategies coming a mile off—they know that in reel 10 the hero will face an insuperable problem, and they know that in reel 11 he will overcome it. Why write it?

My heart is broken about my version of *The* →

THE HOURS

(01–03) Because of the complexity of author Michael Cunningham's multiple story arcs in *The Hours*, the book was considered difficult to adapt. But Hare wasn't concerned. "It kept alarming me how many people said, 'How on earth are you going to do that impossible book?' And I kept going, 'I don't know what's impossible about it—it looks very easy to me.' I was freaked—I felt, 'Oh, I'm missing the point of this somehow because everyone keeps saying how hard it is.' Whereas it seems to me juggling those three stories, wow, that is so filmic." But that didn't mean the adaptation was easy. "One of the problems we had was that we knew that the end was much stronger than the middle," says Hare. "We were always going, 'Well, we know the first 40 minutes are going to be very intriguing, because no one's seen a film like this before. And we know we're heading into a fantastic climax, which is so satisfying.' But that middle 40 minutes was absolute hell. Unless you got it right, the audience would be thinking, 'Oh, now we're going back to that story, and I don't like that story—I want to stay with that other story that's much more interesting.' How do we keep all three stories equally interesting? That was the real challenge." The toughest of the three storylines was Laura Brown's, which Hare calls "the deepest story" and was played by Julianne Moore **(01–03)**. "It's the ultimate taboo, isn't it? The mother who leaves her child—unforgivable, you can't do that. So, okay, we're going to make a film about a woman who leaves her child, and we're going to make you understand why she does it. Even if you're never going to sympathize with her, you're nevertheless going to go, 'That probably is the decision she had to make.' That's what we had to swing there."

Dramatizing Virginia Woolf

(04–06) Hare describes the process of dramatizing Virginia Woolf (who was played by Nicole Kidman) in **The Hours** as "nobody's favorite screenwriting task." As he explains, "You know that a thousand academics are going to descend on you, as well as a lot of people to whom her books mean so much. But the thing I was proudest of when the film came out was that her book, *Mrs. Dalloway*, went to number one in the *Los Angeles Times* fiction list. And, you know, okay, you expect Michael Cunningham's book of *The Hours* to go up the fiction list—that's not so rare. But can you believe that more people in Los Angeles bought a copy of a Virginia Woolf novel written in the 1920s that month than they did any other book? That is an incredible achievement. And when I heard snooty academics and biographers complain about the film, I felt 'You've never persuaded quite as many people to read her work as we have.' That was one of the great achievements of my life, actually."

Working with Meryl Streep

(07) Hare has worked with Meryl Streep in **The Hours** and on the 1985 film version of his play *Plenty*. "I will always go to Meryl's rehearsals," he says. "You're crazy not to. It's hell on your way of life if you schlep out to a studio at nine o'clock in the morning to see the rehearsal, but when you've got Meryl Streep, she's going to tell you so much about the scene by the way she does it. And because I know her a little I can say, 'You don't need that line—get rid of that.' And that to me is the real joy of filmmaking: to watch that first rehearsal and then change it all. When you see what the actor's bringing, then you go, 'Oh, look, you need something from that point of view—let me give you that.' Or, 'You don't need this anymore, and it would be more interesting if you did that.' Meryl will always give you so much that it's impossible not to be inspired by her."

> "Good dialogue is not something that you slap arbitrarily on top of a narrative: Good dialogue is the expression of good ideas and complex feelings. It grows out of ideas, it isn't decoration you add at the last minute."

Corrections not being made. I was on it for 23 drafts. I think the problem was that there was nothing for a director to do but shoot it. Jonathan Franzen has a huge personality—and I don't have a small personality—and by the time we had got what we wanted as a feature film, there wasn't anything for any director to do except turn up and shoot it. That's all they had to do. And now, of course, nobody will do that—that's out of fashion. They all want to say, "What is my unique creative input going to be into this?" To which the answer was, "I'm already taking up a lot of room, Jonathan Franzen is taking up the other side of the bed, and there isn't room for three people in this bed. Just shoot the fucker." Director Stephen Frears is famous for the fact that he regards the script as the thing that he's just there to deliver, but that is not how most Hollywood film directors talk today. And so ultimately I think that's why it wasn't made. A part of me died when I lost all that work.

I think that my interest in writing came from— not a lonely childhood, but I suppose a solitary childhood. I was born 60 miles from London by the sea in a town, Bexhill, with the oldest average age in the country. It was just full of old-age pensioners, and it really was the most boring place on Earth. So I had the classic provincial childhood—exactly that kind of solitariness that fires the imagination. And it's left me for the rest of my life grateful that I'm not in Bexhill. Life has always seemed to me incredibly enjoyable and interesting because it's not Bexhill. But there's no doubt that I dreamed very powerfully from such a background. I mean, come on—suburban setting, semi-detached, it's a classic writer's background. The theater and the cinema were very, very glamorous to me.

PAGE EIGHT

(01–02) For **Page Eight**, a thriller about a veteran MI5 officer (played by Bill Nighy) investigating a political cover-up, writer-director David Hare didn't want to adhere to all the tenets of the spy genre. "There are no guns in my film," Hare says proudly, "because I firmly don't believe that MI5 kill people. And I certainly don't believe they kill their own. So what I wanted to make was what's called a suspense film, which is what Hitchcock made. You know, Hitchcock made suspense films that don't actually depend on people bursting into rooms with guns. I prefer **Vertigo** (1958) to **Psycho** (1960) and always will. And so I deliberately said, 'There will be no physical threat. No punches will be thrown. No bullets will fly.' That was my tiny little protest against genre. I would create the suspense through story, not violence. Even if Nighy's character loses, what's going to happen? He's going to go to prison. Well, those aren't the stakes for which thrillers usually play out. I wanted to make those kind of stakes very, very low, but for everybody nevertheless to be in a state of suspense, just as they are in Hitchcock."

And they still are. I still get an incredible kick out of walking past a cinema and seeing my name on there. That sense that I'm incredibly privileged and lucky to be doing what I'm doing has stayed with me. I'm 64 now, and I still get thrilled at the sight of a marquee because I can't believe it's happened to me. "

03 The interior of Hare's office

Paddy Chayefsky

Paddy Chayefsky's screenwriting career is an inspiration to many because of the quality of his work, which earned him three Academy Awards. But beyond the sharpness of his words, Chayefsky also stands as a writer who focused on his craft, a man uninterested in being romantic about the creative process. Billy Ray, the writer of **Shattered Glass** and a co-writer of **Breach**, said, "The best advice I ever heard about writing was in an interview I read with Paddy Chayefsky, who was a hero of mine even when I was a kid. He said, 'Don't think of it as art—think of it as work. When a writer is stuck and calls another writer, that second writer doesn't say, "What's the art problem?" That second writer says, "What's not working?" And they get under the hood and they fix it. If you approach it that way, at the end of the day you'll be able to say, "I did my job." And if you're an artist, it'll come out as art anyway.' That really stayed with me, and I've tried to approach my writing in that way."

Chayefsky was born in the Bronx in January 1923. His birth name was Sidney—he acquired the nickname Paddy while serving in the Army during the Second World War, where he received a Purple Heart. When he returned to America after the War, he focused on playwriting, eventually transitioning to television in the late 1940s. A celebrated writer during the height of live television in the 1950s, Chayefsky wrote for The Philco-Goodyear Television Playhouse and Goodyear Playhouse, crafting scripts for actors like José Ferrer, Eddie Albert, and E.G. Marshall. One of his TV dramas was entitled **Marty**, which was adapted into the hit 1955 film that won the Palme d'Or at the Cannes Film Festival and four Oscars (including Best Picture and Best Screenplay) at the Academy Awards.

Chayefsky's next screen triumph was very different in tone. If **Marty** was a heartrending slice-of-life drama, **The Hospital** (1971) was a caustic satire of the medical industry, earning the

01

MOSCOW

LOS ANGELES

01 Network (1

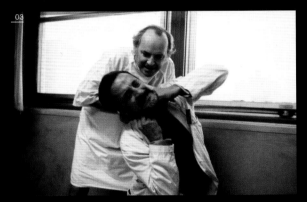

writer his second Academy Award. From there, it wasn't too far of a leap for Chayefsky to tackle television and corporate culture in **Network** (1976), which netted him his third and final Oscar. (The film won three other Oscars, all in acting categories, a testament to Chayefsky's writing.) Years later, **Network** cinematographer Owen Roizman said, "**Network** was the best script I ever read—without question, bar none, no comparison. I called up the producer, Howard Gottfried, and I said, 'This is incredible! I have to shoot this movie!' I would have been heartbroken if I didn't get to shoot that film—that's how much I loved it." Roizman wasn't the only one who loved the script: In the decades since its release, **Network** has become a cultural touchstone, its attacks on the media and the powers that be perfectly encapsulated in beleaguered newscaster Howard Beale's iconic "I'm as mad as hell, and I'm not going to take this anymore" monologue. But for Chayefsky, the movie's point

was never about criticizing television. Speaking with an interviewer after the film's release, he said, "I think what I'm trying to say is, 'How do you preserve yourself in a world in which life doesn't really mean much anymore?' That's what I was trying to say—but the trick, of course, is to say it so that it's a good movie."

Chayefsky died of cancer in the summer of 1981 at the age of 58. And though he will always be remembered for his social consciousness, he insisted that writers don't start a project because they have some message they want to share with the world. "Our obligation in our industry is to entertain people," he said. "That's what we do. We're like football players—we fill up their leisure. We give them a good time and a couple of laughs. If we manage to give them something more than that—if we manage to give them one shred of insight—then we've achieved what is called artistry. And that's bonus."

02 Chayefsky (left) and producer Harold Hecht (right) on the set of **Marty** (1955)

03 The Hospital (1971)

04 Marty (1955)

Anders Thomas Jensen

"I like to make characters come to life. It doesn't matter if it's a drama or a comedy—what makes me do a script is if it has good characters or fun characters. It's interesting when you can go to a place with a new character where you haven't been before. I've never had the same experience twice with a script. The process is new every time because of new people, or working with a new director."

After the Wedding (2006)

One of Denmark's most prominent and celebrated screenwriters, Anders Thomas Jensen began his career making short films, receiving three Oscar nominations in the late 1990s in the process. He won on his third try, for the 1999 comedy **Election Night**, which starred Ulrich Thomsen, who would go on to appear in other Jensen-written projects like **Adam's Apples** (2005) and **In a Better World** (2010). Eventually, Jensen moved on to features, writing and directing the dark comedies **Flickering Lights** (2000), **The Green Butchers** (2003), and **Adam's Apples**, all of which starred his Danish compatriot Mads Mikkelsen. But perhaps Jensen is best known to worldwide audiences for his ongoing collaboration with director Susanne Bier, who has directed his screenplays for **Open Hearts** (2002), **Brothers** (2004), **After the Wedding** (2006), **In a Better World**, and **Love Is All You Need** (2012). As opposed to Jensen's solo films, his work with Bier has been marked by its emotionally charged, intensely dramatic scenarios, often dealing in themes of violence, reconciliation, and coincidence. **Brothers** won the Audience Award at the Sundance Film Festival, and **In a Better World** earned both a Best Foreign Language Film Oscar and a Golden Globe. Jensen, who lives in Copenhagen, was also an early participant in the Dogme film movement, writing the script for both Søren Kragh-Jacobsen's **Mifune** (1999) and **Open Hearts**. His other credits range from the romantic comedy-drama **Wilbur Wants to Kill Himself** (2002) to the period costume drama **The Duchess** (2008). Recently, his career came full circle after he wrote the screenplay for the 2009 dark comedy short **The New Tenants**, which starred Vincent D'Onofrio and Kevin Corrigan and won the Best Live Action Short Oscar.

Anders Thomas Jensen

"I didn't inherit anything creative from my father and mother—there are no artists in my family. I grew up in a very working-class family, but I always wanted to be a director. I always loved films and went to the cinema as much as I could. It started out with American films—I was very much into the Spielberg and Scorsese movies and all the 1970s movies from the States. I was from a very, very little town, so there were no art-house movies at all. I didn't see a French movie until I was 16, but when I got into high school I studied film and discovered Chabrol and Truffaut and the French directors. There's so many films—I keep on discovering new films, so it's an ongoing process. As soon as I could get a job, I actually got a job in a video store—I sound like Tarantino.

I applied to film school as a director, but ultimately I went to university instead and studied rhetoric. I started doing shorts and discovered that it's much more satisfying to write than it is to direct. I still believe that. I started doing scripts without knowing what I was doing. There's a really good energy in doing that. The more scripts you do, you become very much aware of what you are doing, and there's a danger in that: When you've done a lot of writing, it can lose some of the naturalness. You see some scripts where it's really well-crafted, but there's a certain naïvety that's lacking—it's almost too well-structured. That's the hard part, when you are aware of what you're doing, but want to make it seem like you just did it.

Writing is inventing. Directing is finding out the things that it's not possible to do because of the limits of the real world or the financing. I've directed some shorts and three features, and they never turn out exactly the way you thought they would. Filmmaking is really a collective process, where with writing you're your own master, which is really nice. Everything is possible on paper, but when you're starting out you think that a script is like a book or a piece of art. But it's not—a script is a working tool.

I think every writer should actually try to direct. You learn a lot from doing it. Until I

JENSEN ON THE APARTMENT/THE WEST WING
(01–03) As a young person living in Denmark, Jensen fell in love with Billy Wilder's comedies. **"The Apartment** (1960) **(01–02)** I saw many, many times," he says. Perhaps not surprisingly, Jensen (like Wilder) has always had a flair for dialogue. "Dialogue always came very easy to me," he says. "I like words—I always liked them. I think I liked to get attention by saying something funny when I was little. And when I started out as a writer, I got some good reviews: Everybody said my dialogue was good. Here in Denmark, I'm still the guy that can do the funny dialogue." To explain the power of language, Jensen points to the long-running TV drama **The West Wing** **(03).** "Every episode is somebody saying something clever and then another person saying something that is even more clever," he says. "To see people saying something clever or say something funny—you can watch that for hours, you know? Who isn't drawn to that? Who doesn't like to see that? That's a huge part of drama."

> **"Writing is inventing. Directing is finding out the things that it's not possible to do because of the limits of the real world or the financing."**

directed, I turned over the scripts to some directors and I saw the rough cut and thought, "Okay, what the hell did they do?" So when you direct yourself, you think you should be able to control it now and do it better. But then you learn about all the decisions you have to make, and you have such a short time to do it. You have to make a thousand decisions a day. Even if you direct the script yourself, it will not turn out the way that you thought of it as a writer. That's a good thing to learn as a writer because you can understand your director better.

Growing up, I didn't know anything about what a screenwriter did. But the funny thing is, looking back, I realize that in my first scripts all "the rules" were there—three acts, everything. The rules derive from storytelling, which comes from us as people, so it's fun to see that you can do good scripts before you studied writing or knew what you were doing. I see it in my own kids—if they come up to me and tell a story and start with the punch line, they get no attention. They have to learn to structure their story.

Storytelling is all about, "How do you get people's attention?" There are certain rules you need to follow, and you can play with them or stretch their limits. But I truly believe that the basics of storytelling are inside every human being. You can study them and become more aware of them, but it's also a gift that you have subconsciously without knowing what you're doing.

A huge challenge is keeping things fresh. There are so many scenes where I find myself thinking, "I've done this scene before." That's why stories about human relationships are more satisfying to do: They're much harder, but I think there's always a new approach to the scene. Still, I think I've killed 20 people in traffic accidents. You need to find new ways of doing it. And there are typical scenes, such as a meeting where somebody has to tell another person that somebody is dying or sick—you need to keep finding new ways of doing them. It's nice to collaborate with a director on this because the setting and the visual way you do the scene opens up many more possibilities. That's why I →

04

Using drama in comedy

(04) Although his scripts with Susanne Bier are known for their searing drama, Jensen insists that wasn't what drew them to each other initially. "The funny thing is, our whole collaboration started out because we wanted to do a comedy together," he says. But, somehow, they always end up as dramas. "With **After the Wedding**, I sat down and started writing it as a comedy," Jensen recalls. "I mean, the whole set-up—daughter getting married, a father returning—it's a comedy set-up. Then it changed when Susanne said, 'What if he has cancer?' And I thought, 'Okay, we can try that.' It happens every time—she sees the dramatic potential in the comedy. She takes on the characters and adds some real serious problems to them."

JENSEN ON **SOUTH PARK**

(01) "When I'm directing a comedy, I have to admit there's a part of me that wants to see how far I can go," says Jensen, who's directed three features. "Can you have a drooling child in a wheelchair and make fun of it? When you have **South Park** and all these things, there's no taboos left—you can actually do anything now. There's a lot of violence in my dark comedies—explicit violence. But because those movies are in their own universe, it's okay to do it like that—you have to be much more careful with how you use violence in a realistic film. You have so much more free rein in a dark comedy."

always start out with characters—that's what gets me going. I get a lot of energy from letting the story come from the character.

I don't think that my characters are part of me very much, but they're definitely people that I know. I'm a real bastard with that, drawing from everyone I know. But the funny thing is that people don't tend to recognize themselves if you exaggerate them or make them unsympathetic. For instance, in **Flickering Lights**, there's a drunk man called Carl who beats his kids. My father's name is Carl and he drank a lot, but when he saw the film, the only thing he said was, "Oh, he was funny, that guy." He didn't think it might have had something to do with him. If you do a character who's nice, though, people always think it's based on them.

But it's not only people I know who inspire characters—it can be somebody I meet in the supermarket. I really like people who lie to themselves. I think the funniest thing in the world is people where you can see that they're not being honest with themselves. You see it every day. I can see angry people, whether it's in traffic or wherever, and I'll start thinking, "What is his problem?" Almost every time I meet a human being, I start to wonder, "Why are they behaving like they are?" But they have to step out of line somehow. I don't just sit in a café and watch people—that's something poets do, isn't it? But when people do something that they're not supposed to do, then it's very inspiring.

In a Better World actually started that way. I was at this playground and saw a dad hitting his

kid. I was there with my kid, and there was such a bad mood at the playground. Then I started thinking: "If I had said something, that dad probably would have hit me, and what if he did that?" Then I would have to explain that to my kid. From there, the ball starts rolling for that story.

When it's time to collaborate with Susanne Bier, we'll get together and say, "Okay, what if we did this?" Then I will write some scenes and bring it to her. And then together we'll tear it totally apart and she'll say, "What if this happened?" or "What if it wasn't the main character, but what if it was this little character here?" We do a lot of rewrites—we don't do treatments. I like that—I'd rather do many, many scenes and then throw them out to keep that freshness. She doesn't write the scenes, but she's

02 **In a Better World** (2010)

Using darkness in comedy

(03–05) "When I'm writing a drama," Jensen says, "I'm much more aware of not getting emotionally involved, of staying on the sideline of it. If I really get involved with it in my personal life, it becomes crap—it doesn't work. I have too many of my real emotions in it, although of course you need to have those emotions somewhat." By comparison, the films he's written and directed, like **Adam's Apples**, are unapologetic dark comedies. "When I do comedy, it's a playground," he explains. "You know, I just go along with it and laugh and think I'm very funny. Basically the idea for **Adam's Apples** was to take the last 10 years—where I've done dramas with people in wheelchairs or who have cancer or brain tumors or are Nazis—and then take one man, and let it all happen to him. It's a really dark comedy that deals with the same issues I usually write for others. But the same raw material comes out as a comedy when I do films for myself."

really good at making me do what I call "Barbara Cartland-ish scenes." I always laugh because at some point during the script process, she will put the main character in a coma. And I'll say, "It's in such bad taste," but she's really good at saying, "No, no, try to do the scene." And it's really challenging sometimes to do the really, really big emotions, because it risks being in bad taste. I would never think of doing that on my own, so she's good at pushing me. But the challenge is to make it work without people leaving the cinema.

Because I do so many drafts with Susanne, there will be points during the process where we look at each other and I ask her, "What the hell is this film about?" We have a joke that I always say: "I'll find out what this film is about when I read the interviews you do." Our work always has a

> **"Growing up, I didn't know anything about what a screenwriter did. But the funny thing is, looking back, I realize that in my first scripts all 'the rules' were there—three acts, everything."**

theme around it, and I don't need to be necessarily that much aware of it as long as the characters and the story really open up and grip me when I'm doing it. For **Open Hearts**, we wanted to do a film where there was no villain—it was just the coincidental meetings that happen that make the drama. But with **Brothers**, there were so many drafts. The first idea I had for **Brothers** was two brothers changing places: The black sheep →

Drafting and evolution

(01–05) Illustrating how much a screenplay can evolve over time, Jensen did at least three different drafts of his script for the sibling drama **Brothers** in the original Danish. "In draft one, we start out introducing Jannik (Nikolaj Lie Kaas) with a couple of scenes from the prison from which he's about to be released. The tone of the lines is more comedy than drama, Jannik being a bit provocative and sarcastic in the way he talks to the prison guard **(02–03)**. In draft three, we see Jannik leaving the prison in the first scene, cutting straight to the bank where he tries to explain to a bank clerk that he didn't mean to scare her. **(04–05)** We learn why he has gone to prison in the first place, and we see Jannik's attempt to apologize for his violent actions. In this draft, I try to make Jannik's character sympathetic from the very beginning—the general tone is now much more drama than comedy. In the final draft, Michael (Ulrich Thomsen) is now the lead, and it's his story we mainly focus on in the first couple of scenes where we learn that he's on his way to Afghanistan. In a quick scene, we see him picking up his troubled brother Jannik at the prison. The only provocative attitude left in Jannik is that now he asks Michael if he can smoke in the car. Michael replies,

'Go ahead and smoke.'" The script went through several changes, including tone, which explains why the title switched several times too. "Originally, it was **Brothers**," Jensen says. "Then it went from **The Return**, to **Home to Sarah**, and back to **Brothers**."

---

02   -1-

0   INT. FÆNGSEL. CELLE — MORGEN   0

         JANNIK, 38 står inde i en fængselscelle og fylder alle sine
         ting ned i en stor taske. Hans tøj er lagt nydeligt frem i
         små bunker, de pakker han også minutiøst ned i tasken. Så
         kigger han sig omkring, for at tjekke at han ikke har glemt
         noget. Det har han ikke. Han fanger sig selv i et lille
         spejl, betragter sig selv et øjeblik. En LÅS lyder og døren
         går op. En FÆNGSELSBETJENT står der.

                           FÆNGSELSBETJENT
                  Er du klar?

                           JANNIK
                  Ja.

                           FÆNGSELSBETJENT
                  Skal du ikke ha' plakaten med der?

         Jannik vender sig og ser op på en plakat på væggen. Det er en
         filmplakat, AMADEUS.

                           JANNIK
                  Nej, det er ikke min, den hang her da
                  jeg kom. Så den lader vi hænge til den
                  næste.

         Betjenten nikker, giver ham et lille smil. De går, lukker
         døren.

0   INT. BUS — DAG   0

         Jannik sidder i en halvfyldt bus. Han betragter byen gennem
         vinduerne, menneskene, der glider forbi uden for. Han ser
         over på en FAR, der sidder og taler med sine to små BØRN. Så
         tager han sin mobil frem. Ringer et nummer op.

0   INT. MILITÆRBASE. SKABSRUM — DAG   0

         MICHAEL, Janniks 5 år ældre storebror, står og er ved at
         rense og samle sit tjenestevåben. Han har uniform på, er
         officer. Hans mobiltelefon ringer, han tager den, lyser op i
         et smil.

---

03   -1-

0   INT. PRISON. CELL — MORNING   0

         Jannik, 38 is standing inside a prison cell. He's putting all
         his belongings into a large bag. His clothes are placed
         neatly in small piles, which he proceeds to place carefully
         in the bag. He looks around, to make sure he hasn't forgotten
         anything. He hasn't. He catches himself in a small mirror,
         and looks at himself for a moment. The sound of a LOCK is
         heard, and the door opens. A PRISON GUARD appears.

                           PRISON GUARD
                  Are you ready?

                           JANNIK
                  Yes.

                           PRISON GUARD
                  Don't you want to take the poster?

         Jannik turns around and looks up at a poster hanging on the
         wall. It's a movie poster, AMADEUS.

                           JANNIK
                  No. That one's not mine - it was
                  already here when I got got here. So
                  we'll leave it for the next guy.

         The officer nods and gives him a little smile. They leave,
         closing the door behind them.

0   INT. BUS — DAY   0

         Jannik is sitting in a bus that's half full. He looks at the
         city through the windows, the people passing on the outside.
         He looks at a FATHER sitting talking to his two mall
         CHILDREN. Then, he takes out his mobile phone. He dials a
         number.

0   INT. MILITARY BASE. LOCKER ROOM — DAY   0

         MICHAEL, Jannis 5 year older brother, is standing up,
         cleaning and assembling his service weapon. He's wearing a
         uniform. He's an officer. His cell phone rings, he answers
         the call, his face lights up, he's smiling.

BROTHERS

(06) **Brothers** tells the story of two very different siblings. It's a dramatic construction Jensen finds himself incorporating on a regular basis. "I have a brother, and I think I've done 20 stories about brothers," he says. "Of course, it's a good dramatic tool to use brothers, but it's definitely something to do with my brother and me—I never see him, and we're not very close. That's something I should probably see a shrink about, but it tends to sneak into everything I do. A lot of times I've done stories where the characters start out as just friends, and at some point in the process somebody will say, 'Hey, what about if they were brothers?' And I'll think, 'Sure, we can do that.' That is really a theme for me." Asked if he finds writing to be therapeutic, Jensen responds, "I think so. More and more, it dawns on me that it has been. If you'd asked me that five years ago, I probably would have said no. But I think it is, for me."

"I once described Denmark as 'geographically undramatic.' Of course I was exaggerating, but there is some truth in that. Nine out of 10 Danish films are about family, and it's because this is where the drama is in this country—it's within the families."

```
04
1   INT. FÆNGSEL. CELLE — MORGEN                    1

    JANNIK, 38 står inde i en fængselscelle og fylder alle sine
    ting ned i en stor taske. Han kigger sig omkring, for at
    tjekke at han ikke har glemt noget. Det har han ikke. Han
    fanger sig selv i et lille spejl, betragter sig selv et
    øjeblik. En LÅS lyder og døren går op. En FÆNGSELSBETJENT
    står der.

                    FÆNGSELSBETJENT
            Er du klar?

                    JANNIK
            Ja.

    Betjenten nikker, giver ham et lille smil. De går, lukker
    døren.

2   INT. BUS — DAG                                  2

    Jannik sidder i en halvfyldt bus. Han betragter byen gennem
    vinduerne, menneskene, der glider forbi uden for. Så tager
    han sin mobil frem. Ringer et nummer op.

3   INT. BANK — DAG                                 3

    Jannik træder ind i en bank, der står et par KUNDER oppe ved
    skrankerne. Han ser sig omkring, får så øje på en DAME på
    omkring 50 år. Hun sidder nede i et kontorlandskab, bag en
    computerskærm. Jannik betragter hende, hun ser op og da hun
    får øje på ham, rejser hun sig nervøst. Hun begynder at græde
    og trække væk, over til en af MAND. Jannik begynder at gå
    imod hende, signalerer, at han ikke vil noget. Damen græder
    nu meget, folk begynder at kigge på hende og Jannik. Flere
    andre, rejser sig. Damen peger på Jannik, han når næsten over
    til hende, da to unge FULDMÆGTIGE træder ind foran ham.

                    JANNIK
            Jeg vil bare tale med hende.

    Manden træder nu over til Jannik.

                    MAND
            Jeg tror ikke, du har noget at gøre
            her.
```

```
05
1   INT. PRISON. CELL — MORNING                     1

    Jannik, 38 is standing inside a prison cell. He's putting all
    his belongings into a large bag. He looks around, to make
    sure he hasn't forgotten anything. He hasn't. He catches
    himself in a small mirror, and looks at himself for a moment.
    The sound of a LOCK is heard, and the door opens. A PRISON
    GUARD appears.

                    PRISON GUARD
            Are you ready?

                    JANNIK
            Yes.

    The guard nods and gives him a little smile. They leave,
    closing the door behind them.

2   INT. BUS — DAY                                  2

    Jannik is sitting in a bus that's half full. He looks at the
    city through the windows, the people passing on the outside.
    Then, he takes out his mobile phone. He dials a number.

3   INT. BANK — DAY                                 3

    Jannik walks into a bank. There are some CUSTOMERS by the
    counters. He looks around, and catches sight of a WOMAN of
    about fifty. She is sitting in an office environment, behind
    a computer screen. Jannik looks at her, she looks up and she
    sees him, she stands up nervously. She starts to cry and
    pulls away, over to a MAN. Jannik begins to walk towards her,
    signaling that he doesn't want anything. The woman is now
    crying uncontrollably, and people are beginning to stare at
    her and Jannik. Several others stand up. The woman points to
    Jannik, he is almost right by her side now, when two young
    OFFICERS step in front of him.

                    JANNIK
            I just want to speak with her.

    The man now walks over to Jannik.

                    MAN
            I don't think you have any business
            here.
```

02 The opening of Draft One of **Brothers** in the original Danish

03 The opening of Draft One translated into English

04 The opening of Draft Three in the original Danish

05 The opening of Draft Three translated into English

OPEN HEARTS

(01) Open Hearts was the first collaboration between Jensen and director Susanne Bier, which examined the romantic complications that befall an engaged couple after a devastating car accident. "To be honest," says Jensen, "every time I do a film with Susanne, I say, 'We're going to be run out of town this time—this is too much.' But she pushes me—she says, 'You can do this'—and I try my best to make it plausible. But it's not only the writing—it's very much the actors' performances and the director that make it work. I don't think you could do it without involving the actors. What you see when you do these rehearsals is whether something is too much, and then you can go back and do the rewrite and make it work."

learns responsibility, and the perfect wonder-kid ends up somewhere else. But there ended up being so many other things in the movie—that original element is just part of the story now. That happened because of all the rewrites—I would keep writing and thinking that my original theme was what it's about. And then once you get to the sixth or seventh draft, you're not really aware that it's been through so many changes.

I once described Denmark as "geographically undramatic." Of course I was exaggerating, but there is some truth in that. Nine out of 10 Danish films are about family, and it's because this is where the drama is in this country—it's within the families. You can die in a car accident here, but we don't have any natural disasters. We don't have any dangerous animals. It's a society where we take care of everybody, so we don't have anyone who's really poor or starving or other things that you could make into drama. So that's why we do films about family.

When I'm writing the first draft, I go away. I go to a vacation house or a hotel. I lock myself up and do the first draft. There's something about it when people know you're away—they don't call you. I have three children, and we have a rule that they can only disturb me if it's an emergency. But with three children, we have like 10 emergencies every day. So it's great to go away to one of these very boring resorts where there's absolutely

nothing to do: You spend two days by the pool and then you're bored and then you go to your room and stay there for two weeks and get the work done. It's nice to find somewhere where nothing happens at all and where there's nothing else to do.

I'll sometimes act out my dialogue when I'm writing, but I try not to. I'm a really, really bad actor, so actually it's a nice test: If I can say it and it works, then it's a good line.

I quickly found out in the system we have in the US that people are really bad at reading scripts—but treatments are even worse. Every

02 The scene in **Open Hearts** (2002) where two women meet: one (Paprika Steen, left) who has accidentally paralyzed an engaged man; and his fiancée, (Sonja Richter, right), who has fallen in love with her husband

Revising an existing screenplay

(03) At one point, Susanne Bier was pegged to direct **The Duchess**, which starred Keira Knightley and Ralph Fiennes and was based on Amanda Foreman's biography, *Georgiana, Duchess of Devonshire*. Jensen was brought on board to revise the existing screenplay, although Saul Dibb ultimately directed the picture. "It was quite fun," Jensen says of his time working on the script, "because it was like what Bier and I would have done with our own script on the sixth or seventh draft. There was some very good ground material there, and it was just about trying other options and changing some things around. So that process was a great experience." Asked about what he still finds challenging as a writer, Jensen replies, "I still think the hardest part is capturing the whole array of ways people react toward certain emotional situations. The really good films are where humans surprise you—where someone says the thing that turned the whole scene around."

time I turned in a treatment, they said, "We cannot see the characters." And it's obvious you cannot "see the characters" because the characters will come when we get dialogue. So I don't do a lot of treatments. I mean, there are so many films where the treatment would be moronic, you know? **Open Hearts** came out as a book in Japan, and when I read on the back of the book what it was about, I thought, "I wouldn't want to read this book! It sucks!"

I often have the whole story outlined, but I like to start out with characters and see where we can go. The collaboration with Bier is always like that—we never know where it's going and we have 50 endings for the story. I think it's a good thing when you cannot finish a script—it tends to be a good sign because it means the characters are working and their dilemmas are strong.

I like to get involved and be involved with a project through the whole process. I know in the US that that experience is very seldom—there are so many writers on every project, and it's a whole other ballgame over there. In Europe, it's much easier to follow your project the whole way through. But I've done some co-productions— which was a long process—where I got a taste of how it can be in the States. So many rewrites and so many executives making decisions— everybody wanted to get a say. I don't know if it scared me, but it made me realize that it's much more satisfying to stay here in Denmark and perhaps do smaller projects, but keep control.

I have friends that are really good writers, but they hold on to their material. I think that the collaboration process is a part of being a screenwriter—being willing to make compromises and to involve the director at an early stage. I see some writers who don't really want to change their scripts, but it's better for you to change the script with the director than not changing it and the director doing it anyway without you. It's better to swallow some of your pride sometimes and also believe that the director can do what they promised to do.

I like to make characters come to life. It doesn't matter if it's a drama or a comedy—what makes me do a script is if it has good characters or fun characters. It's interesting when you can go to a place with a new character that you haven't been before. I've never had the same experience twice with a script. The process is new every time because of new people, or working with a new director. That's a very satisfying job to have, you know? The worst scenario is sitting there feeling you're doing exactly the same thing you've done before. And I'm not only talking about sequels and things like that. I always want to find something new to do. There needs to be something new to discover every time you're doing a story.

Billy Ray

"At the top of my computer in big, bold letters, it says, 'What is the simple emotional journey?' That's what I look at on my computer monitor all the time."

Billy Ray (center) on the set of Breach (2007)

Growing up in the San Fernando Valley, Billy Ray had an appreciation for screenwriters from an early age—after all, his father was a literary agent. Initially, however, he went to school at Northwestern for journalism before deciding after a year to enroll at UCLA for film. The summer after his sophomore year, he sold his first piece of writing, an episode of **The Jetsons**. Since then, his career has only continued to blossom. His early credits, **Color of Night** (1994) and **Volcano** (1997), were learning experiences, but soon he found more success co-writing the Second World War drama **Hart's War** (2002). However, his two great triumphs are films based on true stories that he wrote and directed. **Shattered Glass** (2003) dramatized the downfall of celebrated *New Republic* journalist Stephen Glass, who had invented dozens of stories that appeared in the magazine in the 1990s. **Breach** (2007), which Ray co-wrote with Adam Mazer and William Rotko, is based on disgraced FBI agent Robert Hanssen, who had sold US secrets to Russia for more than 20 years. Ray has also worked on the screenplays for **Flightplan** (2005), **State of Play** (2009), **The Hunger Games** (2012), and **Captain Phillips** (2013), earning a reputation for being a sought-after Hollywood writer known for his thoughtful, intelligent work. "From a very early age, people were telling me I could write," he says, "which meant a lot to me. I thought writers were heroes."

Billy Ray

"My father was an agent, and he represented so many great screenwriters: Alvin Sargent, Frank Pierson, Ed Hume, Steve Shagan, Carol Sobieski. But my father was not starstruck at all by the business—I don't remember a lot of parties where Hollywood people were around. He was more interested in flying and reading about the Second World War. My parents were divorced, so I would spend weekends with my father, and I remember a lot of times sitting in his bedroom eating sunflower seeds and watching an old movie. That was sort of my education. He had a very healthy level of respect for the difference between something good and something crass, and he tried to impress that upon me all through my life.

I was a grownup kid—I always was very comfortable dealing with adult themes and talking about things in an adult way. I was very precocious. I was the kid, when everyone else was watching **Sesame Street**, I was watching the Watergate hearings on TV. I just was drawn to big, dramatic, grownup stuff. Part of that was just who I was, and part of that was the way I was

brought up. I think I was kind of a peer of my parents in that way. I was a friend of my father's, and I was a friend of my mother's—they treated me in that way ever since I can remember. I filled a role in their lives, which made me conversant in things in an adult way from a very young age.

To me, both movies I've directed, **Shattered Glass** and **Breach**, are about integrity. They are about moral ambiguity at some point giving way to perfect moral clarity, at which point the hero has to decide what the hell to do about it. Those are things that are important to me—I think those are the things that movies are great at examining, when movies choose to examine them. Not in a black-and-white way, but in a very gray way, which I think has more to do with how we actually live our lives. I'm drawn to those kinds of stories.

I'm very competitive—I'm competitive in everything that I do. Every time I work for a director, my goal is for him to come away thinking that every other writer by comparison is phoning it in. When I go into a meeting with a studio head, my goal is to come out of that

The power of film

(01) A pivotal moment in Ray's interest in film came early on. "I had my revelatory moment of what the power of movies could be the night that I saw **One Flew Over the Cuckoo's Nest**," recalls Ray, who wasn't yet a teenager at the time. "I saw it with my mother at a theater that doesn't even exist anymore—it was called the Le Reina Theater, I think it's now a Gap. But my mom took me to the movie, and then we were walking to the car afterwards—she had a pale, yellow Oldsmobile Cutlass— and as I was getting into the car, I was so floored by that movie that I was speechless. For the first time I thought, 'Oh, this is what movies can do.' It had never occurred to me before then that movies could do something other than just entertain you. 'Wow, a movie can take you to a different place and completely rock you emotionally.' That was the first time I realized that."

01

> "Writing is just problem-solving—that's 99 percent of what I do. I don't sit at my computer and think about artistry—I think about problem-solving."

meeting with that studio head saying, "We've got to give this guy everything. Nobody works harder. Nobody's more focused. Nobody's gonna deliver like this guy's gonna deliver." Everything I do, I turn it in faster than they think I will, and I want to turn it in better than they think I will. And by the way, I'm that way with everything: If I go to have a meeting with my son's teacher, I want to be my son's teacher's favorite parent. I just never stop competing, and that's, I'm sure, the product of incredible neurosis and psychological ill-health. But it's what drives me. I want to win several Oscars. When AFI does their next list of the 100 greatest movies of all time, I want my name on at least one of them. I want a legacy. If those are your goals, you've got to work hard. That's just the way it goes.

Having your name on a hit is a lot more fun than having your name on a flop—particularly a flop that deserves to be a flop because it's a bad movie. From the beginning of my career, I wanted to have hall-of-fame credits. But I certainly had an inauspicious debut with **Color of Night**. I didn't write a line of the final film, but

that experience was hugely humiliating. Then I wrote **Volcano**, which, by the way, deserves to be ripped on. But at least that was something I had actually written—I could live with that. But by that point in my career, my credits were a complete embarrassment to me. If you know you're capable of better, and yet the only movies that have your names on them are **Color of Night** and **Volcano**, it's fucking embarrassing. If at that point someone would have shown me the credits of some guy named Billy Ray, I would have said, "That guy's a bad writer." It killed me that people could have come to that conclusion. I knew that I was writing better stuff that wasn't getting made. That didn't change until **Shattered Glass**. **Shattered Glass** changed everything.

Writing is just problem-solving—that's 99 percent of what I do. I don't sit at my computer and think about artistry—I think about problem-solving. In the case of **Shattered Glass**, I knew that Stephen Glass was this really compelling, arresting character, but I thought, "If you make a movie about him, by the end the audience will want to kill themselves, and that's not good." It →

VOLCANO

(02) Ray isn't terribly pleased with how the 1997 Los Angeles disaster film **Volcano** turned out, and he thinks he deserves a bit of the blame. "I think that script came from the most pretentious parts of me," he says. "LA was still recovering emotionally from the Rodney King riots, and I had this super-pretentious idea that the lava could serve as a metaphor for the social ills that were under the city waiting to erupt. And that's what I wanted to write about. And so I infused that script with lots of things about racism and racial tension, and that was probably just a dumb idea, but at the time it seemed like a really smart idea. It seemed like a way to elevate the genre. The one thing I can say in my own defense is there was a draft of that movie that would have cost about 120 million dollars that had lots of subplots in it that I think was good. They shot a movie that was 90 million dollars that had a lot of that textural material cut out, and so it just wound up being a movie about a volcano."

> "There's only one juncture in the development process where a writer actually has some power, and it's at that point where the studio has done a few drafts with other writers and they don't have a script yet that they can make."

required a little bit of sleight of hand, and I never tried anything like it before, but that was a problem that had to be solved: "How can I draw people in with a story about Stephen Glass, but then deliver them a story that actually makes them feel okay?" The trick was to make the first half of the movie about Stephen Glass, and make the second half of the movie about Chuck Lane, the guy who catches him. What that required was putting enough of Chuck Lane in the beginning of the movie, so that he's not coming out of nowhere, and dialing down the story of Glass in such a way that he becomes the bad guy by the end. Those were pretty good writing challenges. And underneath it all was this emotional pulse that was very simple: "What would happen if the least popular kid in high school had to take down the most popular kid in high school?" As heady a movie as **Shattered Glass** is, there's a viscera to that idea that everybody gets, and that was the movie that we eventually made.

I don't think you always have to be concerned with why characters do the things they do. With **Breach**, I wanted to show the audience that our actions define us. It doesn't really matter what you say: Either you handed over secrets to the enemy or you didn't. And in this case, Robert Hanssen did. The "why" is interesting and it's fun to speculate about, but I tried to approach that movie from the point of view that we are what we do. If you murder someone but feel badly about it, the fact that you feel badly doesn't really mitigate the fact that that person's now dead. Thematically, the "why" doesn't matter, so don't go too deeply into the why. But like with **Shattered Glass**, I felt there was a certain journalistic responsibility with **Breach** not to make something up. I didn't have access to Hanssen—the FBI would not let me talk to him, and even if they had, I don't think he would have talked to me. So anything that I said that was definitive or declarative about why he

A complex but subtle structure

(01–02) When Ray first told his agent father that he wanted to be a writer, his father gave him the Oscar-winning screenplay to **Ordinary People** (1980), which was written by his client Alvin Sargent. "That's where my dad was setting the bar," Ray says. "I look at it now, and I realize it's probably the most perfect monster movie ever written. If you go back and look at it through that prism, there's a monster in the house, and it takes Donald Sutherland about two hours of screen time to figure it out. When I saw the movie originally in 1980, I was 16 or 17, and I thought the movie was about Timothy Hutton. But then you read the script and you realize, 'Oh my God, this is about Donald Sutherland. This is about a father who comes to slowly accept the idea that his wife hates their son.' The intricacy of that plotting and the subtlety of it is spectacular. There are some movies where you realize they're constructed like an algebraic equation. Sometimes there's an X, and you apply a certain function to it, and it becomes Y. And in this movie, Donald Sutherland starts out as X, and the movie applies the function to him, and he comes out as this other thing."

01

did it would be a guess, and I didn't think I had the right to do that. So I laid out for the audience what his behavior was, what I thought the circumstances were, and then they can determine why he did what he did. I'm interested in capturing human behavior. In the case of both Stephen Glass and Robert Hanssen, if I got them right, it wasn't that they'd be sympathetic, but they would be compelling. You'd look at them and say, "Ah, that's idiosyncratic human behavior that I recognize. It feels truthful to me. I know people like that." That makes them compelling. I didn't need to put in a scene where they save a drowning puppy.

If you asked people out there who hire me what they think I can do, they won't say there's just one thing—there are different kinds of movies that they would approach me with. When I started my career, I saw that studios were already thinking of writers as "the action guy" or "the drama guy" or "the broad comedy guy." I knew →

Horse or cow?

(03) The erotic thriller **Color of Night**, which starred Bruce Willis, was Ray's first screen credit. He's still never watched the film, though. "That was a spec that I sold," he says. "The studio wanted it to be a horse, and I had given them a cow. They wanted this steamy, sexy thriller because that's what Bruce Willis wanted to do, but that's not what I wrote. So I was taken off that movie and they brought on someone who could write them a steamy, sexy thriller. But because the Writers Guild rules work the way that they do, because I was the first writer, my name was going to be on the movie. It was the most painful creative experience I'd ever had at the time." But although the film was widely panned, Ray's initial idea still sounds quite intriguing. "It was about a shrink who had had a patient kill herself. He decided he was never gonna treat another patient, so he and his wife—who doesn't exist in the final movie—drive out to Los Angeles, and they're staying at the home of his friend while they're trying to restart their life. And his friend gets killed. And it becomes clear that his friend was killed by someone in a therapy group. So the main character, to find the killer of his best friend, has to go do the thing that scares him the most, which is treat patients. I thought it was a good idea." Despite his misgivings about the experience, though, there has been one unexpected bright side. "That movie has brought me a lot of money in residuals," he says, laughing. "I think there's a **Color of Night** channel out there somewhere."

SHATTERED GLASS

(01–03) Ray says that he knows he's attracted to an idea when he wakes up thinking about it. "Then I know it's living in me and that's the thing I should write." For **Shattered Glass (01–03)**, he was inspired by his love for **All the President's Men** (1976), which chronicled the uncovering of the Watergate scandal that led to the resignation of President Richard Nixon. "I grew up in one of those houses where Woodward and Bernstein were heroes," he says. "That movie was about journalism and ethics—those were very real things to me. And so to see Stephen Glass completely pervert the ethos of American journalism, I had a lot to say about that subject." He was hired by HBO to write the project, but by the time he turned in his draft, "the administration at HBO that had hired me was all fired. I turned in the draft to a new administration that had no interest in it. I'm convinced that's why I write so fast now: I can make sure that the guy who hired me is still in power by the time I hand in the script." It took two years for **Shattered Glass** to finally be made, and when he got ready to shoot the film, he screened **All the President's Men** for his cast and crew in a hotel ballroom in Montreal the night before they began filming. "I personally don't believe that **All the President's Men** and **Shattered Glass** belong in the same sentence," Ray says. "I think **All the President's Men** is the third-greatest movie ever made. But I believe in setting the bar pretty high."

Finding the right framing device

(04–06) After Ray finished shooting **Shattered Glass** and started putting the film together in the editing room, there was one major area of concern: the story's framing device. "Originally, the framing device was all the people who had worked with Stephen Glass sitting around a table at the Correspondents' Dinner speaking directly to the camera," Ray says. "I thought it worked, but most people around me did not, so it had to change. The studio wanted to just yank it out, but I knew the movie couldn't exist without some framing device." For a couple weeks, Ray brainstormed different alternatives before the idea of having Glass addressing a high-school class that turns out to be only in his imagination. **(05–06)** "I don't remember where I was when it came to me," he says, "but I remember my first thought was, 'Why didn't I think this up when I wrote it in the first place? This is so obvious, how could I have missed this? What an idiot.' I still feel that way. If I could go back and redo anything about that movie, it's that I would have thought that up in the first place. It was such an obvious idea."

05–06 Script pages showing Ray's final high-school class framing device in place

---

3.

That felt pretty good too.

                                          DISSOLVE TO:

INT. HIGHLAND PARK HIGH - ROOM 12 - MINUTES LATER

This room is FILLED now with MRS. DUKE'S JOURNALISM CLASS: 30
kids, ambitious as hell, the well-heeled children of suburban
money. Megan is in the front row.

We pan along the faces while hearing the voice of:

                 MRS. DUKE (V.O.)
          Contributing writer for Harper's
          Magazine. Contributing writer for George
          Magazine. Contributing writer for Rolling
          Stone...

The kids are impressed.

Glass stands at the front of the room. He's trying to be self-
effacing, but it's tough; the adulation is so thick.

                 MRS. DUKE
          ...and, of course, Associate Editor at
          the highly prestigious New Republic
          Magazine in Washington, D.C.

Beside Glass is MRS. DUKE, (45, been here forever.) Her pride
in him is boundless.

                 MRS. DUKE (cont'd) (CONT'D)
          Sorry if I'm beaming, but I was his
          journalistic muse.

                 GLASS
          It's true.

Mrs. Duke just beamed again.

                 MRS. DUKE
          As all of you know, Stephen will be
          receiving Highland Park's Alumni of the
          Year Award tonight - the youngest
          recipient in our school's history, by the
          way. This is why I am so exacting with
          you people! Seven years ago he was
          sitting--

                 GLASS
          --right there.

He points at Megan's desk. Her eyes go wide. Glass officially
owns her now.

                 GLASS (CONT'D)
          And I was doing the same things you guys
          do: grinding out pieces... and then
                 (MORE)

4.

                 GLASS (CONT'D)
          having nightmares every night about Mrs.
          Duke and her red pen.

The kids laugh. Mrs. Duke grabs her RED PEN and brandishes it
like a weapon, in on the joke.

                 MRS. DUKE
          And look what happens when greatness is
          demanded of you. Now he's at The New
          Republic!

                 GLASS
          Now I'm at The New Republic.

Glass breathes out a smile. The kids lean forward, dying to
hear about life in the real world. And we...

                                          CUT TO:

EXT. WASHINGTON, D.C. - VARIOUS

Images of D.C. **BEGIN CREDITS**

INSERT - A DESK - LOCATION UNKNOWN - DAY

A printed copy of the next New Republic slides across an
unidentified D.C. desk. A HAND grabs the issue, opens it. Feet
go up on a desk. **END CREDITS.**

                                          CUT TO:

INT. TNR SUITE - MAILROOM - DAY

The busy, glamourless nerve-center of TNR. Glass hurries
through in his socks, and re-fills his coffee.

Two other reporters enter. They are ROB GRUEN (26), and AARON
BLUTH, (25.) Both Jewish and a bit high-strung.

                 BLUTH
                 (mid-story)
          ...so I said, "Network news, network
          news, hmmm. Oh, right, isn't that the
          show that's on every night in between all
          those Fixodent commercials?"
                 (Gruen laughs)
          That shut him up.

                 GRUEN
          Hey, Steve.

                 BLUTH
          Hey, Hub.

                 GLASS
          Hi, guys.

They enter the mailroom; Glass continues out.

> **"When AFI does their next list of the 100 greatest movies of all time, I want my name on at least one of them. I want a legacy. If those are your goals, you've got to work hard. That's just the way it goes."**

I didn't want to be pigeonholed like that. So from the beginning, I was trying to do a lot of different things to demonstrate that I had a lot of gears. I would do anything that aspired to be great.

Still, I haven't written a lot of comedies. As much as I love **Blazing Saddles** (1974), I just didn't think I was capable of writing that. Having said that, I just finished the remake of 1934's **The Thin Man**. They were a little hesitant to hire me for that because they wanted the dialogue to be very pithy and urbane and have a certain rat-a-tat repartee to it, which I'd never done before. In those initial phone conversations, director Rob Marshall said, "I've read your scripts, I completely believe in you as a screenwriter, but no one knows if you can write funny or not." And it's very difficult to say to someone, "I'm funny—I promise you, I'm really funny." So, we started to talk about story beats that I thought made sense for the movie, and he thought, "Oh yeah, this guy is thinking in terms of comedy beats that also function dramatically." And, to be honest with you, I made him laugh a couple times on the phone. Thank God he's a good audience. So they took a shot on me and, it turns out, I can write funny. The rules of writing apply no matter what genre you're in.

There's only one juncture in the development process where a writer actually has some power, and it's at that point where the studio has done a few drafts with other writers and they don't have a script yet that they can make. They call you, and you come in and say, "Okay, I've read the other drafts. Here's what's not working about them,

01 Bruce Willis playing the role of antihero Col. William A. McNamara in **Hart's War** (2002)

HART'S WAR

(02) The 2002 Second World War drama **Hart's War** appealed to Ray because of his own feelings about the period. "The Second World War is an odd thing," he says. "The more you know about it and the older you get, the more awe-inspiring it becomes. As a kid you look at soldiers and you think of them as heroes, but in a very superficial way. But as you get older—old enough to be drafted—you realize how many American men just went off and suffered and risked their lives in the most work-a-day fashion possible. Their sacrifice becomes almost inexplicable. **Hart's War** for me was a chance to tip my cap to those guys—that was the thing that I wanted to bring to it. I wanted to do a ton of research, get the way those guys actually talked right, get their behavior right, get the details of that camp right. I knew that I had a lot to say about the guys who fought in the War."

FLIGHTPLAN

(03–04) Ray has a simple answer for what makes him choose to come aboard a studio project: "I'll do it if it's a movie that aspires to be great and if it's a movie that I think I have something to say about." In the case of the thriller **Flightplan**, which starred Jodie Foster, there had already been at least one writer who had taken a stab at it. "When I read that movie, I had a six-year-old daughter," Ray explains. "And I just said, 'How would I feel if I was on a plane and I woke up and my six-year-old daughter was gone—and everyone said to me she was never on this plane?' That was enough to keep me on that movie for two years."

here's what I think we can do to make them work, and here's how long I think it'll take." In that second, you're the grownup in the room. They're all a little bit freaked out because they've tried things and it hasn't worked yet, and you are the one saying, "It's gonna be okay, and I know how to make it okay." For that second as a writer, you have a little juice, and it's fun. It goes away almost instantly, but in that second you do have some power. I first realized that working on **Hart's War**. They had three writers before me, and I remember an executive calling me—you could just hear the panic in his voice. They had invested a lot of money in those drafts and they knew they didn't have something they could shoot, and it was the first time I realized, "Oh, I'm the grownup in this process. If I can go in there and communicate total calm and competence, I'm gonna get this job." You want them to feel like, "We can take a deep breath. There's a pro in here who knows how to help us."

Here's my day. I wake my kids up in the morning, I take my son to his bus stop at 7:30, I'm at my desk at eight. Somebody feeds me at one. I'm back at my desk at 1:30 and I write till five or six. My nights and my weekends belong to my family. I don't surf the web when I'm supposed to be writing—I don't look at porn, and I don't gamble on some offshore site. I don't do anything stupid—I just work all day. If you do that, you can get a lot done. I don't spend three hours a day at Starbucks. I don't consult my muse. I just work. I just try to solve problems all day long. I don't know another way to approach it. And I can feel when the solutions I'm coming up with are functioning, and I can feel when they're not. You know the difference—you can't kid yourself. At the top of my computer in big, bold letters, it says, "What is the simple emotional journey?" That's what I look at on my computer monitor all the time. When I get into a jam I just think, "Okay, what's the story I'm telling? What's the emotional journey that I'm telling?"

Humility and confidence are not competing virtues. You can have both. From the time I started as a writer, I was trying to project →

BREACH

(01) Even though Ray was directing from a script he co-wrote for **Breach**, he discovered that the story he was telling on the page wasn't necessarily what ended up on the screen. "**Breach** wound up making a slightly different comment than I thought we were making," he says. "I thought we were setting out to make a movie about how our heroes keep teaching us, even as they're failing us. That's what I thought I was shooting. By the time I saw the first assembly of the movie, I realized that the movie was about something slightly different. It was about how Ryan Phillippe, as a result of being stuck in a room with Chris Cooper, by the end of the movie had to reevaluate how he felt about his career, his marriage, and his religion. Had he never met Chris Cooper's character, Robert Hanssen, he would have felt one way about those three things. But having been stuck in a room with this guy has made him change completely how he feels about these three things. That's his character arc. He arcs, Hanssen doesn't, which means by definition that Phillippe has to be the lead character of the movie."

Writing and directing

(02–03) "I think that writers who direct to protect their material are just doomed to failure," says Ray, who directed his screenplays for **Shattered Glass** and **Breach**. "They're gonna get too precious, and they're gonna get too rigid. That's going to affect how the actors act, and it's going to affect everybody. I try really hard to beat the page when I go to shoot a movie. I try to do better than what I wrote. I try to find what's living between those words. The risk when you do that is you might wind up with a movie that has evolved. But I think it's supposed to evolve. You're not there to do a staged reading of your wonderful screenplay—you're there to make a movie. Movies are supposed to evolve as you're shooting them."

> "I don't think you always have to be concerned with why characters do the things they do. With **Breach**, I wanted to show the audience that our actions define us."

both, because both feel sincere to me. I have confidence that I can write, and yet I'm humbled by how difficult the prospect of it is and how hard it is to get a movie off the ground. When I go in to a meeting, it's very tough for me to step outside myself and gauge how other people see me, but from what I'm told, people think I'm a pretty serious guy. They know that I love movies. They know that if they hire me, I'm not gonna be out at four in the morning chasing hookers and doing blow. I think they're pretty clear that I'm going to approach this like a job and I'm gonna take my job very seriously. So I think they trust me. I think I've earned it. I was mystified early in my career why they didn't trust me more, because I always felt like I had the kind of intentions that they should have faith in. But you have to earn it. "

THE HUNGER GAMES

(04–05) When Ray came on to rewrite the script of *The Hunger Games*, Lionsgate had a script written by the book's author, Suzanne Collins, but they wanted to fine-tune it before looking for a director. Ray, however, won't take any credit for the film's impressive box office success. "They had a bit of a director derby," he says, "and Gary Ross was the guy that they chose, and Gary Ross went out and made his movie. He went out and rewrote it and shot his movie, and it's very much his. He deserves the credit for it—it's a miracle that my name is on that movie. I claim almost no authorship for what's up on that screen." Discussing what drew him to the script, Ray explains, "That was a story about a girl who made a promise to her sister: 'I'm going to survive.' That is the simple emotional journey of that movie, but that was not the thing that made me want to write that movie. What made me want to do it was the context of the movie—the darkness of that idea, of children having to kill children. I wanted to write a movie that made a comment about totalitarianism, which I think was just in the DNA of the book. I knew that I had such outrage about that idea and about the world that Katniss was placed in."

Whit Stillman

"I don't want to read something just to find out how it turns out; I like to read books where you feel you're getting something worthwhile all along. The writers I prefer are those where it's the journey, the detail, the texture of the piece you value. I don't need propulsive narrative momentum."

Damsels in Distress (2012)

A guiding light of American independent cinema in the 1990s, Whit Stillman is the writer and director of **Metropolitan** (1990), **Barcelona** (1994), and **The Last Days of Disco** (1998). **Metropolitan**, which cast an affectionate, satiric eye on New York's *debutante* scene, won Stillman an Independent Spirit Award for Best First Feature, the Best New Director prize from the New York Film Critics Circle, and an Oscar nomination for Best Original Screenplay. His subsequent features shared with **Metropolitan** a breezy, sometimes bittersweet, comic air that focused on the romantic travails of articulate young people stumbling their way through adulthood. After spending much of the 1990s developing projects, including an adaptation of Christopher Buckley's 1999 novel *Little Green Men*, Stillman returned with **Damsels in Distress** (2012), a delightful college comedy that found a new generation of young actors, most notably Greta Gerwig, expertly executing the filmmaker's ticklish, engaging dialogue. Born in Washington, DC, and the son of John Sterling Stillman, an attorney who served in the Truman and Kennedy administrations, Stillman graduated from Harvard University, where he wrote for *The Harvard Crimson* and the Hasty Pudding Theatricals (unproduced), developing the witty, urbane, lighthearted style that he would later incorporate in his films. Indeed, he has come a long way from the Ivy League graduate who, after taking an aptitude test, was told he didn't have the disposition to be a writer and should maybe think about becoming an architect instead.

Whit Stillman

"After my parents split up I went away to a boarding school in Millbrook, New York. I was attracted by the school zoo—a remarkable operation—but while I was there I got interested in both the drama group and the newspaper, the *Millbrook School Silo*. Senior year, after what seemed like a grueling competition, I got to be its editor, and since there was little real news, we veered off into comedy. We had all been frustrated because we had to go to press long before the paper would come out—eight days or even longer—and by then everything would be stale. So we had the idea of writing articles about events which hadn't happened yet—and then making them happen! The culmination of this was the campaign to elect the next student body president, which fortunately, no one took very seriously—or at least so we thought. We wrote about the campaign and the groundswell of support for an unlikely candidate whom we actually quite liked. Then, after having gone to press, we made the campaign happen—but succeeded beyond our expectations. Our "joke candidate" was elected! It was a funny group writing for the paper—far funnier than I was—and it seemed like our mini-**Saturday Night Live**. None went into comedy, all rather becoming very prosperous—while I'm broke, so the laugh is on me. One of my *Silo* friends later gave me a gig shooting commercials in Jakarta, which was a welcome respite from my feature-film hiatus.

My obsession at that point was to get into Harvard, where all my family had gone. When the Harvard interviewer came to our school, he spent his time with the jocks—he must have written Millbrook off academically, but thought that maybe we'd be good for a soccer star or two. There's something about telling your life story to someone who couldn't care less that concentrates the mind. In the interview, there was the standard question about life goals. I started reciting the litany of what was essentially my father's career—go to law school, be a lawyer active in Democratic politics, get elected to something, etc.—but realized as I was saying it that, actually, that was not what I should do. I was entirely under the sway of F. Scott Fitzgerald, and it was during this fairly disastrous Harvard interview that I changed my sights to writing fiction. I sincerely tried during college, but gave up—I didn't feel that I had the stamina to maintain the solitary life of a fiction writer. But I loved the television comedies then airing—**The Mary Tyler Moore Show**, **The Bob Newhart Show**, **Sanford and Son**—and began to have thoughts of working in film or television without having any idea how to get into them.

But I followed my college résumé into book publishing and then journalism. It was not until one of the publications—which paid us too much, so I had some savings—went out of business that I looked around and tried to figure how I could get into film. Through some odd circumstances, I became a foreign sales agent for Spanish films. The Spanish film industry was delightfully improvised, and in two cases when the directors I was working with needed a "stupid American character" in their projects, I was the guy! It was just two films, but they were pivotal experiences

01 **Metropolitan** (1990)

"I could not do A-B-C-D-E-F logically— everything sort of came out A-D-I-Z, and it all came at random."

for my future filmmaking career. One was an extremely low-budget film shot in New York— total minimal effort, but it turned out very well. And then there was this serious shoot in Madrid—maximal effort, but turned out very badly. And so I saw that in film, effort and money are not necessarily rewarded. It's the right idea—the right treatment—that's rewarded.

When I was getting interested in writing screenplays, I bought a published copy of Lawrence Kasdan's *The Big Chill* script. It was very helpful—it showed exactly how a screenplay was supposed to look. And then I found John Brady's book of interviews with screenwriters, *The Craft of the Screenwriter*. It was the usual suspects—Paul Schrader, Robert Towne, Ernest Lehman, William Goldman—and each of those interviews was just so extraordinary. That book just excited me so much. And I found Syd Field's screenplay book helpful too—to fight with, as well as to respect. When you're trying to understand the architecture of screenplays, there are practicalities: You're gonna aim for a film between 90 and 100 minutes; by page 10, all of this should have happened; and by page 60, this should be happening. I mean, no, it does not have to be that way, and it's very funny that in his next book he changed his mind about what some of his plot points were. I admire people who correct themselves and change their mind. Still, it's a very helpful book—it shouldn't be taken as gospel, but certainly apocrypha.

When I started writing **Metropolitan**, I was so intimidated at the prospect of the loneliness of writing that I invited a friend of mine over, and he sat with me for two hours while I tried to come up with ideas. Finally, I excused him at a certain point—really, we didn't do anything together and it was just to have companionship— and I continued solo. Eventually—very eventually, the script took years as I had a demanding day →

Indie and 1980s films

(02–03) Stillman says he loves 1980s comedies, including **Revenge of the Nerds** (1984), **Bachelor Party** (1984), and **Fletch** (1985). "There's a sweetness to those films," he says. "There's a happy goofiness. I'm not keen on the gross-out films. But I liked that period in comedy because the films had a lot of positive elements mixed into the pot." But there's one actor whom he particularly loves. "Bill Murray himself is almost the entire modern history of indie film comedy," says Stillman. "I mean, any indie comedy that works is usually a Bill Murray film: **Rushmore** (1998) **(03)**, **Lost in Translation** (2003), **Broken Flowers** (2005). For a certain period, the only indie comedies that functioned in the commercial marketplace were those that had the engine of Bill Murray's presence. And he was also in those films I liked in the earlier period, like **Ghostbusters** (1984)." In fact, Stillman traces Murray's influence on contemporary comedy to Doug Kenney, who co-founded the humor magazine *National Lampoon* and was one of the writers on the Bill Murray film **Caddyshack** (1980) **(02)**. "Doug Kenney brought back college humor," Stillman says. "He co-wrote **Animal House** (1978), and he was involved in **The National Lampoon Radio Hour**, and a lot of people from that went on to be on **Saturday Night Live**, like Bill Murray." No wonder Stillman took a lot of pride in **Damsels in Distress** being described by some as Jane Austen's **Animal House**.

Seeing story

(01–02) Stillman's films are known for their dialogue, but how does he determine when a particular exchange or monologue is too talky? "Well, I know it's all too talky—but the 'acid test' becomes whether the talk was 'story' or 'comment,'" he explains. "The **Metropolitan** edit room was our dialogue school. We had two especially talkative characters: Charlie, played by Taylor Nichols, who discussed the sociology of their 'doomed' milieu and Nick Smith, played by Chris Eigeman, who told stories (of, it later transpires, dubious veracity)." To illustrate his point, Stillman cites a key scene in which Nick tells a detailed story about how terrible a person Rick von Sloneker is. (Fans of the film will recognize this as "the Polly Perkins story.") "I remember showing the script to a screenwriter friend," recalls Stillman, "and he said, 'This scene is terrible. You can't have this long a monologue.' And then I showed it to a sort of intellectual mentor, my godfather, a professor who hadn't read any scripts. He particularly liked this long story that Nick Smith tells about Polly Perkins. It was easy to read for people not used to reading screenplays. It's five pages of monologue, but what we found in the film was that there was no need to trim almost anything from that scene—it just played beautifully. It's one of the strongest passages in the film, and it comes back again several times in different ways—it's an important aspect of the overall story. Shorter speeches elsewhere in the movie, although I found them interesting and funny, we had to trim constantly because they weren't story. On the other hand, that long monologue was story, so it could go wherever it wanted to go."

job—this magical thing happened. Suddenly, I had these characters and their voices, and I realized it didn't have to be logical. Previously, I had worked in journalism, and I had been stymied by the fact that I could not construct logical pieces. I could not do A-B-C-D-E-F logically—everything sort of came out A-D-I-Z, and it all came at random. But in dialogue comedy and perhaps screenwriting generally, it's good to skip around and jump ahead. An enlightening moment was seeing the film **Longtime Companion** (1989). At one point it jumps from the impending death of one character to the memorial service for another. The film just skips a whole, huge potential part of the story—the story advances in a very surprising way. An aspect of film narrative I love is that you can jump ahead in this way—perhaps I love that too much. So, slowly, it started to seem that my incapacities as a prose writer were actually helpful in writing a dialogue comedy. Which is good because everything else was still very hard!

BARCELONA

(03) Part of **Barcelona**'s spark comes from its mismatched lead characters: meek, sensitive Ted (Taylor Nichols) and his outspoken, brusque cousin Fred (Chris Eigeman). Asked if it's easier to write from the perspective of a character whose worldview he shares, Stillman responds, "I'm a little disturbed by how much more energy the other point of view usually has—sometimes it's much funnier and more pertinent. The Taylor Nichols character is bemoaning the sexual revolution and says the world has been turned upside down. And then the Chris Eigeman character says maybe the world was upside down and now it's right-side up. And, that's kind of a good point, you know? What can you say? They're probably equal as far as being true. But Chris Eigeman's character has the virtue of going second—and being funny."

While writing **Metropolitan**, I had first concentrated on the Tom Townsend character, the red-haired fellow who is stuck on beautiful, indifferent Serena Slocum when there's a sweet, terrific other girl—Audrey Rouget—who loves him, but who he ignores. Then I started to think, "It's not so good putting the whole weight of the story on a character who's so clueless. The real heart of the film is the Audrey Rouget character—her predicament is more interesting and sympathetic."

So I tried to turn it into more of Audrey's story, having the opening show her worried about her behind looking big in her white dress and her mother reassuring her. If there were going to be any identification with or liking of these characters, I would have to show the pain and the embarrassment they were going through, too.

Then for **Barcelona** I was somewhat beaten up: "Oh, the women characters in this film are ciphers." But, the thing is, that film is about the guys—the women in the film are there in relation to them. The film was not "Barcelona Girls"—though I'd like to make that one, too. And I already knew that my next film was going to be about two young women (and **The Last Days of Disco** criticism would be that the men were indistinguishable).

The idea for making **The Last Days of Disco** grew out of the shooting and editing of the disco scenes in **Barcelona**. We had two scenes with the lead actresses, Tushka Bergen and Mira Sorvino,

> **"I feel writing is like this stream that does not have a lot of gold. I'm prospecting, I'm panning for gold—or, rather, anything of value—and this stream is very weak on precious metals."**

dancing in discos. And the idea occurred to us that for our sort of film—basically built around a romantic storyline—beautiful women dancing in discos would be about as "cinematic" as one could get. So for **The Last Days of Disco** I knew I'd be doing female characters, and while writing those characters really enjoyed it. The romantic predicament of women seemed far more interesting to me than that for men which, in that period, was pretty much staring at a phone trying to get up the nerve to make a phone call, and the likely awkwardness that would follow.

Damsels in Distress was inspired partly by stories I had heard of women trying to sanitize the atmosphere in formerly all-male bastions—and partly by my own craziness when I first got to college. It's ostensibly a women's story, but really could apply to lots of students—I saw it as the girl **Rushmore**. During the writing, my two daughters did either enter or leave college, but the story was more my own retro-utopian fantasy of how college might or should be—though they claim to endorse the notion that I got it right.

In terms of deciding whether to focus on male or female characters, it's a bit the luck of the draw. →

> **"There's this joy, this happiness, when you get some fantastic piece of material. Normally, it's not when you're sitting in front of your laptop—it's when you're shaving or you're going down the stairs or going for a swim."**

I hope one day to do a male-focused story again and look forward to being lambasted for not having female characters in the foreground.

If I'm reading a novel and I feel that the only thing that's pulling me forward is plot—if I'm only reading to find out what's going to happen—I just skip to the end. I don't want to read something just to find out how it turns out; I like to read books where you feel you're getting something worthwhile all along. The writers I prefer are those where it's the journey, the detail, the texture of the piece you value. I don't need propulsive narrative momentum.

Very often with my favorite books, I can put them down and I don't need to go back to them for a very long time. I'm just very, very happy with the experience of being within them. I love Raymond Chandler—I mean, I'm not that concerned about his plots—but I love the world of Raymond Chandler and think it's fascinating. So when it comes to my own films, I guess we're prisoners of our preferences—maybe I just don't know how to make my plots terribly propulsive. Still, it really amazes me when some critics go on and on about the "narrative momentum" in a story and complain that it "slows down" at a certain point. I mean, God, are they children? Essentially, substituting a reductive standard for a higher aspiration. If the observation is right, and funny or interesting things are happening right along, yes, it's not gonna be fast-paced, edge-of-your-seat entertainment. But it can be working.

I nearly always write to music, headphones, and the modern equivalent of mix tapes. The music has to be familiar enough not to be distracting, but without getting wearisome. While I was living in Europe, there was a flood of very inexpensive box sets of classic tunes. There was both a great Gershwin three-CD box set and a Fred Astaire three-CD box set, and one of the songs on both was Fred Astaire's version of the Gershwins' "Things Are Looking Up," which I adore. It was the perfect song for **Damsels in Distress**; as university-age depression was our subject, the song is a wonderful depression antidote. It became a true guide and inspiration

for the film, and it was a huge relief we could negotiate the license for it just before the shoot.

Writing to music brings a lot of pleasure, which is good because I find scriptwriting pretty painful until enough of the world and characters are in motion—which can be a very long time. At the start, I find it's all lame and bad—it's just bad, bad, bad, bad, bad, and then more bad. I don't like to write too many hours in any one session because I find, after a few hours, I just keep going down the pike of some bad idea. The scripts that worked and became films took me years to write—18 months at least. I feel writing is like this stream that does not have a lot of gold. I'm prospecting, I'm panning for gold—or, rather, anything of value—and this stream is very weak on precious metals. Look at Woody Allen's productivity versus my productivity. Or, rather, don't look at it! I mean, he really is a comic genius—incredibly fecund with ideas. I feel that I don't have that many ideas and I really have to work them. It's the tortoise and the hare—and I'm a total tortoise. →

01 The Last Days of Disco
(1998)

THE LAST DAYS OF DISCO

(02–03) One of the highlights of **The Last Days of Disco** concerns a disagreement among the characters about the message of the Disney film **Lady and the Tramp** (1955). Prosecutor Josh Neff (Matt Keeslar) argues that Lady would have been better off with her loyal Scottish Terrier friend Jock than the egotistical scoundrel Tramp. The opposing views are so memorably aired that one might be tempted to assume that Stillman based them on a real-life exchange. That wasn't the case at all. "That came from anger and rage," he says. "At the time I wrote that script, I identified with the 'Scotty dog' and I couldn't stand the whole 'Tramp' glorification happening in our culture." He laughs. "I just felt I was the guy not getting the girl, and I was mad about it. So that scene was essentially written by the Scotty dog—it was dictated by a Scotty. Now, frankly, I identify with Tramp."

"Writing to music brings a lot of pleasure, which is good because I find scriptwriting pretty painful until enough of the world and characters are in motion—which can be a very long time."

I had zero sense of humor as a child—it's something that developed very, very late. At Millbrook, for example, I was herding funny people more than being funny myself. But you know if something's funny when you hear it. I don't think I ever try to be funny in a script—it's just the absurdity of the characters. I like material that starts off as odd or funny and just gets funnier as one of the characters does something with it. But there's a huge peril when you get into patterns you like that work. I don't really know about the world of comedy writers, but I've met a few in recent years, and they'll talk about doing "much more" with something. I sent a comedy writer my script for **Little Green Men**, which I thought had some really funny stuff, and he said, "No, actually you can do much more with this. You got to take this much further." That kind of scared me. If I tried to do that, I'd end up on Mars. So I guess I like the idea that you're not trying to be funny—you're trying to tell a story, and then the comedy just gets in the way. From there I suppose comes the charge of "no forward momentum."

Anthony Minghella was talking about the screenwriting process, and he said that it's like a drawer that opens and there are these wonderful things inside the drawer: Each time the drawer opens, you get to take one thing out. It's a great remark. You're working on your material, but then the really great thing is when the drawer opens and you're allowed to take out some really great piece of material. I can't remember which script it was for, but I was at the seaside in Spain, on the Costa Brava, and I was coming back from swimming, walking back up the hill to the house we were staying in, and I got this great idea for the script. There's this joy, this happiness, when you get some fantastic piece of material. Normally, it's not when you're sitting in front of your laptop—it's when you're shaving or you're going down the stairs or going for a swim. So I guess it's important to have breaks in your day when your mind is not going to be clogged with a lot of other concerns. The walking, the swimming, the shaving—that's when that hallelujah-material rainfall can occur.

01 Damsels in Distress (2012)

I'm accused of lack of productivity and that's pretty true, but also, for the screenwriter, so much of what we do, including some of our best work, is not and will never be seen. That a film hasn't come out, that we don't have a credit, reflects hardly at all the reality of our writing lives.

I've never been able to sell myself at all. I can't do it—I can't pitch. And it's a little dispiriting. I suppose I've been lucky knowing that no one would ever buy one of my projects from a pitch. So I just made a film. And then once I made the film and it was reasonably successful, I could say, "Well, I'd like to do a film on this other subject," and extrapolating from the earlier film, the executives could do the pitch themselves. But, in fact, that's only worked with one buyer so far—and I was fortunate to have a three-film run with him.

Sydney Pollack once said that filmmakers are divided between those whose movies had guns and those that had love stories. I hope to put both together in a film someday. But, you know, so far I'm stuck with love stories—usually with some identity crises thrown in.

Cutting it—then putting it back in

(02–03) "When you're writing a script," Stillman says, "you're getting all kinds of ideas, and some of them are good, but they're not really good enough or they're not taking you where you need to go. I have an easy time cutting things out—in fact, I have a too-easy time cutting things out." For example, during the writing of **Damsels in Distress**, Stillman had decided to significantly trim down the role of Depressed Debbie, one of Violet's (Greta Gerwig) chief adversaries. "I thought the trajectory of the Depressed Debbie character was kind of familiar and depressing," he explains. But when Aubrey Plaza expressed interest in the part, she was curious if the character could be fleshed out more. Stillman went back to earlier drafts and reinserted some of her scenes, including a memorable moment where Debbie chastises Violet during her tailspin as not being "clinically" depressed—she hasn't been to a clinic. "I put that back in," he says, "and was later glad I had. It helped having that conflict with Debbie and showing more of the resistance and hostility Violet was up against. And it also got laughs."

Ben Hecht

When film lovers imagine the prototypical screenwriter from Hollywood's early years—the hard-drinking, sharp-witted cynic who was part poet and part *bon vivant*—they're probably picturing Ben Hecht. Nominated for six Academy Awards and winner of two, including one at the very first Oscar ceremony, Hecht was a playwright, journalist, and novelist before moving west to write for the movies. In the process, he helped to shape the popular perception of the screenwriter as the one voice of urbane intelligence amidst a sea of greedy, moronic suits whose sole mission was to dilute the brilliance of the writer's work.

Hecht was born in New York in February 1894, the son of Russian Jews, and moved with his family to Wisconsin during his childhood. Although he studied the violin and spent some time in the circus as an acrobat, Hecht eventually turned his talents to writing, first in Chicago and then later in New York. But by 1926, he had decided to give screenwriting (and its promises of easy money) a try, moving to Los Angeles and winning an Oscar for director Josef von Sternberg's silent gangster film **Underworld** (1927).

From there, Hecht went on to have a dizzyingly prolific period during the 1930s. His play (with Charles MacArthur) *The Front Page* was adapted into a successful film in 1931. Meanwhile, Hecht adapted Armitage Trail's gangster novel into the iconic **Scarface** (1932). He was easily one of Hollywood's most in-demand writers, famously doing a feverish one-week rewrite of **Gone With the Wind** (1939) after the studio closed down production less than a month into the shoot, terrified the film was going to be a disaster. But despite his success and riches—Hecht was paid a lavish $15,000 for his work on **Gone With the Wind**—he never stopped disparaging Hollywood. "I have always

01

01 Scarface (1932)

considered that half of the large sum paid me for writing a movie script was in payment for listening to the producer and obeying him," he recalled in his memoir *A Child of the Century*. "I am not being facetious. The movies pay as much for obedience as for creative work. An able writer is paid a larger sum than a man of small talent. But he is paid this added money not to use his superior talents."

His cutting wit was as apparent in his screenplays, where he refused to water down his superior talents. With MacArthur, he wrote the Best Picture-nominated **Wuthering Heights** (1939), which is generally considered the definitive screen version of the Emily Brontë novel. *The Front Page* was adapted yet again into the beloved screwball comedy **His Girl Friday** (1940)—Charles Lederer wrote the terrific screenplay. Hecht worked on **Spellbound** (1945), Alfred Hitchcock's underrated thriller, and then followed it up with **Notorious** (1946), one of the master of suspense's finest films, equal parts espionage thriller and romantic drama. Easily illustrating his versatility, Hecht co-directed and co-wrote (with MacArthur) a 1935 film adaptation of Noël Coward's drama *The Scoundrel*, which

resulted in Hecht's second screenplay Oscar, and a 1957 film adaptation of Ernest Hemingway's classic war novel *A Farewell to Arms*.

Beyond his many screenplays, though, Hecht stands out as a larger-than-life personality, a romantic vision of the suave, sophisticated screenwriter trying to bring a bit of art and entertainment to the masses. When he died in April 1964, one Hollywood golden age was ending, with the exciting renaissance of the 1970s just around the corner. But Hecht spent the final years of his life convinced that his contribution to film was rather minor. "Maybe out of 70, I've written about eight or nine movies that I could tolerate if I were a member of the audience," he said in 1958. And he also never stopped having a low opinion of movies in general. "My reason for disliking the movies is a little odd," he said during the same interview. "I really don't dislike them—I have no interest in them, anymore than a plumber has any vital interest in his product. He has to know how to make his stuff, do it well, collect his money—he doesn't have to admire what he makes." Ben Hecht may not have admired his movies, but generations of audiences absolutely have.

02 Notorious (1946)

03 Spellbound (1945)

Robin Swicord

"What I'm looking for is a really rich experience. I don't always find it, but what I'm looking for in a project is a really rich collaboration. In a meeting, what's most important is to find out whether we agree. If I come in and I have a strong take on something, what am I seeing reflected back to me that makes me think we're going to have a good work experience and make the same movie together?"

Memoirs of a Geisha (2005)

When Robin Swicord was a girl living in the small town of Panama City Beach, Florida, in the early 1960s, her hometown television station wasn't affiliated with a network. Luckily, a local film buff who worked at the station would broadcast his black-and-white 16mm prints of his favorite movies, which allowed Swicord to grow up on the films of Alfred Hitchcock, John Ford, Bette Davis, and Barbara Stanwyck. "I wanted to break into film, but I didn't see the path," Swicord says, "so I wrote a play instead. After my first play was done on Off-Broadway, I met an agent who helped me sell my first screenplay, which was called *Stock Cars for Christ*." Later, she was one of the writers on **Shag** (1989), an ensemble comedy that offered breakout roles for young actresses like Annabeth Gish and Bridget Fonda. Since then, Swicord has established herself as a reliable adapter of popular novels, first with **Little Women** (1994), which earned three Academy Award nominations, including Best Actress for Winona Ryder. With her husband, screenwriter Nicholas Kazan, she wrote **Matilda** (1996), based on Roald Dahl's novel. In 1998, she co-wrote **Practical Magic**, which starred Sandra Bullock and Nicole Kidman. Her next great success came with **Memoirs of a Geisha** (2005), turning Arthur Golden's novel about a Japanese geisha during the Second World War into an Oscar winner. She wrote and directed **The Jane Austen Book Club** (2007), based on Karen Joy Fowler's book, and received "story by" credit for **The Curious Case of Benjamin Button** (2008), which was adapted from an F. Scott Fitzgerald short story. Even as a child, she knew she had a future in visual storytelling. "In class after I finished an assignment," she says, "I would draw on a piece of paper and make these boxes. Essentially, I was making graphic novels—there would be dialogue and narration and prose in between. It was like storyboarding. People would look at me and say, 'What is this?' I had no idea what to say except, 'These are my stories.'"

Robin Swicord

"Reading was a refuge for me when I was young. Because my father was in the Service, we traveled quite a bit. We were stationed in Barcelona in the 1950s when I was a little girl. Before we came back to the US, I got sent to an English-speaking school for 10 days to get me ready to go back into an English-speaking world. They put everybody from different grades in the same room, so even though I was a beginning student, I was with kids who already knew how to read and were reading aloud in class. When it came to be my turn, I would always let my eyes rest on the page and just say whatever the girl next to me had said. Then one day, my teacher called me up to her desk and said, "I want you to read this for me." She held out a page in front of me, I looked at it, and I had this phenomenal experience. My vision went completely white— I felt this heat pass over the crown of my head. Suddenly, I could read every word. I read the entire page, and then I turned the page and I read that page aloud, and then I turned the page and I read that page aloud. After that, all I wanted to do was read. From then on, it didn't really matter where I was because I was in books. I would read a book, and then I would make paper dolls of the characters—I would make sets and enact the book on the floor. I played with dolls seriously well into high school. It was just what I did—I was a complete creative oddball.

A screenwriter is the first person to "see" the movie. My husband, who's also a screenwriter, will start an idea from hearing dialogue in his head, but I'll see pictures—I become curious about the people that are in those pictures. Ever since college, I have been shooting photos all the time—I could just as easily be working as a photographer in terms of how much I care about it. Very often, the pictures that I'm taking contain the mood or visual elements that relate to the seed of the film I'm thinking about. Every now and then, though, an object might inspire me. That happened to me this year—I was at a thrift store, and saw a little object of a mouse. It triggered a memory of when I was a child hearing the story of Cinderella. I never imagined

"...if there's been a book like *Memoirs of a Geisha* that's a hit, people are more inclined to make that movie than the movie that I'm sitting at home writing with a female protagonist no one's ever heard of."

myself as Cinderella—I never thought that my prince would come or any of that. I always identified with the mice. I was worried about them because they were corralled into being horses—they went to the ball, but they didn't get to go into the ball, and when it was over, all of a sudden they had to go back to being mice. And I remembered all that when I saw that mouse. So now I'm actually writing something inspired by that object.

My first screenplay was *Stock Cars for Christ*. It's a comedy—it was an odd little script and not a very good script. Generally speaking, I don't think first screenplays are very good unless you're a complete genius, which I'm not. It was about this kid, Ulysses, who revered a stock car driver named Sonny True, who was the baddest guy in the world. The kid went to jail for a manslaughter charge—he tried to emulate Sonny True, but went off a bridge and landed on a float and killed some bathing beauties. Ulysses eventually meets Sonny, and he ends up doing this crazy Passion Play in which they reenact the crucifixion as a kind of prelude to the prayer section before stock car races. You can tell from what I'm describing that it was a completely outlandish idea for a movie. Uncommercial beyond belief. Who would even see it, much less write something like that? But I wrote this thing, and it just proves that, starting out, you should write what's on your mind and write it with conviction, personality, and voice. Certainly that movie will never be made, but someone might say, "You're a writer—come and write." That's what happened to me—I sold the screenplay, and I got to come out to Hollywood.

I do like adaptations. It's not the only thing I like, but I think that particularly when you're dealing with movies with female protagonists, if →

THE CURIOUS CASE OF BENJAMIN BUTTON

(01–03) It took about 20 years from the time Swicord started working on the screenplay for **The Curious Case of Benjamin Button**, which was based on the F. Scott Fitzgerald short story, for the film to finally hit the screen. "I wrote the first draft of that, I think, in 1988," Swicord says. "I wrote like 16 drafts for four different directors and two or three different studios. And then it was dormant, until David Fincher started carrying the script around for a while. He hired Eric Roth to come on and rewrite my screenplay." Among the many changes, the finished film—for which Swicord received "story by" credit—was set in New Orleans as opposed to Baltimore. "I would say that there were numerous small differences," she says. "In mine, Benjamin was less of a jack-of-all-trades. I really wanted to make a kind of millennial movie that would contain all of the 20th century in the life of one man. And I chose music as a way to do that, so I made him a musician." Additionally, in Swicord's version, the character of Queenie (played by Taraji P. Henson) didn't work in a nursing home, but instead was a freed slave who worked for the Button family, caring for the elderly patriarch of the family. She hides Benjamin and for several years raises him in the attic of the Button home, inhabiting a shadow world. "There's a lot of dysfunction in the Button family," Swicord says of her screenplay. "There was a family business, but it was not a button business—in my millennial theme, their fortune was tied to the fortunes of the United States. So, they were in a foundry business, which expanded later to weaponry. I was tracking the economic thread of the US in the 20th century, but my film was essentially the story of this outcast. I departed substantially from Fitzgerald's story, which began during the Civil War, and ended in the Jazz Age. At its core, the story I wrote was a love story between Benjamin and Daisy, who he knows from infancy—that wasn't at all in Fitzgerald's short story, it's something I invented so I could show what endures in a life lived backward. This guy looks different on the outside than he is on the inside—people can never really know him. And, really, his story is a quest to know himself. A lot of those things are still there thematically in the film—some of the scenes that I wrote are still kind of intact—but they're used differently."

03 The timeline that Swicord wrote for her version of the script. Note the recurring focus on music

03

How Old He Looks	How Old He Is	Year in History	Important Relationship
80	newborn	1910	grandfather Uremiah; Queenie, former slave
75	5	1915	Uremiah teaches him music
70	10	1920	Uremiah dies; 1st mortality
65	15	1925	baby girl cousin born; Daisy
60	20	1930	Thomas is father=age 60; new-found friendship
55	25	1935	Marries Helene, 30
50	30	1940	Son James is born Too "old" to go to war
45	35	1945	Plays music with USO; meets Daisy (20); Father dies; marriage ends
40	40	1950	Exiled in Paris; parity with age; reunited with Daisy, they begin affair
35	45	1955	Hears electric guitar; forsakes jazz for rock and roll
30	50	1960	Returns to New York
25	55	1965	Daisy is 40; beginning of youth cult era; drift apart Reunited with son James, 25.
22	58	1968	Summer of Love; Benjamin on the road with rock and roll
20	60	1970	Vietnam draftee; never gets out of boot camp/school
15	65	1975	Son takes him in; son=40 son=father;music "prodigy"; resumes serious work on opus
10	70	1980	Granddaughter born; losing some musical ability, hands small
5	75	1985	Age parity with grandchild. Daisy (60) rescues him.
0	80	1990	dies

THE JANE AUSTEN BOOK CLUB

(01) Swicord made her directorial debut with **The Jane Austen Book Club**, which she adapted from the 2004 novel by Karen Joy Fowler. "I loved reading her book," Swicord says. "I loved every page of it. When I thought about how I would do it as a movie, I felt I wanted to contrast the way we live—which is so often without real beauty around us; it's mini-malls and traffic signals and urban life—with the English countryside and walks in the shrubbery. You know, the whole Jane Austen thing. Other than her people going to Bath and the occasional party, by and large Austen's novels are very bucolic. In Karen Joy Fowler's book, I saw her modern-day characters finding refuge in these Austen novels and sharing these romantic ideas with each other. Visually I wanted the film to contrast their romantic conceptions about Austen's world with their own unbeautiful, present-day lives."

Women as audiences

(02) **Little Women** was one of Swicord's first writing successes, but it was a project that took a long time to develop. "When I first came into the business in the early 1980s," she recalls, "people weren't making period movies. I would talk about *Little Women*, and they'd say, 'Well, can you make the contemporary version of it? We just don't want to deal with those long skirts.' I walked around with it for about 12 years like that." A break came through Sid Ganis, then head of marketing at Sony, who had four daughters who had all read *Little Women*. Swicord sold him on why audiences would want a new film. "I met with him and said, 'There's an audience for this. Women are half of every audience for a **Lethal Weapon 2** (1989), and they're most of the audience for **Last of the Mohicans** (1992). So stop pretending that women don't go to the movies. They do, and if they really love a good movie—like **Beaches** (1988)—they go to the movie multiple times. They come back with their daughter, they come back with their mother, they come back with their grandmother—they go in groups repeatedly. If we do it right, they're going to come.' Sid Ganis believed my marketing argument—he absolutely shared it, and he became a strong proponent of the film." **Little Women** opened to strong reviews on December 21, 1994, and, as Swicord had predicted, became one of the biggest hits of that holiday season.

"In a sense, in adaptation you're having a conversation with the author— you track through their traces to get a very deep understanding of the book so you can try to make the movie that the author would want."

there's been a book like *Memoirs of a Geisha* that's a hit, people are more inclined to make that movie than the movie that I'm sitting at home writing with a female protagonist no one's ever heard of. The famous books make it to the screen, while the "original stories" are much harder to get made—and if you have a female lead character, it's virtually impossible for the movie to be made. You really have to have everything line up magically for that to come true.

After I had broken into screenwriting, what I wanted to do was the thing I'd wanted to do since I was a child, which was a proper version of *Little Women*—the actual adaptation of the real book. I had seen all of the films when I was young, and I read the book for the first time when I was eight—I read it every year until I was 16 or 17. I knew the book very well, and I knew that the movies that I was seeing were not the book. My understanding of the book was so different from the movies' understanding. All of them were about "Who will Jo marry?" That is not a question that the book ever asks. The book is about female ambition—that's quite clear from the very beginning. The book is so much about "Can we keep this family together, and can we make our individual dreams come true?" Even when Louisa May Alcott was writing the books that would become *Little Women*, she was in receipt of pressure from her readers: "We want Jo to marry Laurie." She was not even interested in marriage herself (she never married) as this was a time when to be married was to become someone else's property, literally. Legally, a woman had the same rights as a slave when she married. Alcott didn't want to aim Jo toward marriage because Jo was her representative in the book, which is semi-autobiographical. I had to come to understand all of that really deeply, because what I wanted to write was the screenplay that Alcott herself would have written. In a sense, in adaptation you're having a conversation with the author—you track through their traces to get a very deep understanding of the book so you can try to make the movie that the author would want.

I'm sure some novelists are concerned their books will be ruined being turned into movies. But I find that if they have reached the point where they are selling their book, they're usually pretty happy. It's hard to make a living as a novelist, and one of the things that I think novelists hope will happen is that they'll get this extra boost of having their book be acquired for a movie or television series. It buys them a lot more writing time, and it gives them a broader audience. People who never would have read *The Jane Austen Book Club* read it because they saw the movie. So, it's a good thing for the novelist, generally speaking. In the case of *The Jane Austen Book Club*, that was a beautiful collection of essentially six different short stories from Karen Joy Fowler, with each story delving into the distant backstories of each character in the book club. For the film's narrative, I was only dealing with the present day—only what happened during the book club meetings, and in between. Karen probably could have said, "But that's not my novel," but she didn't—she was very generous. I think that she knew, from our early conversations, that I was only taking the present-day material and then inventing stuff that's not there to connect it all up into something that makes it into a dramatic shape. With an adaptation, you want something that conveys the intention of the author. Karen Joy Fowler went at the story from one direction, and I came at it from another, but our intentions were the same. If the author is sophisticated, they don't get that upset. Or if they do, they do it very privately and I never know about it.

With **Memoirs of a Geisha**, I really wanted that writing job. I went and interviewed, and I knew that the director, Rob Marshall, was continuing to meet other writers—I don't know if it's true, but I heard that he met 44 writers. I just knew that I wanted to do the project. So I just started working. I sent him pages and pages of notes of my thoughts about the novel after we met. After he hired me, Rob said—he started his career as a choreographer—"I always feel like in an audition process that there's some dancer who →

Female hierarchy onscreen

(01–03) Swicord had plenty of reasons to be passionate about adapting the novel *Memoirs of a Geisha*. "First of all, I loved the world of it," she says. "My first apartment in Los Angeles in 1980 had Shoji screens. I loved them—I went out to Little Tokyo in LA and found a traditional person who made those screens, and had shojis built for my little apartment, so that I could divide off my work area with them. I've always been drawn to that Japanese aesthetic. But specifically with *Memoirs of a Geisha* what I felt was that here was a book that was honestly about hierarchy among women. That's not something that gets depicted in the movies almost ever. Over and over again we see movies about hierarchy among men, but here in the book was a world where women are warriors and abusers and queens—you got the feeling that this is what 'girl world' looks like when you clear the patriarchy out of it. And yet that same world is weirdly in service to a traditional Japanese culture in which the women are there to serve the men. The dichotomy between those two things I found to be completely involving. And I loved that it was a survival story—that here was a girl taken out of a fishing village who goes on this enormous journey that could have destroyed her many times. Many times she could have died—either physically or emotionally or psychically, she could have just been crushed. In the book, she's always associated with water, which is why I used water all the way through the film. That ability to just flow between the rocks and not be destroyed—I identified so much with her. I felt that here was an amazing story that had never been seen on screen before and would probably never be seen again."

02 Swicord gave a lot of attention to the movie's opening as the audience had to understand and feel for Sayuri as she goes through enormous changes

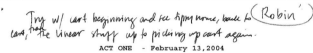

> ## "You really do have to have others read the script aloud so you can hear people responding in the room . . . The ear can tell you so much more than the mind can."

comes in and claims the role. By sending me these pages and showing me that you had continued thinking after our meeting, you claimed this." But I never think about having to sell myself in those situations. What I'm looking for is a really rich experience. I don't always find it, but what I'm looking for in a project is a really rich collaboration. In a meeting, what's most important is to find out whether we agree. If I come in and I have a strong take on something, what am I seeing reflected back to me that makes me think we're going to have a good work experience and make the same movie together? I don't worry so much about getting the job. Maybe there are people who are competitive in that way, but I can't imagine anything more painful than competing for a job, getting it, and then finding that you have to write something that's really contrary to your every instinct.

How do I know if something I wrote is funny? Oh, I'm tremendously self-amusing. Tremendously. I'm confident in the moment, but it's a completely misplaced confidence. In life, I'm always laughing at stuff that no one else thinks is funny, so why would it be any different when I'm writing? It's terrifying. You really do →

<u>04</u> **Memoirs of a Geisha** (2005)

Aesthetics of a world

(05–06) On the day Swicord was hired to adapt *Memoirs of a Geisha*, she met the film's production designer, John Myhre, who had also just been hired. "We both agreed that we needed to understand a lot more about this culture to be able to make a film about it," she recalls. As luck would have it, because the film had been in development for several years before Swicord came aboard, the producers already had a wide range of art books for the project in their offices. "John Myhre and I were given keys, and he and I did everything except sleep there for four days as we combed through these books. He and I went through this full visual immersion. We marked any page that attracted us, and then we would talk to each other about it." When they were finished, they put together a book of images they felt represented the story they wanted to tell. "When I flew to New York a couple of weeks later to start working with Rob Marshall to break down the novel and the story together, I brought him that stack of images. Many of the film's images came out of that stack of pictures. It became the common language for everyone, from the costume designers to the DP. The movie got green-lit on the strength of a 70-page outline that I made—which was essentially the screenplay without dialogue—and that stack of photographs."

SHAG

(01) One of Swicord's first produced screenplays was the period comedy **Shag**, which starred Phoebe Cates, Bridget Fonda, Page Hannah, and Annabeth Gish as best friends who get away for a girls' weekend at Myrtle Beach in 1963. "It was kind of an answer to **Porky's** (1982)," says Swicord. "There were a lot of movies at that time about guys getting drunk and going out and getting girls, and I was just like, 'Okay, let's do something more interesting than that.' It was a female response to the objectification in all those kinds of movies where the men are bonding, but it's at the expense of making the women not really human beings. For me, it felt essential that there be a cultural response in which women were given their moment to show what it was really like to come of age, in a comic way. There were so many wonderful actresses that I would see on the screen and there would be no roles for them—other than, say, 'The Girl in the Towel.' I mean, hats off to Judd Apatow, who got behind **Bridesmaids** (2011), but when I came along with **Shag**, there was no Judd Apatow. So the counter-response had to come from the outside—from the fringe, really. **Shag** had to be independently financed. There were very few women who were directing film, and no man was going to make that movie."

01

have to have others read the script aloud so you can hear people responding in the room. It's one of the things that should be institutionalized with screenplay writing: Just as in the theater, there should be ample opportunities for read-throughs. The ear can tell you so much more than the mind can. On **Matilda**, which I wrote with my husband, we did a table read in our little country kitchen with some friends who were visiting. They read it aloud to us, and we made changes based on that reading. Then later, when Danny DeVito was sending us casting tapes so we could see who he was thinking about for the Trunchbull, we got to hear the script read aloud by professional actors. We'd finish the tapes, look at each other, and say, "We don't need that line—we've got to cut that." That process of shaping for the actor is wonderful, but it's sad that you have to wait until you're casting to get the thing read aloud so you can make it better. The script is a performance piece—you need the performance to inform it.

Screenwriters have very little control. There are so many hands that touch a movie that you have to hold onto that period in which you were

> ## "Screenwriters have very little control. There are so many hands that touch a movie that you have to hold onto that period in which you were writing the script as being the most precious time."

writing the script as being the most precious time. That's when the movie is most alive for you personally—because, immediately after that, things start to happen. For instance, I really wish that the great experience that I had writing **Practical Magic** had been the audience's experience watching the movie. What happened was that after I finished the script, the studio said, "This is your director—we already have a deal with him, and this is how it is." And so you try to make it all work, even though you're not on the same page and you're never going to be allied. Everything after that is hard. When people are not essentially agreed, it just exponentially develops more and more disagreements. Later, when you read the film review, the screenwriter is heaped with all the blame because it's impossible

to tell what really went wrong and where. We never get a chance to take the reviewer aside and say, "Well, you should have been there on the day when this idiot person on the set came up with this suggestion . . ." You just have to live with your experiences and say, "You know, I was happy with this film, and I wasn't happy with that other film." You don't look at the ones that make you unhappy—you just keep moving.

Probably if I were smarter and more strategic, I would be reading books to see if they should be turned into movies. But for me, they're separate things. Unless somebody specifically puts a book in my hand and says, "We've optioned this and we want to make it into a movie," I don't think that way—to me, it's wonderful to read for pleasure. Of course, I've right now got two pieces—one's for television and one's for film—that are from E.L. Doctorow, and I did have the experience reading these two short stories where I thought, "Wait a minute, this is too good—this one has to be a movie!" So it does happen, but it's not foremost for me. In college, I just thought he was a fantastic writer. And now, I get to be friends with E.L. Doctorow and talk to him about short stories and go out and have tea with him. How good is that? That's amazing.

02 **The Perez Family**
(1995)

An idea ahead of its time

(02) Swicord chose to adapt Christine Bell's *The Perez Family*, about Cuban immigrants living in Miami, because she loved the novel so much. "It's so beautifully constructed," she says. "It is structured in three acts—it has a natural dramatic structure. And it has a really unexpected protagonist in Dottie Perez," who was played in the 1995 film by Marisa Tomei. "It's so full of this certain kind of offbeat humor all the way through, just line upon line—I used to be able to quote them. Christine Bell has such a beautiful, dry sense of humor. She had written many drafts of the novel, and one of the reasons why it was so well structured is that she'd done about 15 drafts of the novel. It's beautifully written—and in my opinion so much better than the movie that was made." Swicord had hoped to make **The Perez Family** with emerging director Alfonso Cuarón, but because he was still an unknown at the time, the Samuel Goldwyn Company, which was distributing the film, decided to go with Mira Nair, whom they had worked with on **Mississippi Masala** (1991). "Mira Nair's sensibility is really different from Cuarón's," says Swicord. "Her natural sensibility is completely different from the novel and different from the screenplay. Working from her own experience growing up in India, she saw the movie as being about exile. She made a more romantic movie than I wrote, that didn't really convey my sense of the Cuban community that I had already spent quite a lot of time exploring. I had stayed with Christine Bell for some time, and Christine gave me a window into the Cuban culture in Miami. But understandably, Mira had her own personal, very strong viewpoint that she brought to the film." Though Swicord was unhappy with the final film, she thinks its central idea might be timelier today than when the movie came out in 1995. "We were way ahead of ourselves with that movie," she says, referring to the movie's immigration plotline. "We were almost 20 years ahead of our time in terms of our intention toward that project. I could start again right now and make a movie from the same script with Alfonso Cuarón, and it would be sufficiently different from the movie made before. And I think it would be the right time now. We just weren't in the zeitgeist."

Caroline Thompson

"I'm not romantic at all about the creative process. More than anything else, I've felt like a plow horse—just one foot in front of the other. I do believe that when it's working really well, it's not me—it's coming from someplace else, and I don't know where that place is."

Edward Scissorhands (1990)

A writer of films populated with children, animals, and fantastical creations, Caroline Thompson saw her first movie at the age of four. It was 1960's **The Time Machine**, and it utterly frightened her. "Movies terrified me after that," she recalls. "I think that actually made them very powerful experiences for me. I take them really seriously." After growing up outside Washington, DC, she moved to Los Angeles in her early twenties, hoping to make her name as a novelist. In 1983, she published her first book, *First Born*, which was structured like diary entries written by a mother to the child she aborted who comes back to life. The book helped open the door to a screenwriting career when she collaborated with director Penelope Spheeris on a possible adaptation. No movie was made from their efforts, but it led to her meeting director Tim Burton, whose idea for a character with scissors for hands inspired her script for **Edward Scissorhands** (1990). With Larry Wilson, she then wrote the screenplay for **The Addams Family**, which was one of 1991's biggest commercial hits. Her love of the 1963 family film **The Incredible Journey**, which was based on Sheila Burnford's novel, stirred her to write the script for **Homeward Bound: The Incredible Journey** (1993). That same year saw the release of **The Secret Garden**, based on Frances Hodgson Burnett's children's novel, and **The Nightmare Before Christmas**. In subsequent years, she turned her attention to directing her screenplays for **Black Beauty** (1994) and **Buddy** (1997), and in 2001 she wrote and directed the television film **Snow White: The Fairest of Them All**. More recently, she was one of the writers on **Corpse Bride** (2005)—her third collaboration with Burton—and adapted Jeanne DuPrau's science-fiction novel for **City of Ember** (2008). Currently, she lives in Ojai, California, with her husband and beloved animals.

Caroline Thompson

❝ I grew up in Bethesda, Maryland, and my particular neighborhood was a strange place because it was mostly old people—there weren't a lot of kids there. I envied a friend of mine who lived in what now I would be appalled by: a tract-housing neighborhood where all the houses were identical and were so recently built that there was almost no landscaping. But every house contained a family—the kids would come home from school, and they'd all play touch football in the street, including the girls, and the parents would have their cocktails and sit in lawn chairs. I just thought it was the most amazing, gorgeous, heartwarming neighborhood. I based the **Edward Scissorhands** neighborhood on that neighborhood. Of course, by the time I wrote **Edward Scissorhands**, I had a different perspective—I was an adult living in Burbank, which was the kind of neighborhood where whenever anything happened, everybody would come piling out of their houses and watch the disaster. So, I put all my feelings about that suburban world through Edward's eyes—it got to look amazingly beautiful and enchanting at first, but as the people tried to suck the life out of him, it became a darker and darker place.

As a kid, I wasn't allowed to have pets—my mother was terrified of dogs. My first word was "aminal," and all I ever wanted was a "googie," which is what I called dogs. I got to go to a summer day camp at the age of five. The camp bus stopped at the riding stables, and I never went any further onto the campgrounds—I just sat on the fence and looked at the horses. There was this one called Stonewall Jackson, which I would lure over and hop on his back and just sit there all day long. I've loved horses ever since—the smell of them is so vivid for me. People

05 **Edward Scissorhands**
(1990) starring Johnny Depp as the titular hero

01

11

```
                    PEG
                  (blurts)
            Look at your face... What in
            the world happened?  Where are
            your parents?

                    EDWARD
            My parents?

                    PEG
            Yes.  Your mother.  Your father.

                    EDWARD
            My father's dead.

        Anxiously he scratches himself and slices a fresh gash in his
        nose.  Peg winces.

                    EDWARD
            I didn't ever have a mother.

        Peg kneels beside her samples case.  She opens it.

                    PEG
            Well, no wonder.  You poor
            thing.  The idea of you living
            up here all by yourself...

        She studies the bottles and pulls one out.

                    PEG
            A good astringent should at the
            very least prevent infection....
            No.  On second thought,
                  (she snaps the case closed and stands)
            I think you should come with me.
            Put those things down and...

                    EDWARD
            What things?

                    PEG
            Those...uh...
                  (nods toward his hands_
            weapons or whatever they are.

                    EDWARD
            They're my hands.  He didn't
            get to finish me.

                                        Continued
```

02

12

```
                    PEG
            Oh...

        As he steps fully into the light, Peg can see that they are in
        fact his hands and that his clothes are in tatters all about him,
        hanging in shreds from his thin body.  She shakes her head pityingly.

                    PEG
            We'll work on that.  And on
            your skin.  And certainly on
            your wardrobe.

                                        CUT TO:

        EXT. PEG'S STREET. LATER.

        As Peg drives by, with Edward in the passenger seat, WOMEN'S
        FACES -- Joyce's among them -- appear at the windows of the
        various houses she passes.  "Who's that with Peg?" each one
        wonders aloud -- almost like a chant.  Peg pulls into her

        DRIVEWAY as

        ALL UP AND DOWN THE BLOCK

        women's heads pop out of their front doors for a better look.
        Their dogs' heads poke out, yapping excitedly, noses between
        their mistresses' legs.  Nothing goes on here that not everybody
        knows about.  Curious, eager to be sprung from boredom, the women
        oogle and gawk.

        AT THE BOGGS' HOUSE.

        the front door closes behind Peg and Edward.  The house is a
        variation on the others in the neighborhood -- fifties ranch
        style, slightly bungaloid; a bland face, efficiently, but
        unimaginatively landscaped.

        THE OTHER WOMEN

        slam their own doors and dart INSIDE to the telephone.  Each
        giddily punches in number after number until she finds one that
        isn't busy.  Amidst the chitter-chatter about what's going on --
        or what might be going on:

                                        Continued
```

> "The character of Edward Scissorhands was based on the best dog I ever had, who I got when I was 18. She's long gone now, but we had one of those telepathic connections . . . [s]he was just with me wherever I went . . ."

misunderstand and think it's a dominant/submissive relationship between the rider and the horse. In fact, it's much more like dancing partners—the cooperation and union of it has always hooked me. They're amazingly generous creatures, and they certainly mirror your emotional state. Even when you have no idea what your emotional state is, they'll let you know.

Dogs are my soul mates. The character of Edward Scissorhands was based on the best dog I ever had, who I got when I was 18. She's long gone now, but we had one of those telepathic connections where I didn't have to say, "Let's go this way, let's go that way." She was just with me wherever I went—no leash, no nothing. She even made eye contact, which is very rare for a dog. She didn't have the equipment to talk, but she was just enormously interested in everything, and everything was magical and mystifying to her. →

Letting a strong story speak for itself

(01–04) Initially, director Tim Burton had an idea that the romantic fantasy **Edward Scissorhands** should be a musical. "His rationale was that musicals can be out there," Thompson says. "People can accept the reality of a musical more easily. So what I did—because I was still primarily a prose writer at that time—was I wrote it in prose in three weeks. It was 75 pages, and it just came out." As part of her original prose version, Thompson also included lyrics for possible musical interludes. "The only song I really remember was one called 'I Can't Handle It.'" She laughs. "I don't know if it was because the songs were so awful or because the story was so great, but Tim looked at it and said, 'You know what? I don't think we need to do it as a musical.'" Thompson's first draft of the screenplay **(01–03)** was completed on October 21, 1987, a little more than three years before the film was released.

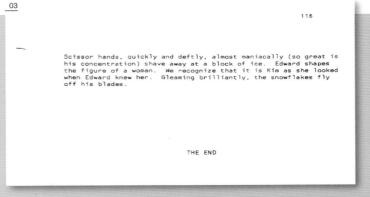

On co-writing and keeping control

(01–02) When producer Scott Rudin, who had championed **Edward Scissorhands** at 20th Century Fox, approached Thompson about writing a film version of **The Addams Family**, she was incredibly reluctant. "I said, 'No, I can't do that—I can't do a big commercial movie,'" she recalls. "I mean, I know who I am—I'm not interested in tentpoles or whatever they call it now. But Scott is very charming when he wants to be: He wined and dined me and sent gifts, and then he finally said, 'What if you had a writing partner?' And I said, 'Well, it depends on who it is.'" Rudin introduced her to Larry Wilson, one of the writers on **Beetlejuice** (1988). "Larry is one of the most charming, most funny, loveliest, kindest people," Thompson says, "so, I relented and said okay." When the two writers started working on the script, Thompson didn't draw much inspiration from the TV show, instead returning to Charles Addams' original comic strips. "We wanted it to be witty and dark," she explains. And although Thompson usually doesn't collaborate with a writing partner, she loved working with Wilson. "We just laughed for 18 months. I thought, 'I can't make a living doing this—I can't laugh for 18 months.' But that's how long it took us to write our first draft." Asked how the division of labor worked between them, Thompson admits, "I know that I am too much of a control freak not to have my hands on the keys. I haven't collaborated much, but whenever I have, I've gotten my hands on the keys so that whatever idea the other person has, I can always say, 'Yeah, I don't know—let's keep working.'"

When I was trying to imagine who Edward would be, it was she who came into my brain.

But, of course, Edward was also inspired by a drawing Tim Burton had made in high school of a character with scissors for hands. He and I had been introduced by our agents because they didn't know what to do with either of us—we met and really fell for each other on a work level. We shared the same sensibility, which is kind of gothic and whimsical at the same time. We love graveyards, and we love ghoulish things, and we're terrified of death, but we're also obsessed by it. We wanted to do something together, and so in our conversations, he told me about this

drawing, and I said, "Stop right there—that's it." The story just fell out of the sky, into my head and out my hands. It was my love poem to Tim, and I think one reason it was so powerful is because I was really writing it out of genuine affection for him. It was a gift to me from him, and a gift from me to him, and a gift from God to both of us. Sometimes, you just get lucky.

During the first preview for **Edward Scissorhands**, I had the most amazing experience—it might never happen again. I rode with Tim and the composer, Danny Elfman, to Orange County—it was my first limo drive—and we went to this suburban movie theater. Every

HOMEWARD BOUND: THE INCREDIBLE JOURNEY

(03) Thompson's involvement with **Homeward Bound: The Incredible Journey** began with a meeting at Disney: "I said to them, 'You made one of my favorite childhood movies, **The Incredible Journey**: You should remake it.' And they thought that was a good idea, and they hired me to write it." But although she loved the original 1963 film, she wanted to make some changes. "I just thought it was so dated," she says. "Kids would never see it, and I wanted people to see it. And hearing the animals talk wasn't part of the original—they had a narrator, that Disney voice, telling us what they were thinking. It was just kind of folksy." Interestingly, **Homeward Bound: The Incredible Journey** is the only movie Thompson has written that still makes her cry—although she didn't intend for that to happen. "I still cry at the end of that movie—director Duwayne Dunham did such a great job. Even though I know exactly what's going to happen, that moment when the old dog Shadow returns to Peter—oh, Duwayne milked it for just the right length of time. I just start to weep."

kid that had been recruited to see the movie looked like the character of Jim, who is the bad kid in the movie. Tim immediately went to the men's room to vomit, and he stayed there the entire screening. Now, this is my first experience to find out if what I've written plays—I'm watching the movie, and people are laughing at the beginning like I hoped they would, and they're really enjoying it, and they're laughing and laughing and laughing. And then, right when I hoped, I start to hear [*imitates people sniffling*]. And by the end, I'm hearing people sobbing. My face was gonna break, I was smiling so hard. It was just a magical experience. That's a structure that I love—you laugh in the beginning, and then you cry. Not very many movies get to do that. I'm not sure why I love that structure so much— maybe because it's got everything. To me, it's what the experience is supposed to be—you soften them up with the laughs, making them more vulnerable. It's really hard to find stories that earn both laughs and tears, so I feel blessed to have been able to do that.

My first produced screenplay was such a great experience, but I had no idea what the business was really like. There weren't studio notes on **Edward Scissorhands**. That movie would never get made today—it's too odd. I feel so grateful for

> "To me, it's what the experience is supposed to be—you soften them up with the laughs, making them more vulnerable. It's really hard to find stories that earn both laughs and tears, so I feel blessed to have been able to do that."

Edward Scissorhands, but then I went into the movie business and experienced the reality of it. I was working on **The Addams Family**, which was produced by Scott Rudin, and I was at a table reading with my co-writer, Larry Wilson, and Raul Julia and Anjelica Huston—it was a thrill since I'd never been to one of those. But there's also another writer sitting at the table, Paul Rudnick. Larry's going, "Yeah, I think Scott is going to have us collaborate with Paul." I was like, "I don't think so, Larry. I think we're getting fired today." Well, we got fired that day after working on the script for 18 months. Scott was very rude about it—he was like, "Get the fuck outta here." He and I had words—he's very opinionated and so am I.

I have a reputation with some people for being difficult, but I think it's just because I stand up for the work. I mean, my scripts are my babies, and I fight for them—I fight for what I believe in. If I think someone's got a terrible idea, I have a bad →

poker face, and so I tell them. I'm not very politic. It's one reason I was so unhappy as a director—I'd spend my energy fighting with people, and I'd wear myself out. The powers that be really want to push you around, and I don't care for it. For me, it's not personal—the movie itself is personal to me, but it never means I hate you forever because you misbehaved. I just wouldn't work with that person again. But it's a very personal business—everybody's so childish. I've always stood up for what I care about. I remember when I lived in Boston and my dog wandered off into a construction site. One worker said to the other, "Throw that brick at that dog." I said, "You touch that fucking dog, and I'm gonna bring my baseball bat and break your knees."

If I'm going to write something original, I write it on spec. I just can't pitch. I don't even know how to begin—I need to go to one of those classes. It's just not who I am—I'm not a salesman. It's a gift, and it's not a gift I have. But I can write, which is what I thought my job was. When I started out, I'd be intimidated by the executives, so I'd pretend it was my party and that my job was to make them comfortable—I'm

a good hostess. But I also wanted them to know that they didn't own me and that my whole life wasn't saying, "Oh, please, please, please . . ." So, I would wear my riding clothes to meetings—I would literally be on the way to ride my horse, but I wouldn't change for the meeting. So, I'd have my jodhpurs on, and the men, of course, were like, "Did you bring your whip?" But it telegraphed that I had another life and that I didn't really need them, which I think they were alarmed and charmed by.

Films may not always be autobiographical, but there is always an element of projection. For example, **The Secret Garden** was a very difficult

01   **The Secret Garden**
(1993)

BLACK BEAUTY

(02) Thompson made her directorial debut with **Black Beauty**, which starred Alan Cumming as the voice of the horse. Some critics complained about Thompson's choice to anthropomorphize the animal, but for her, it was an easy decision. "My husband and I always have this argument: He says that movies are about people, and I say that movies are about emotions—movies are about a character. There are all these studies they're doing now with animals—there used to be this big injunction against anthropomorphizing animals and thinking they have feelings and emotions. Guess what? They do. All you have to do is have a dog or cat, and you know that they have feelings. People to this day say to me, 'Horses have personalities? One's different from the other?' Oh yeah. I bet even flies have personalities."

On creating a character that speaks to you

(03–04) When Thompson was brought in to work on **The Nightmare Before Christmas**, the central character of Jack Skellington had already been well-formed through Danny Elfman's songs. But when she traveled to the San Francisco studio where the animation was being developed, she was drawn to the character sketches for Jack's love interest Sally. "Sally at that time was more like the **Corpse Bride** character," Thompson explains. "Tim has a thing for the hourglass figure, which was hard for me to relate to since I'm tall and thin. But I realized that Sally's a character whose story the songs weren't telling yet. Tim had always had her sort of stitched-up, so she was obviously a creation. But I said, 'You know, she has to be more like the Little Match Girl—she can't be this sort of vamp. I wouldn't know what to do with her.' So they said, 'Okay, go do it your way.'" She had a week to complete the script, which ended up being roughly a 50-page document, not including Elfman's songs. In the process, she made Sally a sweeter, more sensitive and resourceful heroine. "With **The Nightmare Before Christmas**, I've always said I built a house that people were already living in," Thompson says. "I just built Sally's story."

adaptation. The novel was written by Frances Hodgson Burnett, who supported around 15 people on her writing. I spent more time writing the script than she spent on the novel—she blazed through that thing, and it's so repetitive. She was a devout Christian Scientist, so it has all this kind of proselytizing in it. I ended up honoring the book I loved as a kid rather than the book I was now reading. Sometimes I find myself writing for an aspect of myself that used to be—it's like I'm writing for that child I was. Another interesting thing happened with that film. →

"I have a reputation with some people for being difficult, but I think it's just because I stand up for the work. I mean, my scripts are my babies, and I fight for them—I fight for what I believe in."

"Sometimes I find myself writing for an aspect of myself that used to be—it's like I'm writing for that child I was."

Agnieszka Holland directed the movie—I'm tall and thin, and she's short. There were two girls up for Mary, and one was tall and thin and willowy, and the other was short and wide. I was all over the tall, thin, willowy one, and she went for the short, wide one. And she's the director so, of course, she should decide who should be cast, but it was just fascinating. It was at that moment I realized, "Oh, yeah, right—we're projecting."

My first decade in the business, practically everything I wrote got made—after that, it's been such a struggle. One that has gotten made in the 2000s, **Corpse Bride**, was a huge disappointment to me. **Corpse Bride** is and will be the end of my association with Tim Burton—it was a very difficult situation. He was off directing **Big Fish**, and he hired a co-director, Mike Johnson, for **Corpse Bride**, but he told me to write the script I wanted. The young director met with me over lunch, and he told me a bunch of his ideas, all of which I didn't like. I just said, "Oh, that's nice"—I was very flip with him, and I'm sure that it pissed him off. I didn't mean to be so flip—I would be nicer today, but I was very sure of my relationship with Tim. So I wrote a draft. Tim saw it, told me he loved it, and said, "You just keep doing what you're doing." I said, "Well, Mike wants this and that." Tim said, "Just ignore it." So I wrote my next draft, and I turned it in and didn't hear anything. Finally, two months later, called the producer. He said, "Oh, didn't you know you got fired? You've been replaced. We've rewritten you completely." So I contacted Tim, and I gave him a piece of my mind, and he wrote me this email like you can't even believe—he said that I had betrayed him. Basically the young director's idea of what the movie should be is what the movie became. But I got my name on it, which is very important in our business since you're only as valuable as your credits. I never saw the movie—I started it and was just appalled. My film had gravitas. The structure, I think, is somewhat the same—it was based on a Russian fairy tale—but with mine, you got to cry at the end. My script wasn't gold, but the movie just turned out to be a really bad experience. It's very odd to have my name on a movie that I've never seen. A producer came up to me once and said, "**Corpse Bride** is so undervalued—you did such a great job." All I could do was say, "Thank you." There's no point in explaining to people what happened. I just feel sad for the movies that Tim Burton and I never got to make and never will make.

I'm not romantic at all about the creative process. More than anything else, I've felt like a plow horse—just one foot in front of the other. I do believe that when it's working really well, it's not me—it's coming from someplace else, and I don't know where that place is. I only do one project at a time, and I only do one a year. In the morning, I go to my office and write five script pages every day. People think, "That's not very much." Well, if I write more—if I get into a big blaze and I write 15 pages—my brain's exhausted, so then I don't write for four or five days, and my rhythm gets completely thrown off. So I've learned over the years that if I do my five pages a day, I have a first draft in about a month.

Usually, my writing day ends around 2 p.m. The rest of the day is my horses. I have five at my home full-time. Most of them are retired, but all of them have personalities—I could write stories about them. Being with my horses, it's like meditation. You can't think about other things— if your mind wanders while you're dealing with the horse, something bad could happen. They're a whole different kind of focus. They ask of you to be a stronger and braver person than you actually are, so then you become that stronger, braver person.

THOMPSON'S OFFICE

(01–03) Thompson's writing space is in a small cabin in her backyard. "I go in there at eight in the morning, and I'm usually done by lunch," she says. "That routine is how I've been happiest ever since I started out. I'm not on the phone—I just go in there, and that's all I do. I'm really lucky to have the focus, and I'm also really lucky that I can leave it in that room when I'm done for the day. People will say, 'Well, I'm sure you're thinking about the project,' but not really—I don't think about it when I'm away from it. Every now and then, an image will float into a dream or while I'm driving, but generally speaking, it stays in there." A picture of her beloved dog Ariel **(01)**, upon whom she based the character of Edward Scissorhands, hangs on the bookcase to the right of her desk. She also has a French poster for the film in her office **(02)**. "Tim's assistant at the time gave me this," Thompson says. "It hangs behind me and to the left. If I'm feeling really insecure, I'll look around at it and recall myself. But I don't keep it in view all the time. That would be creepy self-aggrandizing like those people who line their office walls with photos of themselves and celebrities." As for the crucifix she has on the wall, Thompson explains, "Sometimes I look up at him when I'm struggling and we share our pain. I consider myself a spiritual atheist, but I sure do love this crucifix, especially the nasty hair and the intensity of his pose. He's a perfect office buddy **(03)**."

The impact of film that reflects experience

(04) After Thompson finished her first novel, *First Born*, she asked her agent to get it to director Brian De Palma—for one specific reason. "**Carrie** (1976) is one of my favorite movies," she says. "I just think it's a brilliant metaphor for what it feels like to be a teenage girl. Later, I met Brian De Palma and I tried to tell him how brilliant I thought he was and asked him a bunch of questions about **Carrie**. He looked at me like my hair was on fire—I don't think he realized how special a movie he'd made and how viscerally accurate about the teenage experience he'd been." Asked if she encounters a similar experience when fans tell her how much her movies have meant to them, Thompson responds, "Well, when I meet people who talk about **Edward Scissorhands**, I know that it was a very important movie for them—especially for people not comfortable in their own skin. It doesn't surprise me in the least. And when I was adapting this one author's novel, I noticed on the back cover, in her author picture, she's wearing a **The Nightmare Before Christmas** sweatshirt. That was great for me. And for her. Happily, she was enormously pleased to have me doing the adaptation."

David Webb Peoples

 "... if you write a really good script, that is in itself an accomplishment. That was something I picked up from William Goldman: I've never met him, but he has always been one of my mentors. He was able to make the script itself a finished thing— you could read it and see the movie."

Unforgiven (1992)

Starting his career as an editor, David Webb Peoples began writing screenplays in the 1970s, producing a series of scripts that eventually brought him to the attention of director Tony Scott. Through Scott's encouragement, Peoples became involved with **Blade Runner** (1982), the seminal science-fiction film directed by Scott's brother Ridley. However, one of Peoples' greatest successes came more than 15 years after he first conceived the idea: Director Clint Eastwood optioned his script of *The Cut-Whore Killings*, eventually turning it into his Best Picture-winning **Unforgiven** (1992), which netted Peoples a Best Original Screenplay Oscar nomination. That same year, he wrote **Hero** (a.k.a. **Accidental Hero**), a Preston Sturges-style comedy starring Dustin Hoffman, Geena Davis, and Andy Garcia. He and his wife, screenwriter Janet Peoples, also co-wrote director Jon Else's Oscar-nominated documentary **The Day After Trinity** (1981), an in-depth account of J. Robert Oppenheimer, the so-called father of the atomic bomb. In 1989, he made his directorial debut with **The Salute of the Jugger** (a.k.a. **The Blood of Heroes**), a post-apocalyptic thriller with Rutger Hauer, Joan Chen, and Delroy Lindo. In the mid-1990s, Peoples retired as a solo writer to collaborate full-time with his wife, Janet Peoples. Together, they adapted Chris Marker's heralded 1962 short film **La Jetée** into **Twelve Monkeys** (1995), which earned Brad Pitt a nomination for Best Supporting Actor. At the 2012 San Francisco International Film Festival, Peoples received the Kanbar Award for excellence in screenwriting. Unerringly modest, Peoples incorrectly insists that he doesn't have anything noteworthy to say about his process. "An interview implies that the subject is interesting," he told the *Los Angeles Times* in 1992. "I'm not. As a writer, I never intended to be either Frank Sinatra or Howard Hughes. It's all there in the screenplay."

David Webb Peoples

"I started getting into movies in my late teens, but I didn't think about movies as writing. In fact, movies at that time made me think contemptuously of writers. I thought the creative world was about images. I didn't have much respect for the written word. I was sort of a young brat and liked movies from Europe. Somehow, I didn't think people wrote those scripts—I thought those images just collected themselves. I was very naïve.

Instead of writing, I became a film editor, which was manipulating images. I was mostly editing documentaries, and in documentaries you are more of a storyteller as an editor than you are if you're editing a feature. In a feature, the writer and the director are telling the story, and the editor is putting it together, which is not to diminish in any way the editor's role, because the editor makes it magic. But the actual storytelling is often more on the shoulders of an editor in documentary films. The documentary maker

doesn't know what's coming and what he or she is going to put on film, so you and the director are important in finding the story in the material.

Still, I did from time to time keep trying to write a screenplay, but I couldn't finish it and didn't understand how it was done. Plus, back when I was in college, I was an English major, and one of the negatives was that they taught you to be critical of the great writers. You analyze all these magnificent writers, and then, of course, if you sit down and try to write yourself, it doesn't come out as good—you immediately feel that you can't write. But later I found myself editing a very low-budget, exploitation kind of movie. The script didn't seem to me all that good, and I noticed that the filmed scenes were coming out like they were in the script. So, I thought, "Well, I could do better than this." So instead of trying to write better than Dostoyevsky or James Joyce, I tried to write better than this particular script, and that was doable. That low-budget script was

Sometimes words aren't necessary

(01–03) When director Clint Eastwood made **Unforgiven**, he barely deviated from Webb Peoples' screenplay, except in one place. "There was one scene before the very ending that Clint Eastwood shot that he then left out," Peoples says. "It had to do with the rhythms and the feel of the movie, and I think Clint made the right choice." The excised scene involved William Munny (played by Eastwood) returning to his children after killing Little Bill (Gene Hackman). "They're digging up some dirt in the henhouse, and the little boy's mentioning that the Schofield Kid came by and left them some money. William Munny's digging up this money, and the kid says, 'Uh, Pop, did you . . .' and he can't get the words out. Munny says to him, 'Steal it? No, I didn't steal it.' And the kid says, 'No. I mean, did you kill anybody?' Then Munny looks at him for a moment and says, 'Nope.' And that was the scene. It was a flat-out rip-off of the end of **The Godfather**, where Michael's wife asks him if he had Carlo killed, and he says no. It's the same scene, in a way." **(02–03)** The script pages showing the dialogue marked for cutting.

"You analyze all these magnificent writers, and then, of course, if you sit down and try to write yourself, it doesn't come out as good—you immediately feel that you can't write."

just trying to do a job, which was to entertain the audience. Suddenly, I understood what the job was, and I stopped trying to self-consciously imitate the masters. Before, I had just been writing scripts because I thought I wanted to be a director, but then I started liking writing scripts—I liked putting that stuff on paper and hoping that it would be entertaining to others.

I was one of the writers on Jon Else's documentary **The Day After Trinity**, about Robert Oppenheimer and the atomic bomb. When we were making it, we had an idea that if we did the research and figured out what everybody Jon was going to interview would contribute to the story, we could figure out how he could ask them the right questions and get them to say what we wanted them to say. We wrote what we called a "toy movie"—it was a movie in which all the participants said more or less what we wanted them to say. When the time came to do the interviews, they didn't say exactly what we wanted them to say—they said much better stuff—but at least we had a guide. There's an interesting similarity there with screenwriting. One of the more difficult things in screenwriting is that you very often have something in mind you want your characters to do, but somehow you have to get them to want to do it. If you think back on the history of movies—think of those expensive writers from the East Coast locked in their rooms at MGM or at Warner Bros., and then the producer comes in and gives them some story point, like "Hey, let's have the professor rob a bank." That can actually be a good idea— maybe it really would be interesting if the professor suddenly robbed a bank—but if you're going to write a good script, you have to make it appear that the desire to rob a bank really comes from the professor. What you're trying to do when you write a script is to make the characters behave like they have the plan rather than they are just doing what the writer wants them to do. →

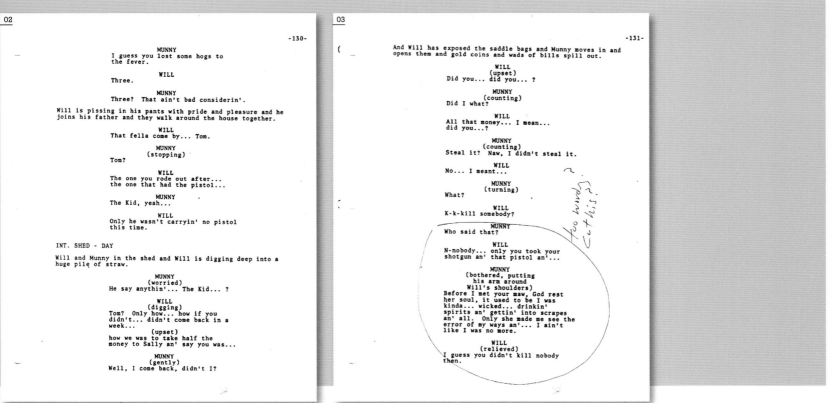

A new angle on an old story

(01–02) Initially, Webb Peoples and Janet Peoples were so impressed with **La Jetée**, Chris Marker's original short film that inspired **Twelve Monkeys**, that they were hesitant to take on the writing assignment. But after some convincing by the producers, the couple tried a thought experiment they like to do at such moments. David explains: "We say to each other, 'Well, if they kidnapped our children and we had to write this in order to get our children back, what would we do?' We got the vision of a man in a world with nothing but animals left. The post-holocaust business had been so done so well—Jim Cameron had been there a couple of times already and just masterfully handled it—that it just seemed old. But as soon as it was biological, well, it was the same thing, but a fresh way of looking at it. And that's what you want—a fresh way to look at something. And then, because Janet and I come from Berkeley, which has a number of people who are different, we started imagining one of those people who tells you that the world's gonna come to an end. They actually believe it, but what if we looked at the world from their point of view? So, that was a fresh way of looking at that everyday part of life. And then we found the key piece—there's this psychiatrist who's sure the protagonist is crazy. Partway through the picture, she convinces him he's crazy, and then he convinces her he's really from the future. So, we said, 'Okay, we'll get on board and do this.'"

Finding out that Ridley Scott wanted me to work on **Blade Runner** was a very thrilling phone call. Michael Deeley, the producer, called me up, and they got me to go to LA and put me up in this fancy suite at the Chateau Marmont. They sent Hampton Fancher's script over by messenger. After I read it, Michael Deeley and Ridley Scott came over to talk to me. It broke my heart to say, "I can't make this any better. I think this is a fantastic script." I didn't want to say that—I thought, "It would be so cool to say, 'Oh, this is a piece of shit. I can fix this.'" But it was a wonderful script, and there wasn't anything I could think of that I could do that would make it better. Michael Deeley sort of chuckled and said, "I think Ridley has a few ideas . . ." I was a very naïve young man: I didn't realize the issue wasn't what the writer could do. It's what the director wants done.

"What you're trying to do when you write a script is to make the characters behave like they have the plan rather than they are just doing what the writer wants them to do."

Blade Runner got mixed reviews at the time, but I always knew I was part of something special. I knew **Blade Runner** was extraordinary. I was frustrated by some of the narrative issues, because narrative is my thing, but I certainly didn't help it narratively. So I had some qualms. But as time went by, I began to realize just what a great film it was. It talks to people—it's a vision. Ridley's vision superseded the narrative demands, and it made the movie special and exceptional. It's a more European movie than American movie, and I'm totally an American writer—very American. Hampton and Ridley had this great →

BLADE RUNNER

(03–06) When Webb Peoples came on board to rewrite Hampton Fancher's screenplay for **Blade Runner**, director Ridley Scott instructed him not to read the original Philip K. Dick novel, *Do Androids Dream of Electric Sheep?* "I've never read it to this day," says Peoples. "At the time, I wasn't eager to read it, and it was easy to not read it, so I didn't. And, of course, Hampton had already adapted it and made those decisions." Peoples had heard that Scott was a taskmaster, and the two men discussed the many changes that Scott wanted implemented. "There was a lot of stuff," Peoples recalls. "He's got a very imaginative and creative mind. I'm not nearly as imaginative, but I am a junkie for narrative, so I think there was a little clash there to a certain degree. But my main thing was to satisfy his very imaginative desires. But at the same time, I can't tell you how much I admired Hampton's writing—I literally tried to copy it and write in the style that he'd written everything in. I wanted to make it seamless in that sense."

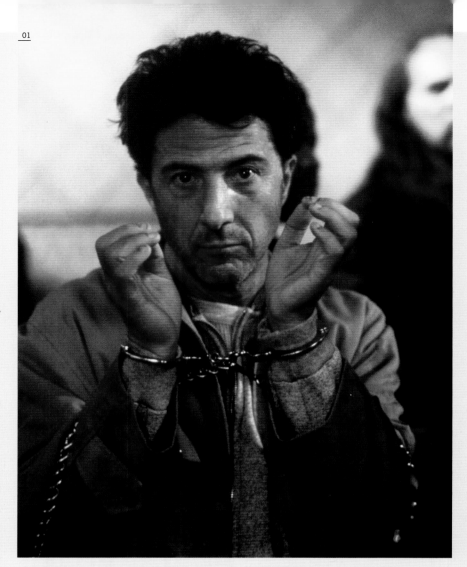

HERO (A.K.A. ACCIDENTAL HERO)

(01–03) The germ of the idea for **Hero**, a comedy about a conniving pickpocket named Bernie LaPlante (Dustin Hoffman) who behaves unexpectedly heroically during an airplane crash, came to Webb Peoples through writer Alvin Sargent and producer Laura Ziskin. "They brought me a different story," he recalls. "It had something to do with a senator. Alvin had received a pocketknife somehow, and it had a name on it: Bernie LaPlante. This is what writers do—Alvin got this name, and he wasn't going to let that go. So he starts doing this story about Bernie LaPlante that was pretty different, but I'd also had an idea of my own that I'd been working on, which was much, much darker but with the same idea. It wasn't a comedy—it was a very dark story about a guy who was not a particularly admirable person who did something heroic." With their blessing, Peoples combined the ideas. "Since it was a comedy, I was thinking Preston Sturges, because there is no greater comedy writer as far as I'm concerned. Which is not to say that **Hero** ever achieved that level of greatness, but it was certainly the intention." Asked if he was drawn to the movie's satire of hero worship and disposable celebrity, Peoples responds, "I just thought it was a good story about a guy. Basically, you want to write a story about an interesting character and here's this guy Bernie who's stealing money out of his very young lawyer's purse and then later paying her with her own money. I mean, that's an interesting guy. One of the most interesting things about writing is that, in real life, you don't know what the person next to you is going to do when, say, suddenly a bomb goes off. You don't know if the person next to you is going to act in a heroic way or an abject way. And you don't know how you're going to react. So to me, it was just exciting that here's this lowlife who goes into a burning airplane, and he didn't know he'd do anything that nutty and was shocked that he had. That appealed to me tremendously and still does."

A rewrite is not necessarily a fix

(04) **Soldier** arrived in theaters in 1998, but the script was written more than a decade earlier. "When I wrote it," David Webb Peoples recalls, "I was so energized by seeing the first **Terminator** (1984). I'd always had this idea of the monster tough-guy being the hero, and in the first **Terminator**—which is absolutely a brilliant movie, one of the greats of all time—the Terminator played by Schwarzenegger wasn't technically the hero. At that point, I didn't think James Cameron had exactly licked what I was trying to lick. I had in my mind a story where a guy as bad as the Terminator was the hero of the story. Cameron had almost done it, so I said, 'I've got to do it—I've got to make the Terminator the hero,' which Cameron then did even better in **T2**." **Soldier** was finally made with Kurt Russell and director Paul W.S. Anderson. Asked if having years away from a script helps create a greater objectivity about the story's problems, Peoples responds, "You can see some of the flaws more clearly, but one of the problems that I always find is that just because something doesn't seem great anymore doesn't mean you can make it better." He laughs. "Very often, I just make it worse when I rewrite it, even though I can see what's wrong."

vision. I made some really good contributions to the script—I'm not being falsely modest—but it's certainly not my movie in any sense of the word. It's a movie I was lucky to work on.

I recently got an award at the San Francisco Film Festival, and somebody wrote what a modest, self-effacing guy I was. So I've been going around bragging to everybody what a modest, self-effacing guy I am. The fact is, there's no point in pretending that everything you write works. It doesn't, right? It's a struggle. I'm aware there are writers who are not as good as I am—but I'm very, very aware of a bunch of writers who are much better than I am.

When you work on a spec script, you're working on your own time. And when I was writing spec scripts early in my career, I couldn't work at a day job and do the spec script at night. I had to carve out a piece of time and write very, very fast. When you write for pay, the whole thing is changed. You're no longer writing to surprise anybody, because everybody's already talked all about it. And also, nowadays, when you write for the studios, you're writing for a committee that's →

<u>05</u> Unforgiven (1992)

THE SALUTE OF THE JUGGER
(A.K.A. THE BLOOD OF HEROES)

(01–03) Webb Peoples made his feature directorial debut with 1989's **The Salute of the Jugger**, a post-apocalyptic drama starring Rutger Hauer about a vicious sport played by "Juggers." "The script was largely inspired by the original short story 'Roller Ball Murder' that appeared in *Esquire* magazine," says Peoples. "This was long before the **Rollerball** (1975) movie happened. The original story was what energized me—I liked the rambunctiousness of the sport, and I started thinking about some characters in a very rough sport. The key to writing it was my admiration for athletes who endure and put themselves into these very tough places and show their heart. Now many years later, there are actually teams and leagues that play the game in a big annual tournament in Berlin. MMA and the UFC reflect the violence and the heart of the game that's in the movie. I wasn't as interested in the skills as much as I was interested in the determination and the will and the courage and the character that the characters showed." Asked to assess the experience of directing, Peoples replies, "It was humbling," and then laughs. "It was a terrific experience—I met some of the best friends of my life working on that—but it was a discovery that I'm not particularly talented in terms of being a director. It wasn't a bad piece of directing, but I would have to direct five or 10 more pictures to get to be a pretty good director. It taught me that I'm not a director, so that was enlightening."

Dystopian societies focus us on our own

(01–03) Although Webb Peoples has worked on several dystopian science-fiction films, such as **Blade Runner** and **Twelve Monkeys**, he confesses that he's not a sci-fi fanatic. "I don't read a lot of science fiction," he says. "Science fiction is a way to write and to talk about some things, and it can be terrific. I just like telling stories. You can tell a story better in a particular time and place, and I'm open to doing science fiction, but I don't feel a need to do science fiction." Of course, science fiction does allow for certain liberties a writer may not have in other genres. "There's all sorts of specifics in everyday life that get confusing, and you can avoid that realism by going into the future and creating a world in which you can write about the things you want to write about and leave out the things you don't want to write about." As for his interest in dystopian societies, Peoples says, "I think there was a period where I was drawn to this kind of scenario, and I think it was in the gestalt. I find myself not quite there at the moment, but I still admire it when it's done in a fresh way, as in **Children of Men** (2006). I didn't care for the premise, but by gosh the movie was terrific, because it resonated. It said, 'Let's take what's in the world today and look at it from an angle that's a little different.' That's what science fiction lets you do— it makes the story you're telling resonate with what's happening in the world today."

going to parse it and look it over and critique it. So, the positive side is that you really have to polish things and work them over—the negative side is that this process takes out a lot of the creative energy and spark. Those old pictures that people used to crank out, like Roger Corman pictures, they had a lot of heart and spirit to them. Working for the studios, everything has to be polished to some degree—you can't just bang out something that's all spirit and heart. So there's a compromise there.

I wrote *The Cut-Whore Killings*, which became **Unforgiven**, around 1976. I've always been drawn to what are called the revisionist Westerns instead of the big John Ford movies. I like things like **The Culpepper Cattle Co.** (1972) and **The Great Northfield Minnesota Raid** (1972), which I consider a masterpiece. But I was also influenced by **Taxi Driver** (1976), which I thought was an amazing movie. Paul Schrader

just opened up the world with that movie. When I first started writing, I didn't want to have anybody get killed in any script I wrote because I was just so put off by the unreality. When people get killed in the movies, it's like in James Bond, which is perfectly legitimate because James Bond is James Bond, and that's the reality they set up. But even in other movies, you kill 10 people and then you go have breakfast—it's as if it didn't have any impact whatsoever. But all of a sudden I see **Taxi Driver** and people are getting killed, and the characters maintained how they would be in real life. But at the same time, it's an entertaining movie, and that was always important to me—I wanted to write things that were entertaining. I didn't want to write obscure art pictures with little lessons in them—I wanted to write entertainment. **Taxi Driver** opened up what entertainment could be. It said, "Yeah, you can write this kind of stuff and it'll be entertaining."

> "I think there are a lot of screenwriters with projects that are their best work that don't get made—I don't think it's unique in any way."

All writers work to a large degree like actors. There's an actor in all writers, but I found I was operating more like an actor than a lot of other writers were—which is to say I get into the thing I'm working on and I'm not able to get out of it. You're struggling to stay in this world you're creating, but you've got a life to live with a family, so you can't just be totally in that world. So, I found I could no longer read any fiction, because what I love about fiction is it sucks you in, and you become engrossed in that world. Well, I couldn't handle three worlds—I could only handle the writing world and the daily world of my family. I needed all that focus. Even now, I don't read much fiction unless I deliberately and with great care take six-to-eight weeks off, which I never do. I took a vacation once, and after like a week or 10 days of not thinking about writing, suddenly I could read like I was in college again. I used to be able to just lose myself in a book—it's very hard to do that now.

My wife Janet Peoples and I began writing together around 1995 as a practical consideration. We'd been writing screenplays separately, and it played havoc with the rhythms of our life—I'd be finishing one and want to take a week off, and she'd be just starting one, and it was just madness. So we thought, "Well, we'll write together and we'll be on the same schedule." Chuck Roven and Robert Kosberg came to us with **La Jetée**, which became **Twelve Monkeys**, and since then Janet and I have been working together. Initially, maybe there was some concern about how that would work— we both have very strong ideas—so one of the conditions we put on writing together was we wouldn't do original work. We wouldn't do my idea or her idea—we'd do something that was brought to us by a third party. That way, neither one of us was the chief authority on that particular piece of material—our viewpoints were equally valid. That's not to say that it's not a real struggle sometimes, but it's a level playing field: We're working on what we've decided to do together.

We've written good stuff, but it doesn't get made, and we've also written uncredited stuff on other pictures. But the bottom line is, we have a pile of scripts that are just not in sync with the times. We haven't had a lot of success because we tend to write a lot like the 1970s and early 1980s films we loved. Those movies were what inspired Janet and myself to be writers. Here was a time when you could pull out all the stops and write something that was entertaining, that would dazzle people, that would be enormously successful, and that you could feel good about. It was a very exciting time, and it's hard getting those pictures made now. Clint Eastwood still does really strong, wonderful character movies, but he's not going to do everything you write.

The best thing that Janet and I have ever written has never been made, an adaptation of James Dickey's *To the White Sea*. I think there are a lot of screenwriters with projects that are their best work that don't get made—I don't think it's unique in any way. But a movie is much more than a script. You have to have a good director and actors who get it, and there's not somebody out there to get everything that's been written. So I don't think it's that unusual, and I don't think it's necessarily the end of the world. A lot of movies do get made, and it's wonderful the good ones that do get made.

I'm not eager to see the movies that I've written, and I don't think Janet necessarily is either. It's not that we've never seen any of them, but if you write a really good script, that is in itself an accomplishment. That was something I picked up from William Goldman: I've never met him, but he has always been one of my mentors. He was able to make the script itself a finished thing—you could read it and see the movie. That's what Janet and I are doing, and when other people make the movie, good for them. That's great, but the part that we did is on paper. It's an enormous thrill to see **Unforgiven** and to see the performances—the magic those actors put into those parts is a pleasure to see. But I didn't do that. That's what they did.

Born in 1906, filmmaker Billy Wilder won six Oscars, along with an Irving G. Thalberg Memorial Award, but his wonderful movies weren't the product of his fruitful imagination alone. "I always collaborated with somebody," he said in the late 1990s after his career was over. "If you think that I am speaking lousy English now, you should have heard it then. I felt I had to have a collaborator [because of language]." Growing up in Vienna and working on films in Europe before moving to America in his late twenties, Wilder found superb collaborators when he began making Hollywood movies, including Raymond Chandler on **Double Indemnity** (1944) and Charles Brackett on **The Lost Weekend** (1945) and **Sunset Boulevard** (1950). But with all due respect to those two fine writers, Wilder's greatest partnership may have been with I.A.L. Diamond.

Born in 1920 in Austria-Hungary (now Moldova), Diamond moved to Brooklyn with his family when he was nine. Before teaming up with Wilder, he spent over a decade writing scripts, including **Monkey Business** (1952), which he co-wrote with Ben Hecht and Charles Lederer, and starred Cary Grant, Ginger Rogers, and Marilyn Monroe. His partnership with Wilder began with **Love in the Afternoon** (1957), but their first masterpiece came two years later with **Some Like it Hot** (1959), the celebrated comedy that brought together Tony Curtis and Jack Lemmon as 1920s musicians disguised as women and on the run from the mob. Beyond all its other attributes, the movie is forever remembered for its terrific final line. Lemmon explains to fiancé Joe E. Brown that he can't marry him because he's actually a man, to which Brown matter-of-factly responds, "Well, nobody's

01

01 Some Like it Hot (1959)

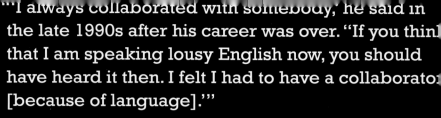

perfect.'' It was all Diamond's idea. Years later, Wilder recalled that Diamond had suggested it for the final line and that Wilder had decided to stick with it until they could come up with something better. They never did—but it turned out to be just right. "The audience just exploded at the preview in Westwood . . . And it wound up being our funniest last line," Wilder said.

Their hot streak continued with the next film. A sublime mixture of romance, comedy, and drama, **The Apartment** (1960) won five Oscars, including Best Picture. Wilder had the idea for the film after watching David Lean's **Brief Encounter** (1945), which was about an affair between a married man and a married woman. But it wasn't until Wilder and Diamond heard a news story about a woman's husband who killed his wife's clandestine lover that they figured out the plot. "The interesting thing was that [the lover] was using the apartment of one of the underlings at [his] agency," Diamond recalled. "That was what gave us the relationship— somebody who was using somebody lower than he in a big company, using his apartment."

The two men continued to collaborate over he next two decades on hits like **Irma La Douce**

(1963) and superb comedies such as **The Fortune Cookie** (1966). Together, they were nominated for three writing Oscars, and won one for **The Apartment**. And while Wilder had worked with several writing partners, it was clear that Diamond was someone very special to him. "If I ever lost this guy," Wilder claimed, "I'd feel like Abercrombie without Fitch." That moment came April 21, 1988, when Diamond died of multiple myeloma at the age of 67. Their final onscreen pairing was 1981's **Buddy Buddy**, and true to his word, Wilder effectively retired after that. "I wanted to quit when I was 80," Wilder said. "I quit when I was 82."

Wilder lived 14 more years, dying at the age of 95 in March 2002. He continues to inspire new filmmakers. When director Michel Hazanavicius accepted the Best Picture Oscar for **The Artist** in 2012, he concluded his comments with "I want to thank three persons—I want to thank Billy Wilder, I want to thank Billy Wilder, and I want to thank Billy Wilder." Wilder is buried in Pierce Brothers Westwood Village Memorial Park, and his tombstone is further testament to his eternal connection to Diamond. "I'm A Writer," his grave reads, "But Then Nobody's Perfect."

02 The plot of **The Fortune Cookie** (1966) centers on a crooked lawyer (Walter Matthau) who convinces his brother-in-law (Jack Lemmon) to fake a serious injury for profit

03 I.A.L. Diamond (left) and Billy Wilder (right) on the set of **The Front Page** (1974), a witty newspaper caper starring Jack Lemmon and Walter Matthau

04 **The Apartment** (1960)

Glossary

Act A major story section in a traditional Hollywood screenplay. The typical script consists of three acts. Act One introduces the main character and the central conflict, Act Two shows the main character trying to reach his or her goal, and then Act Three resolves that central conflict. While there are no set rules on structure, in a traditional 120-page script Act One would be approximately 30 pages long, Act Two would be around 60 pages, and Act Three would be about 30 pages.

Adaptation A screenplay based on an existing piece of literary material, such as a novel, short story, television show, or play.

Agent A person who represents a writer, director, actor, or other creative talent. The agent negotiates contracts and other business deals for his or her client.

Antagonist The character who opposes the main character. This character is often the villain of the story.

Arbitration The process by which the Writers Guild of America determines final writing credits on a feature film.

Backstory A character's background and history. This information may be revealed through flashbacks or dialogue, but it represents the important life history the character has lived through before the screenplay's story begins.

Beat An important individual moment in a screenplay. Writers will refer to these as story beats, action beats, or emotional beats, depending on the purpose they serve in the script.

Coverage An analysis, written by someone at a studio or production company, that synopsizes a script's story and evaluates its strengths and weaknesses.

Credit Official designation of who contributed to the writing of a screenplay. Specific credits include "written by" and "story by."

Description The text in a screenplay that describes what the audience will see in the final film.

Development The process by which a studio or producer asks for changes to an existing screenplay before it can be made into a film. (When this process drags on with no end in sight, it is often referred to as "development hell.")

Development executive An employee at a studio or production company whose job it is to suggest changes to an existing screenplay. These individuals also read material with an eye toward possibly turning the work into a film.

Dialogue The words that the characters speak.

Draft A completed version of a screenplay. Screenplays often go through several drafts before a film is made.

Ensemble A screenplay with several central characters who may be part of the same story or who may inhabit their own separate story.

Flashback Moving backward in time to show an event that happened prior to the present-day scenes in a screenplay.

High-concept A movie idea, meant for a mainstream audience, which can be summarized succinctly and dynamically in a sentence or two.

Independent film A movie made outside of a studio.

Outline A preliminary writing step in which the screenwriter puts down initial ideas about the characters, storyline, and themes. Outlines are written in numerous ways, but the principal purpose is to help clarify the approach that will be taken when writing the screenplay.

Manager An individual who, like an agent, represents the interests of a writer. However, unlike an agent, a manager does not negotiate contracts. Instead, a manager works as a form of advisor for the writer, helping them shape their career.

Nonlinear A story that doesn't develop chronologically, but instead bounces around between different time periods or realities.

Option The agreement by which a studio or producer owns the rights to a screenplay or other creative property, such as a novel or play.

Period A film set in the past. These movies are often referred to as period pieces.

Remake A screenplay based on an existing film.

Pitch An oral presentation of a story delivered by the writer to producers or studio executives with the aim of getting them interested in buying the movie idea.

Preview A screening for a finished film that's carried out by the studio before it releases the film. At the preview, an audience is brought in to evaluate the film and offer feedback. From the preview, studio executives can determine if anything needs to be changed in the film before its release.

Producer An individual who helps shepherd a screenplay from the page to the screen. Producers do many different jobs on a film—from technical to financial to creative—but their principal responsibility is to help the writers, stars, director, and studio execute their visions.

Produced screenplay A script that is turned into a film. By comparison, a script that has not been turned into a film is referred to as an unproduced screenplay.

Protagonist The main character, often the hero of the screenplay.

Rewrite In its simplest meaning, a rewrite is the process by which a writer makes changes and edits to his or her screenplay. In studio terms, it refers to the period during which a new writer is hired on an existing project to rewrite scenes, characters, or dialogue.

Set piece A sequence that is intended to be one of the focal moments in the screenplay. Set pieces are often action sequences, but they can also refer to any major emotional or dramatic scene or series of scenes.

Spec script A screenplay that has been written in the hopes of being sold to a producer or studio.

Table read The time when the actors and director sit together, usually at a table, to read through the screenplay out loud. A table reading is done to help the filmmakers and actors get a sense of how the script's dialogue and story are working. (It can also help the writer learn what can be changed or removed in the script.) This process can also be called a read-through.

Theme The underlying philosophical, intellectual, or political ideas within the screenplay.

Through-line An element of the narrative that carries through from the beginning of the script until the end. Usually, the protagonist's story is the central through-line for a screenplay. Likewise, an important thematic component that recurs during the story can be said to be a thematic through-line.

Turnaround A situation in which the ownership rights of a script are transferred from one studio to another.

Voiceover The thoughts of a character, usually in the form of narration, that are heard on the soundtrack of a film.

Index